WORLD WAR II FROM ORIGINAL SOURCES

THE U-BOAT WAR IN THE ATLANTIC
Volume II : 1942-1943

EDITED BY BOB CARRUTHERS

Pen & Sword
MARITIME

This edition published in 2013 by
Pen & Sword Maritime
An imprint of
Pen & Sword Books Ltd
47 Church Street
Barnsley
South Yorkshire
S70 2AS

First published in Great Britain in 2011 in digital format by
Coda Books Ltd.

ISBN 978 1 78159 160 4

A CIP catalogue record for this book is
available from the British Library

Printed and bound by
CPI Group (UK) Ltd, Croydon, CR0 4YY

Pen & Sword Books Ltd incorporates the Imprints of Pen & Sword Aviation, Pen &
Sword Family History, Pen & Sword Maritime, Pen & Sword Military, Pen & Sword
Discovery, Pen & Sword Politics, Pen & Sword Atlas, Pen & Sword Archaeology,
Wharncliffe Local History, Wharncliffe True Crime, Wharncliffe Transport, Pen &
Sword Select, Pen & Sword Military Classics, Leo Cooper, The Praetorian Press,
Claymore Press, Remember When, Seaforth Publishing and Frontline Publishing

For a complete list of Pen & Sword titles please contact
PEN & SWORD BOOKS LIMITED
47 Church Street, Barnsley, South Yorkshire, S70 2AS, England
E-mail: enquiries@pen-and-sword.co.uk
Website: www.pen-and-sword.co.uk

CONTENTS

CHAPTER 4
JANUARY-JULY, 1942

CHAPTER 5
JULY - DECEMBER 1942

CHAPTER 6
JANUARY - MAY, 1943

APPENDIX

- C H A P T E R   4 -

JANUARY-JULY, 1942

AMERICA ENTERS THE WAR

164. Situation on 7th December, 1941

Already in July, 1941, the German Naval Staff appreciated that America was determined to do all in her power to help her Anglo-Saxon partner to win the war. After listing the various resources that the United States had already put at Great Britain's disposal, the appreciation concluded with these words: "Thus in effect the United States has become Great Britain's ally without declaring war, and in consequence the odds in the Atlantic have become weighted against us" (245)[1]. Since the summer of 1941 the tempo of this American aid had continuously increased, for her naval and air forces had extended their activity across the Atlantic, and several U-boats had been attacked by them. The U-boat Command no longer doubted that U.S. warships were helping to escort Atlantic convoys, or that U.S. merchant ships were calling at Freetown. All this constituted a severe handicap to the U-boat campaign. Attacks on darkened escort vessels were forbidden, and U.S. merchant ships were still immune from attack. U-boat operations in the Pan-American safety zone were forbidden, yet enemy merchant ships had made increasing use of that zone. The German Naval Staff's repeated representations, including a proposal in September, 1941, that action should be taken against American vessels carrying supplies to Britain, were rejected by Hitler on political grounds.

It was evident that the United States intended to gain time. A large part of the American people was averse to active participation in the war; international developments foreshadowed a U.S. war on two

---

1 Numbers in brackets refer to the author's notes and sources, which will be found at the end of this volume.

fronts - the Atlantic and the Pacific - for which their armed forces were inadequate. In the autumn of 1941 Roosevelt was therefore still at pains to avoid an open conflict with Germany (246). Even a number of incidents in the Atlantic had failed to move the Washington Government from the " short-of-war " policy. In October, 1941, the House of Representatives decided to arm U.S: merchant ships. In that month a German Naval Staff study on the prosecution of the war against Great Britain contained the following passage:

"… It is expected that America will repudiate Article 2 of the Neutrality Act which forbids neutral ships to enter belligerent ports north of 30 degrees North on the eastern side of the Atlantic, and north of 35 degrees North on the western side. She is also expected to renounce her declared War Zone, to enable her ships to call at British, Irish and Canadian ports. These steps follow naturally upon those already taken and are tantamount to direct participation in the war. The Naval Staff considers that delay in intensifying the war against merchant shipping is no longer justified, unless we are to dance to the tune of American politics. Our Eastern campaign can no longer be terminated this year. Our successes in this campaign have not deterred the United States from continuing support to Britain" (247).

In November U.S. legislation permitting American ships to use British ports became operative. But before the German Naval Staff could obtain the Supreme Command's approval for retaliatory measures, the wholly unexpected Japanese attack on Pearl Harbour precipitated full-scale intervention by the United States. In some respects this development was regarded with relief in naval circles. Referring to Pearl Harbour in his diary of 9th December, 1941, Dönitz wrote: " This event will have immediate consequences in the lifting of the restrictions hitherto imposed on U-boat warfare in the Atlantic."

165. New Requirements of U-Boat War

The new situation made it imperative to sink more shipping than ever before, since much of the American merchant marine and shipbuilding potential would now be at the disposal of Great Britain. If Germany and her Axis partners could sink more tonnage than the Allies could replace, then victory would be certain.

In June, 1941, our Naval Staff had estimated that if U-boats could achieve a monthly sinking rate of 800,000 tons, this would constitute a mortal blow to Great Britain, who could not hope for anything more than 100,000 tons per month of replacement construction from her own and American shipyards (248). But we estimated that during 1941 our boats had sunk ships at an average rate of only 230,000 tons[2] per month, or a quarter of the desired rate. F.O. U-boats hoped, however, that it would be possible to show greatly improved results in the coming year. His optimism was occasioned by the fact that we had started 1941 with a mere handful of 22 boats available for operations - a figure that showed no considerable increase until the year was half over. In the first half of 1941 there had never been more than six to nine boats in the North Atlantic at any one time; during the second half the number averaged from fourteen to seventeen (249). The following table is also revealing (250):

1941	New Boats Commissioned	New Boats Operational	Losses
Average for first half	13 per month	7.5 per month	2 per month
Average for last half	20.3 per month	9.5 per month	2 per month

The promise of many more operational boats in the early months of 1942, and of new and favourable areas in which to operate, seemed to warrant our hopes of much greater sinkings in the near future; but for reasons which will be given later, these hopes were to prove somewhat illusory.

166. Prospects in Western Atlantic

How could we achieve the greatest destruction of shipping in the shortest possible time with the smallest loss of U-boats ? Naturally we were attracted to the weakly defended points in the vast net-work of routes, where the volume of shipping made attacks worth

2 British records show that the avergae for 1941 was only 180,000 tons per month.

while. On the other hand, operations in remote areas, involving long outward and return passages, would have to show better results than those nearer home. American waters fulfilled this condition, for our intelligence showed that traffic between the American Atlantic ports and the departure points of the Atlantic convoys was very heavy, and most of these ships were sailing independently. Here then was an opportunity which no longer existed elsewhere. Our boats would operate close to the U.S. ports, where the local defences would be ineffective. After two and a half years' war experience our crews were at the peak of efficiency, while the American A/S and air forces would lack experience. The conditions seemed somewhat similar to those in British waters during the first year of the war.

The approximate distances from the Biscay coast to the chief U.S. Atlantic traffic centres are as follows:

	miles		*miles*
Sidney Roads	2,200	Trinidad	3,800
Halifax	2,400	Key West	4,000
New York	3,000	Aruba	4,000
Bermuda	3,000	Galveston	4,600
Cape Hatteras	3,400	Colon	4,600
Charleston	3,600		

According to our first estimate - which later proved short of the mark - fuel capacity permitted the Type VII (Medium) boats to operate in the Nova Scotia area, Type IXB (Large) as far as the Florida Strait and Type IXC (with larger tanks) as far as Trinidad. More distant areas such as the Panama Canal, New Orleans and the south shore of the Gulf of Mexico, could not be considered until March, 1942, when the first U-tankers were expected to be in service. As long as no replenishing facilities existed in the Atlantic, the Type IXC U-boat was the most suited to American waters.

As single ship traffic could be expected along the entire American seaboard the best results would be obtained by spreading our boats. But in covering these large areas the distance between boats had to be carefully considered. If too close, a diversion or suspension of shipping would leave them without targets ; if too far apart, the shipping might never be located. After an attack at one place the enemy would have to be kept guessing as to where the boats would strike next. We believed that the Americans would anticipate the U-boats' arrival by introducing traffic control and the convoy system, and by quickly expanding their A/S forces. We should therefore strike soon and hard before their measures had been fully developed.

167. Delays due to Mediterranean Commitments

Before describing the first action off the American coast, it is necessary to explain the delays which marked the commencement of these operations. The day after Pearl Harbour Dönitz sought the approval of the Naval Staff to dispatch twelve large U-boats (Type IX) for the initial strike off the U.S. coast. Six of these were already somewhere between the Western Approaches and Gibraltar, heading for the Mediterranean. Their prospects of sinkings would be much greater if they were diverted to America. But the Naval Staff, while appreciating this, was slow to abandon the previously planned support for the Mediterranean operations, and conceded only that these six boats should assemble instead near the Azores, as Group Seydlitz. They were eventually ordered westward on 2nd January, 1942, when it was also decided that only six of the Atlantic U-boats were to be allocated to Mediterranean tasks. Of these, three were to be sent into the Mediterranean to replace losses, while the other three would patrol between the Azores and Gibraltar.

168. End of Mediterranean Concentration

These three boats west of Gibraltar were ordered to patrol towards the Strait. Their purpose was to conceal the withdrawal of the remainder, so that the enemy should be induced to maintain his extensive A/S organisation in those waters. On 11th January they were ordered to attack HG 78, whose anticipated sailing from Gibraltar was known through agents. The convoy was shadowed for four days with the help of air reconnaissance, but the three U-boats were inadequate for the task. One was destroyed by the A/S screen.

Meanwhile the three boats detailed as replacements for the Mediterranean had left their base and were waiting off the coast of Spain for the beginning of the new-moon period before breaking through the Gibraltar Strait. Two succeeded in their first attempt, but the third, U.572, commanded by Lt.-Commander Hirsacker, finding the defences too strong, gave up after the second attempt, and remained west of the Strait.

On 16th January U.402, a relief boat for the Gibraltar group encountered a southbound convoy west of the Bay of Biscay, and torpedoed the troop transport *Llangibby* Castle. The damaged vessel put into Horta in the Azores. Timely intelligence of her arrival and expected date of departure enabled U.402 to be ready for a further attack on leaving territorial waters. The *Llangibby* Castle sailed on 2nd February escorted by two destroyers and a corvette. For three days U.402 tried to attack but the escort always repelled her. U.581, also in the vicinity, made one attempt which was also beaten off, and was sunk by depth-charges close to Pico Island. One of her officers survived by swimming ashore and later reached Germany. He provided details of the depth-charge damage, which resulted in modifications to the glands in the pressure hull of this type of U-boat.

By the beginning of February it was obvious that much better results could be achieved in the Western Atlantic than by hanging about near Gibraltar. It was therefore decided to send no further boats in support of the Mediterranean area.

JANUARY - MARCH, 1942
FIRST THRUST TO U.S. COAST
AND CARIBBEAN

169. Operation *Paukenschlag*

With practically all the Atlantic boats again at his disposal, Dönitz on 2nd January ordered those of Group Seydlitz having sufficient fuel to the Newfoundland Bank. Boats en route from Germany to the Azores and those leaving Biscay bases were also diverted westward. The plan was to occupy the North American coastal area with those large boats which had been at sea since mid-December, and with further large boats when available. Two more were destined for Trinidad and two for Aruba. All Type VII boats based on the Biscay coast were to move to the south of Newfoundland where Britain's main supply line was most dense and not too strongly protected. It will be recalled that there had been a discussion at Hitler's Headquarters in the autumn of 1941 about America entering the war (251). Experience having shown the great effectiveness of the sudden appearance of U-boats in new areas, Dönitz had insisted that he should be given ample warning of such an eventuality. If only he could have his boats ready off the U.S. coast at the outbreak of war, he would be able to deliver a tremendous and sudden blow - *einen kräftigen Paukenschlag*. This latter word was in fact used as a cover name for the first operation in American waters. That it could not be launched until five weeks after the two countries were at war shows that Pearl Harbour took Germany completely by surprise.

Operation *Paukenschlag* was carried out by five boats disposed between the St. Lawrence and Cape Hatteras which were free to move southward should weather or traffic conditions render this necessary. As a simultaneous strike by all five promised the best results, they were instructed to move unobserved from the Newfoundland Bank to the U.S. coast. Their progress westward was plotted at U-boat headquarters, and it was not until 13th January that they were ordered to launch the attack. The object was to sink vessels over 10,000 tons. Despite the delayed start and the small number of attackers, results were excellent. Traffic between New York and Cape Hatteras was so dense that it was impossible to seize all the opportunities.[3] The

---

3 There were each day between 120 and 130 ships requiring protection within the boundaries of the U.S. Eastern Sea Frontier. (S. E. Morison, *History of United States Naval Operations in World War II*, Volume I, *The Battle of the Atlantic*, p. 255.) In subsequent footnotes this book will be referred to as "Morison p..."

U-boat Command realised the effectiveness of the attack from the numerous intercepted SSS and SOS calls, and at once decided to assemble every available large boat in this rewarding area. U.103, 106 and 107 arrived in the vicinity of Chesapeake Bay before the first boats had to return, and thus the continued occupation of the coast between New York and Cape Hatteras was temporarily assured. Two medium boats, which refuelled from a larger boat, were added to the force, so that during February four or five boats were always in the area.

170. Medium Boats off Newfoundland

The medium boats worked independently of Operation *Paukenschlag*. They comprised seven Type VIICs, of which three had been in, and the remainder bound for, the Azores area. Re-routed on 2nd January, as described in the previous section, they arrived off Newfoundland between the 7th and 9th. To obtain an idea of the traffic situation they were disposed between the south coast of the island and latitude 43° North, in contiguous attack areas. This disposition proved effective, as most of them found targets in single vessels and small, weakly escorted convoys near the coast. But the intense cold and the heavy ground swell on the Newfoundland Bank, caused considerable discomfort. The increased proportion of misses due to fog, snowstorms and heavy seas, and the torpedo failures adversely affected results, each boat sinking not more than two or three ships. The enemy took counter-measures in this area much more speedily than off the American coast. Probably bad weather prevented stronger air patrols, without which the surface A/S forces were unable to drive the U-boats from the Newfoundland Bank. Suspicion was aroused on several occasions by what appeared to be a cable-layer, apparently invulnerable to torpedo attack. The strange behaviour of this vessel and her escort caused the Commanding Officers to suspect a trap (252). Most of the sinkings occurred close to the coast at Cape Race, so that from 22nd January onwards no rigid dispositions were ordered, Commanding Officers being free to choose their own areas. Towards the end of January the intense cold created difficulties through the freezing up of the diving mechanism, and it was left to the Commanding Officers to decide whether to return to base or move further south.

171. The Boats move West

At the end of January there was in fact a gradual movement into the area south of Halifax, which in February became the battle ground of the medium boats. Again operations were affected by the cold and rough weather. Frozen exhaust valves sometimes imperiled crash diving, as can be seen by the following extract from the log of U.130. Having made two surface attacks on a ship off Cape Breton in the early hours of 18th January, with ice forming on his upper deck, the Commanding Officer was turning to make a third attack when he saw an American destroyer coming towards him at high speed.

"… By putting one engine full ahead and the other full astern I manage to evade her and she misses me by about 10 metres. I order "Crash dive !" As I enter the conning tower a second destroyer appears astern of the steamship. About eight tons of water enter the boat through the frozen diesel exhaust valves, causing us to hit bottom. Here I remain bumping uncomfortably on the rocks. It is better to lie here for a while with everything stopped. There is no sign from the destroyer ; presumably her depth-charge dropping gear has frozen up. I leave the bottom at 0210 and continue submerged…"

Freezing up could only be avoided by diving every two or three hours. Much trouble was caused in this area by fog, which restricted opportunities of attack and forced the boats to the West. They began to arrive in the New York area at the beginning of March, and the middle of that month saw them off Cape Hatteras. This move proved profitable, for targets were plentiful and the boats were able to expend all their torpedoes. The formerly occupied areas on the Newfoundland Bank and south of Nova Scotia were still used by boats on passage to and from the American coast, and by those which, because of defects or inadequate fuel were unable to make the American coast.

It was considered that the medium (Type VII) U-boats had sufficient endurance to reach the American coast, but no thorough tests had ever been made. The operation off that coast now showed that the endurance exceeded our expectations. This increased range was achieved partly through the initiative of the crews and flotilla staffs. Fuel was put in drinking and washing water tanks, trimming tanks, and even compensating tanks. While appreciating the efforts of those concerned, F.O. U-boats had to forbid the use of compensating tanks for fuel. Though the contents would be expended early on the outward passage, there was a danger that the oil trace from these tanks would reveal the track of an escaping U-boat.

At sea every endeavour was made to save fuel. Lengthy trials were carried out with different combinations of diesel and diesel-electric drive at various engine speeds, the details of which were reported to Headquarters. Great circle sailing was used ; unfavourable tidal streams and bad weather fronts were avoided ; gales were avoided by passing under them submerged, with motors at about half speed, and surfacing only to recharge batteries. In the medium boats these expedients saved about twenty tons of fuel, which enabled them to remain in the remote operational area for two to three weeks.

Endurance was achieved at the expense of comfort, for every compartment was filled with additional spares, stores and provisions. In the early weeks of a sortie there was no seating accommodation for the crew in the bow or stern compartments, and it was almost impossible to stand upright. Messes and bunks were stacked with cases, leaving only a narrow gangway. Loading capacity was limited by the quantity of compensating water carried. This was normally nine tons ; but on these long-range operations it was often reduced to less than half that amount.

172. Initial Weakness of U.S. Counter-measures

New York was no further from the U-boat bases than Freetown, and could be reached by U-boats at economical speed in about three weeks. The U.S. Navy might therefore have expected the first attacks in American coastal waters at the beginning of January, 1942.

We thought they would use the period of grace to institute traffic control and organise their A/S defences, for our operations off the American coast did not begin until 13th January - five weeks after war had been declared - but the results in the first weeks surpassed our best expectations. The inadequacy of the initial U.S. defence organisation is vividly shown by the log of U.123, commanded by Lt.-Commander Hardegen, which was operating off Cape Hatteras on the night of 18th-19th January. On 18th January she had lain submerged, and surfaced at 0046 (G.M.T.) on the 19th, making for a position close to Cape Hatteras in 7 to 8 metres of water. At 0304 the first target, a ship of 4,000 tons, was torpedoed and sunk off the Wimble Shoal. Three further ships were sighted but were soon out of range, and at 0542 a small coaster was not worth attacking. The channel was well marked by light buoys, which were left to port by all ships proceeding in either direction. By hugging the line of buoys the U-boat encountered more targets than she could engage. Torpedo control was simplified by having to estimate only the speed of the targets. At 0930, after sinking a vessel of about 4,000 tons, several lights were sighted astern, which proved to be a string of five merchant ships. The leading one, S.S. Malay, a tanker of 8,207 tons, was engaged by gunfire and left burning. The U-boat then turned her attention to a 6,000-ton ship, which however was steaming at about 15 knots, and could not be overtaken. Another ship approached from the opposite direction, but again U.123 failed to come within range. It was now nearly dawn, and the U-boat commander, with only two torpedoes left, was wondering if he could get in another shot before daylight, when the Malay reported by radio that she had been attacked, and later that the fire on board had been extinguished so that she was able to proceed. The U-boat intercepted this intelligence, and decided to sink her by torpedo. At 1200, while making for the Malay's estimated position, a freighter of about 5,000 tons was encountered, torpedoed and sunk. Shortly afterwards two vessels were sighted hove to. One of these, the Malay, got under way and headed towards Norfolk. The other, the City of Delhi, 7,443 tons, was hoisting a boat. U.123 used her last remaining torpedo to sink the tanker. Lt.-Commander Hardegen concluded:

"... Our operation has been most successful: eight ships, including three tankers, totalling 53,860 tons, within 12 hours. It is a pity there were not a couple of large U-minelayers with me the other night off New York, or ten to twenty U-boats here last night, instead of one. I am sure all would have found ample targets. Altogether I saw about twenty steamships, some undarkened ; also a few small tramp steamers, all hugging the coast. Buoys and beacons in the area had dimmed lights which however were visible up to two or three miles."

The extensive shallow U.S. coastal waters were not regarded with favour by our boats, which for safety preferred to have at least 100 metres of water under their keels in case of pursuit. They would certainly not have operated, as they did, in 40 metres or less if the local A/S measures had been in any way effective. But shipping continued to approach Cape Hatteras direct from the South Atlantic, despite reported U-boats. Yet this traffic could have been diverted to more southerly landfalls, such as Cape Canaveral or Cape Fear, which were still unmolested by us. No effective action was taken against U-boats whose positions were known through the SOS calls of torpedoed ships, and succeeding and unprotected victims would pass through the same waters.

Apart from occasional temporary stoppages of traffic, it was more than two months before appropriate A/S measures were instituted.[4] In these early weeks the conduct of many merchant ship captains revealed complete ignorance of the U-boats' methods. Their careless use of radio is shown by Lt.-Commander Hardegen's report in March, 1942, during his second operation in U.S. waters:

"... A most important contribution to the success of this and the previous operation was made by the enemy's unrestricted use of the

---

4 It was not until 1st April, 1942, that a partial convoy system was inaugurated, whereby ships were moved from anchorage to anchorage escorted by such local craft as were available in the various districts controlled by the U.S. Commander, Eastern Sea Frontier (Morison, p.254).

600 metre band. Emergency calls were intercepted every day, often giving the position, course and speed of the ship. By plotting these, a good idea of the traffic routes could be obtained, so that targets could be easily found."

At U-boat headquarters also these intercepts were used to great advantage, and they enabled us to obtain a picture of the comparative ineffectiveness of the American A/S forces. The U.S. air patrols were strong at the focal points of Halifax, New York and Cape Hatteras. But the air crews were not as experienced in attack as those of the British A/S aircraft, and this gave the U-boat crews confidence to undertake actions which would have been impossible off the English coast even in 1939. The combined efforts of the U.S. sea and air defences failed to drive the attackers from the coastal waters. During daylight the U-boats lay only a few miles from shore, bottomed in depths of 50 to 150 metres. At dusk they proceeded landward submerged, and surfaced on the shipping routes after dark. Generally they had not long to wait for their first victim to appear, and they had no difficulty in finding targets for all their torpedoes.

173. Convoy Operations on Passage to U.S. Coast

The Atlantic convoys encountered on passage to the American coast were fewer than anticipated. On two occasions only were they attacked by more than two boats. The first was on 31st January when U.82 sighted two troop transports escorted by two destroyers 60 miles southeast of Sable Island, and sank the British destroyer Belmont. In an endeavour to get in her two remaining torpedoes U.82 pursued the convoy for three days, during which time she was joined by three other boats. But the convoy was steaming at 14 knots and could not be overtaken.

"… This illustrates the difficulty of attacking fast convoys. In such cases it is always questionable whether the remote chance of a successful attack justifies the large fuel consumption involved…" (253).

A successful major convoy operation took place at the end of February. U.155, on her way to the American coast, sighted ONS 67

600 miles northeast of Cape Race. Another U-boat was a little to the southward, and four more, outward-bound from the Biscay bases, were 200 or 300 miles further south. U.155 was ordered to transmit shadowing reports every four hours until the nearest boat arrived. During a three day chase the U-boats claimed seven ships totalling 54,000 tons sunk, and four totalling 23,000 tons damaged. British figures confirm the sinking of eight ships and damage to another. Six large tankers were among the casualties.

As the boats were approaching the Newfoundland Bank the mysterious vessel with the cable-laying bow was again sighted. U.587 scored a hit without any visible result, and it was surmised that she was protected by torpedo nets. A report from another boat strengthened this belief. That the enemy had introduced something new was confirmed when two tankers in a convoy were observed to be fitted with protective nets.[5] All U-boat commanders were ordered to look out for such devices and to report them forthwith. At the same time the Torpedo Development Organisation was ordered to devise counter-measures.

174. First group Operation in the Caribbean

After the initial dispositions for Operation *Paukenschlag*, it was intended to send all subsequent large (Type IX) boats to the Caribbean. In order to form a " wave " as soon as possible, several of this type leaving German bases in January were ordered to Lorient to be equipped for operations in the tropics. There was little fresh intelligence on the traffic and defence situation in the Caribbean. Reports from neutral sources showed that in some ports booms had been rigged, and sea and air patrols instituted. In the absence of up-to-date intelligence, pre-war data had to suffice. It was known that Port of Spain was an increasingly important fuelling station ; this

5 This refers to A.N.D. (Admiralty Net Defence), introduced in January, 1942, for the protection of freighters and tankers. It consisted of wire nets supported by booms stepped inboard ; the nets being brailed on the curtain principle. The first ship to receive this equipment was the S.S. *Empire Celt*, a tanker, which, with streamed nets, was torpedoed on 24th February, 1942, in position 43° 50' N., 43° 38' W. She subsequently sank. Altogether 732 freighters and 36 tankers were equipped with A.N.D. during the war, but there is no Admiralty record of a cable-laying vessel having been so fitted.

area together with Curacao and Aruba seemed to offer the greatest promise.

The Caribbean operation (cover name *Westindien*) was fixed for the new-moon period of February, 1942, by which time five boats (Group Neuland) could be in position. The attack was to commence simultaneously with one U-boat each at Aruba, Curacao and the northwest coast of the Paranagua peninsula, and with two boats off Trinidad. The boats sent a short signal on passing the fortieth meridian, reporting the quantity of fuel remaining. These reports were of such importance to the timing of the intended surprise attack that it was decided to accept the risk of enemy D/F. The attack was ordered to commence on the morning of 16th February. In view of the favourable navigational conditions at Aruba and Curacao it was hoped also to bombard the oil installations at these places, but only if the torpedo attack on shipping had met with initial success. If no ships were encountered the bombardment was to be deferred until the evening.

All five boats arrived in time to start operations according to plan. U.156, after sinking two tankers off Aruba, attempted a night bombardment; but failure to remove the tampeon caused a premature, which split the gun and seriously injured an officer and a rating, who were landed at Martinique. Later the gun was repaired, and used to sink two ships. U.502 was moved from the Paranagua peninsula to Aruba, and with U.67 (which had been operating off Curacao) attempted to bombard the shore installations; but the harbours had meanwhile been blacked out, and local patrol vessels frustrated the attempt.

Operations were at once concentrated against tankers, of which a considerable number - chiefly small tenders - was sunk in the first two days. Enemy reaction was quicker here than off the American coast; traffic was suspended for a time, and shipping was instructed to avoid certain areas and to pass others at given times. But these measures had little effect during the new-moon period, when the U-boats could move about freely at night. Enemy instructions to shipping, made in plain language, were intercepted by our boats; those in cypher were intercepted by our Y Stations. They took a few days to unravel, and were then transmitted to the U-boats.

The defences developed as anticipated. Air patrols, though inexperienced, were from the very outset so strong and persistent that when the first full-moon period occurred it was no longer possible to operate continuously off the principal ports. Our original dispositions were not long maintained. If the boats were tied to certain limited areas, temporary closing of a port would have left them without targets. Hence after remaining in one place for a week, they were allowed to change their location if necessary. They continued to operate principally in the Caribbean, with the exception of U.129 which made a successful sweep southwest along the coast of Guiana. An attempt to find targets off the bauxite ports, Georgetown and Paramaribo, failed owing to the air patrols and the shallow coastal waters. Though traffic was often suspended and diverted, all boats were able to expend their torpedoes and ammunition in a reasonably short time.

The effect of these early operations was enhanced by the bold actions of Lt.-Commander Achilles, commanding U.161, who penetrated into the harbours of Port of Spain and Port Castries on the nights of 17th February and 9th March respectively. The entrance to the roadstead of Port of Spain was shallow, narrow and well protected, and the attack called for a high degree of courage and skill.

The only available relief boat, U.126, arrived a fortnight after the commencement of the operation, being stationed between the Windward Passage and the Old Bahama Channel. In 14 days she sank nine ships, returning home simultaneously with the first wave. No further Type IXC boats were available to relieve the first wave as had been intended. Admiral Raeder complained of the resulting interruption of operations, and ordered that the Caribbean should be occupied continuously. But this could only have been done by keeping back boats of the first wave, which would have resulted in alternate periods of idleness and congestion at the bases (254). This problem was eventually solved by the appearance in April, 1942, of the first U-tankers - a most important development which enabled U-boats of all types greatly to prolong their operations in distant areas.

175. Investigation off Freetown

Up to the summer of 1941 the bulk of British shipping to and from South Africa and South America had beea routed via Freetown, but thereafter it was diverted west into the Pan-American safety zone, where it was safe from U-boat attack. After our abortive operation in October, 1941, no further U-boats had been sent to the Freetown area. With America's entry into the war the safety zone no longer afforded protection, but became rather more dangerous than Freetown, so that a shift back of at least some of the traffic to the African coast was to be expected. In mid-February, 1942, our Radio Intelligence seemed to confirm this eventuality, and U.68 and 505 (Type IXC) were therefore sent to reconnoitre off Freetown (255). They arrived at the beginning of March, having encountered no shipping to the west of Sierra Leone. But to the south and southeast of Freetown traffic was considerable, though spasmodic. U.68 happened to meet such traffic off Cape Palmas, and sank seven ships, while U.505 sank four. These results were better than those achieved in the previous autumn. But it was important to exploit the even better conditions in the American hemisphere while they lasted, and no further U-boats were sent to West Africa, which could always receive our renewed attention at a later date.

THE NORWAY SCARE

176. Medium Boats in the Atlantic

The original plan of operations in the Western Hemisphere envisaged using mainly the Type IXC U-boat, reinforced by Type VIIC from the Biscay bases. To send the latter type all that way from German bases in the winter months would have left them with little fuel. So those becoming available in January were sent to the North Atlantic. As the precise area could not be decided, they were first assembled west of the Hebrides, where shipping had recently been frequent. Four boats were stationed here from 15th January. For a brief period on the 18th they formed a patrol line 40 miles east of the Outer Bailey Bank in an attempt to intercept 10 transports, which, according to radio intercepts decrypted on the 16th, were proceeding from Reykjavik to England. This and other reports indicated that the Allies were making increasing use of Reykjavik; but because of the seasonal gales and the long arctic nights it was decided that one boat only should watch that area.

Between 18th and 21st January another " wave " of medium boats arrived in the Atlantic from Germany. They assembled west of Rockall to commence a southwesterly sweep across the Atlantic convoy routes. Now however the first reports were reaching us of the exceptional opportunities off the U.S. coast, so the sweep was abandoned and the boats recalled to Western France for a short overhaul before leaving for American waters. Meanwhile an order was suddenly received from the Naval Staff that eight boats were to be sent forthwith to the Iceland-Faroes-Scotland area for the protection of Norway. Five of the boats that had been recalled to Western France were therefore instructed to disregard the previous order and return to the North via Iceland (256).

177. Hitler requires U-Boats for Defence of Norway

The idea of employing U-boats in the defence of Norway was not new. A proposal by Naval Group Command North that for this purpose some boats should be stationed permanently between Bergen and Stadtlandet had been turned down by the Naval Staff on 27th December, 1941. This time however the demand came from a higher quarter. On 22nd January, 1942, Admiral Fricke, the Deputy Chief of Naval Staff, had attended a meeting at which Hitler had expressed acute fears of an Allied attack on Norway. The Führer had suddenly decided that "the outcome of the war would be decided in Norway, and for its defence every available surface craft and U-boat would be needed" (257). But before the necessary orders could be issued he had modified his views. Reference to this is found in a marginal comment in the Naval Staff Diary of 23rd January, 1942:

"… Captain Puttkammer (Naval Aide to Hitler) telephoned this afternoon that the Führer had noted with satisfaction the mounting sinkings in American waters. After enquiring about the number of U-boats engaged, he said that he wanted these operations to continue. This is in significant contrast to his instructions - given only yesterday - about defending Norway" (258).

The Naval Staff made it clear that with the boats available, both commitments could not be fully met.

On 25th January, after the return of Fricke from Hitler's headquarters, the Naval Staff ordered eight boats to be stationed in the Iceland-Faroes-Scotland area. The final Norway defence plan early in February envisaged a total of 20 medium boats, of which eight were to be stationed in the Iceland-Faroes-Scotland area, six in Northern waters, two in Narvik or Tromso, two in Trondheim and two in Bergen. In addition four captured Dutch U-boats were assigned to the transport of war supplies to Norway.

178. Norway Requirements prejudice Atlantic War

Excellent results were attainable in the American theatre, but the provision of 20 boats for the defence of Norway would seriously prejudice this effort. The Naval Staff therefore suggested that a part of the operational boats based on Norway should be replaced by training boats from the Baltic, where the ice conditions were interfering with training. The U-boat Command regarded this transfer as impracticable because off Norway there were no areas sufficiently large or safe for tactical training and convoy attack exercises, while the fjords were unsuitable for torpedo firing practice. Moreover, the northern latitude permitted only day firing in summer and night firing in winter. The scheme was therefore dropped.

The Naval Staff wanted the dispositions for the defence of

Norway to be completed by 15th February, but owing to the freezing up of the Baltic dockyards only six boats became ready in February, and 10 in March, which was just sufficient to meet this requirement. Meanwhile nofurther boats were going to the Atlantic, and Dönitz, who refused to believe that the Allies had any intention of landing in Norway, was seriously perturbed at this misdirection of the U-boat campaign.

"… The Allied problem is chiefly one of shipping and escort vessels. The more ships that are sunk, and the more protection the enemy is obliged to provide for his vital supplies from across the Atlantic, the less he will be able to spare for a landing (in Norway) which, without adequate supplies would be foredoomed to failure…" (259).

But the Naval Staff was adamant:

"… There can be no doubt that every ton of enemy shipping sunk diminishes the enemy's potential for operations overseas, but the Naval Staff considers that despite losses, the enemy still has sufficient ships for action against Norway. The transportation of 100,000 troops with full equipment would require about 1,250,000 tons of shipping space, and 30,000 to 50,000 tons a month would be needed to keep these troops supplied. The enemy mercantile marine is already fully occupied with civil and military commitments, so that additional demands could only be met by diverting shipping from other tasks. However, if the enemy really wishes to land in Norway, he will probably accept a temporary diminution of non-military imports. If the additional tonnage thus made available is not used for other purposes, such as the reinforcement of the Middle East, then the danger of an attack on Norway persists, despite the recent heavy losses in American waters" (260).

The Naval Staff evidently saw no reason to oppose Hitler's continued obsession about Norway.[6]

---

6 Though there had been British raids at Vaagso and the Lofoten Islands between 26th and 29th December, 1941, Hitler's apprehensions over a possible British landing in Norway were premature. But by April, 1942, they had some foundation. In that month Mr. Churchill instructed the Chiefs of Staff to examine the prospects of a landing in North Norway, for he believed that this would not only relieve the serious danger to convoys bound for North Russia, but provide an opportunity for dislodging the Germans from the north. In

179. Unremunerative Activity between Iceland and North Channel

Of the boats in the Iceland-Faroes-Scotland area on 25th January, one was stationed off Reykjavik and three off Seydis Fjord (east coast of Iceland) in an attempt to locate a suspected northern convoy assembly area. It was observed that the inner anchorage at Seydis Fjord was patrolled, and protected by searchlight and net barrages. But no shipping activity was discovered, and the boats were withdrawn. Their task was defined by the Naval Staff on 10th February:

"… They are to operate in the area between the enemy bases in northern Scotland, northern Ireland and Iceland, and on the probable routes from these bases to northern Norway. They will give early warning of the approach of enemy transports, and inflict damage on the forces engaged in these operations. They will keep this area under constant observation…" (261).

If a landing appeared imminent the boats would be subordinated to Naval Group Command North.

The boats patrolled chiefly to the northwest of the Hebrides, making occasional sweeps to the east coast of Iceland, also into the Atlantic for weather reporting in connection with the movements of the German surface forces. This latter duty, which took them towards the North Channel, produced a number of minor convoy attacks. The boats were drawn away from their allotted areas through these attacks on ON and ONS convoys[7], but the Naval Staff raised no objections. On the chance sighting of a convoy all boats within range, including those on outward passage, were ordered to attack, but on no occasion were more than four involved. An attack by three boats on ONS 63 between 4th and 7th February when 300 miles west of the North Channel resulted in the sinking of the British corvette *Arbutus*. From 10th to 12th February SC 67, which was first sighted 500 miles to the west of the North Channel, was attacked by two

September, 1942, he still had the strongest political and strategic reasons for wanting to seize North Norway, but the Chiefs of Staff considered the scheme impracticable. (See Churchill's *Second World War*, Volume IV, pp. 288-91, 312-16, 510.)

7 For designation of Allied convoys, see page 118.

boats, which sank the corvette *Spikenard* and a motor ship of 4,000 tons. HX 175 was attacked by four boats between the 22nd and 24th when 800 miles westward of the North Channel. In this attack U.154 missed with 14 torpedoes, although they were well aimed. On return to base it was discovered that her torpedo control system was badly out of adjustment. A more experienced commander would have been quick to detect this defect, and would have resorted to firing by direct observation, with a reasonable chance of hitting. Between 18th and 20th March four boats took part in an operation against ONS 76,200 miles westward of the North Channel, but the sighting boat was unable to keep touch long enough for the others to close her.

For reasons already stated, reinforcements from Germany were not available during February and only four to five boats were in the operational area. At the end of the month, after repeated injunctions from the Naval Staff, six more boats arrived from French bases. These included U.553, 569, 701 and 753, commanded by well-tried officers, who had been earmarked for American waters in March. Their sole achievement in this unremunerative northern area was the sinking of one small freighter and three patrol boats off Seydis Fjord.

The emergency order placing the boats under the control of Naval Group Command North came into force for the first time on 11th March, 1942. This was occasioned by the sighting, on the 10th, of British heavy units northeast of the Faroes, and also because U-boats were needed to cover the movements of the Tirpitz. Four boats only were transferred under this order and disposed, as Group York, between the Shetlands and Faroes on the probable return route of the British forces. They waited here in vain for fourteen days, and on 26th March were ordered back to Western France.

180. New Tasks in Northern Waters

During February, as the periods of daylight lengthened, the danger of an enemy landing in Norway was regarded at Hitler's headquarters as having decreased, and it was realised that the use of U-boats for purely defensive purposes was not only wasteful, but might have been deliberately encouraged by the enemy. The disposition west of the Hebrides served no useful purpose, neither was the occupation of the area east of Iceland justified. If the U-boats were to contribute effectively to the protection of Northern Norway and to assist our military operations, they should be used against enemy shipping. In the Arctic, between North Cape and Bear Island, for instance, conditions were excellent for attacking supplies to North Russia. Accordingly, on 12th March, 1942, the policy was altered, and the Naval Staff ordered four boats from the Hebrides area to be placed under the command of F.O. Northern Waters for attacking the northern convoys and the shipping off Murmansk and Archangel. The other four boats were placed under Group North for intercepting shipping in the waters bounded by Jan Mayen, the east of Iceland and northern Scotland (262). These new tasks were to commence on conclusion of the operation begun on 11th March by Group York. The boats coming from Western France were not equipped for the Arctic, having neither the requisite charts nor winter gear. Dönitz therefore suggested that the transfer should be postponed until they could be relieved by new and suitably equipped boats from Germany. The change occurred on 26th March when F.O. Northern Waters took over control of operations in those waters and the administration of U-boat bases in Norway, Dönitz remaining responsible only for providing the requisite numbers - that is, about 20 boats.

MARCH AND APRIL, 1942
CLIMAX OF THE AMERICAN
COASTAL BATTLE

181. Effectiveness of Attacks

The first two months of operations off the American coast and in the Caribbean had shown that even the medium boats could give an excellent account of themselves in those waters. It was now a matter of urgency to fling every available large and medium boat into the battle before the enemy could organise his counter-measures.

But there were few boats available at this period. Six Type VIIs originally due in the Caribbean at the beginning of the new-moon period between 10th and 15th March, had been diverted, as we have seen, to Northern Waters in the latter half of February. From mid-March until 20th April there were only six to eight off the American coast; yet sinkings in March were bigger than ever, partly because of individual achievements by such " Aces " as Hardegen (U.123) who sank no less than eleven ships, Mohr (U.124) nine ships ; Topp (U.552), Miizelburg (U.203) and Lassen (U.160), all of whom sank five to six ships. Their quest for the best targets started off New York and ended at Cape Hatteras. During four weeks the waters between Cape Hatteras and Cape Fear, frequented by shipping at night, were the scene of numerous attacks by both gun and torpedo. U.123 continued southwest along the shipping route, sinking several tankers between Savannah and St. Augustine in depths from 10 to 20 metres. Occasional attacks were made at considerable risk in only 8 to 10 metres of water.

Another U-boat concentration was established 300 miles east of Cape Hatteras. On her way there, U.105 in seeking better weather, had taken a route 500 miles south of the great circle, but owing to excessive battery temperatures she could only use her diesel-electric drive for short periods, and had to weather a strong westerly gale on the surface. Unable to reach Cape Hatteras through shortage of fuel, she occupied a position 300 miles to the eastward, where she found the junction of three busy routes - from the northeast, southeast and northwest. This area proved very profitable up to 20th April, being occupied by various boats during the full-moon period.

182. U.S. Defences Improve

At times as many as seven boats operated off Cape Hatteras. There was no rigid control by Headquarters, who relied on the commanders to find the best area from New York southwards. From the U-boats' reports it was clear that good results were being achieved, but also that the American A/S organisation was warming up to its task. Shipping still used the Cape Hatteras area during the day, but now passed either singly or in bunches and at irregular intervals. As the U-boats ventured close to the coast at night, the partially marked inshore channel, which was navigable by steamships, became as dangerous as the remaining area. The enemy realising this, varied his routes. For example, if one bunch of ships proceeded along the 20 metre line, the next would appear on the 60, 80 or 200 metre line. Though these measures resulted in fewer opportunities for attack, they could never be as effective as the full adoption of controlled convoys. After two months' war experience, the captains of merchant ships were becoming familiar with the U-boat's tactics, and sometimes fired on their attackers. The log of U.123 for 26th March records one such engagement with the American steamship Carolyn, a suspected " Q " ship, 270 miles from Cape Hatteras. This vessel was sighted at 2000 (G.M.T.) and at midnight U.123 attacked on the surface, firing one torpedo which hit under the bridge. The Carolyn opened fire with gun and machine guns, and attacked with depth-charges. The U-boat was badly shaken, one midshipman being killed by a machine gun bullet, and hauled out of range. At 0429 she returned for a submerged attack. One torpedo was fired, which hit the Carolyn in the engine room. When U.123 surfaced at 0527, the vessel was in a sinking condition and the crew had taken to the boats. Twenty minutes later she blew up.

The enemy was tackling the problem of eliminating the U-boats from the shallow waters and was reinforcing his coastal defence forces. Besides regular patrols by destroyers, coastguard cutters and small patrol vessels, close escort was now provided for shipping passing through the dangerous areas. The fighting power of the A/S vessels was still low. They were partly without Asdic and Radar, and all lacked experience. The high speed of their exploratory sweeps precluded the effective use of their location gear, and sometimes after obtaining contact they went on without attacking. Their first kill was made on 14th April, when U.85 was sunk east of Cape Hatteras; but their successes were few because attacks in shallow water were not pressed home. Many of the enemy's A/S measures bore the stamp of improvisation. Small calibre guns were mounted in very small fishing boats and yachts - a measure that seemed of no practical value.[8] The first airships were appearing, and also a host of land planes little suited to A/S work, which seemed to be under training. This activity hardly impeded U-boat operations, but it extended the enemy's reconnaissance and facilitated his traffic control.

183. Inshore Operations limited to New-moon Periods

U-boats usually needed two to four hours on the surface to recharge their batteries. But with air patrols extending their activities this recharging at night became dangerous during the period from nine days before until five days after full moon. Recharging had to be done even further from the coast. This had also been the problem for our boats off Gibraltar and Freetown in 1940 and 1941.

From April, 1942, we found it unsafe to attack near the American coast except during the new moon periods, and this factor also influenced the timing of further operations in the Panama zone, off the Brazilian coast, and at Capetown.

184. Anxiety about British A/S Measures

While we could be well pleased with results in American waters, there was some anxiety about the cause of the loss of several U-boats nearer home in the early months of 1942. U.82 on 6th February, U.587 on 26th March and U.252 on 15th April had all been lost while on their way home. Each had encountered a small and apparently weakly escorted convoy in the Bay of Biscay. Each had made shadowing reports for a short period, but never any further signals. As the reported convoys did not tally with any Gibraltar or WS convoys plotted by Headquarters, we began to suspect that these were special "Q" convoys or hunter-killer groups. On 19th April it was therefore decided that U-boats leaving the Biscay for American waters were to avoid attacking convoys met between 10 and 15 degrees W. and 43 and 50 degrees N., but were to lie off and report anything peculiar (263). The order remained in force for several

8 The early and admittedly inadequate A/S measures taken by the United States are described in Morison, Chapter X.

months, for we did not wish to hazard the boats on their way to the remunerative American zone. The mystery was not cleared up.[9] We knew that British air patrols in the Bay of Biscay had increased, but we did not then suspect that these were already using A.S.V. Radar to locate our boats.

APRIL AND MAY, 1942
PROBLEMS IN THE WEST ATLANTIC

185. Radio Control of U-Boats

The ensuing months were characterised by a progressive strengthening of the American A/S organisation, culminating in the introduction of the convoy system. It was necessary to counter these measures step by step, and U-boat tactics and dispositions were adjusted accordingly. While still outward-bound, the boats had to be diverted to fresh operational areas in the American zone. They could no longer be permitted to rove, but were confined to prescribed areas. This control was in any case essential after the arrival of the U-tankers when we could maintain many more boats in the zone. In order to identify the frequent rerouting of shipping, the U-boat Command required as complete a picture as possible of the traffic situation in the whole area.

The planning of Operations *Paukenschlag* and *Westindien* had been based mainly on pre-war data of shipping routes and traffic density, and on interceptions of SSS calls and navigational warnings. Later most valuable data were also obtained from the logs of boats returning from operations ; but as they were not available for three to five weeks after the event, the intelligence was often out of date. Hence it was necessary to include much information in the current radio reports from U-boats on the spot. A typical report would read:

---

9 The Germans were mistaken in attributing these losses to unusual causes. All three U-boats were sighted and sunk by convoy escort vessels before having a chance to attack the convoys, which were OS 18 (U.82), WS 17 (U.587) and OG 82 (U.252).

"23rd March, 1942. U.123 (position). Considerable traffic off Hatteras, mainly tankers, spasmodic morning and evening. Night traffic from there to Cape Fear. None between Cape Fear and Charleston. Ships steer straight courses between buoys. No mines off Hatteras. Any traffic diversion probably due to wrecks or because of suspected mines. Route patrolled at regular intervals by single destroyers, with air patrols towards evening."

Each observation was plotted on the Headquarters chart, and new directions were transmitted to the U-boats at the first opportunity. These numerous reports by radio exposed the U-boats to the danger of being fixed and hunted by ships fitted with H.F./D.F., but the resulting intelligence was so vital to the proper control of operations that the risk was accepted.

186. Briefing of U-Boat Commanders

Before sailing, all German warships, including U-boats, were issued with written operational orders containing all available intelligence of the enemy. In the early months of the war the provision of written orders for each individual boat entailed considerable work at U-boat headquarters. After 1941, when U-boats covered the whole of the Atlantic, a general Atlantic operational order was introduced, and amended from time to time. Additional orders were issued for special minelaying operations, and for the South Atlantic. By 1942 these orders were superseded by a special loose-leaf folio in which were inserted all the radio reports from Headquarters and from boats. To ensure that signals of operational importance reached boats while on outward passage, they were transmitted on all Atlantic wave-lengths. On the boats' return their folios were sent to flotilla headquarters. The latter came within Shore Headquarters W/T Network, which embraced F.O. U-boats, the U-boat Administrative Headquarters, the Operations Division of the Naval Staff, Naval Group Commands North and West, all U-boat flotilla headquarters and U-boats in the transit areas. The flotilla headquarters kept the folios up to date while the boats were in port.

On return from an operation each commander immediately

reported at U-boat headquarters, where the whole cruise was fully discussed in session with Dönitz, his Chief of Staff and the various specialist officers. Before sailing the commanders reported again, and were briefed in the latest developments. Such tasks as minelaying, the opening of a fresh area, the landing or picking up of agents were discussed with the relevant staff officers or with merchant service captains who might have special local knowledge. Their sailing orders, teleprinted from U-boat headquarters, contained a naval grid square position beyond the Bay of Biscay to which the boat had first to proceed. The operational area was assigned later by radio.

187. U-Tankers allow Extended Operations

Owing to a certain loss of freedom in the movements of the U-boats, operations off the American coast had gradually become more difficult. This difficulty was ascribed by F.O. U-boats to our policy of confining the attacks to certain well-defined areas, such as between Nantucket and Hatteras, which enabled the Americans to concentrate their A/S forces. From the German viewpoint the time was therefore ripe to extend the attacks to various nodal points of shipping along the U.S. coast and in the Caribbean. This was made possible by the arrival in the Atlantic of the first U-tanker - a vessel of 1,700 tons, armed with one 37-mm. gun and two 20-mm. flaks but no torpedoes, and known to the Service as the " milch-cow." The tanker, designated Type XIV, carried 700 tons of diesel fuel, of which up to 600 tons (depending on the time spent at sea) was available for replenishment of the operational boats. This quantity was sufficient to allow twelve medium boats to carry out a further operation in the remotest parts of the Caribbean, or in the case of the larger boats off Capetown, it would allow five to renew their operations. The tanker also carried spare parts, stores, ammunition, a doctor and spare specialist ratings.

Since the disastrous sinking of the raider Ship 16 and of the supply ship Python in November, 1941, there had been no possibility of U-boats replenishing from our surface vessels, and they had sometimes to help each other out by transferring fuel while at sea. In March, 1942, the ex-Polish U-boat UA had been used while on passage from France to Germany to replenish three operational boats. Now, however, with the appearance of the U-tanker, it would be possible to extend the operations to widely separated areas, thereby dispersing the American A/S forces. Moreover, the U-boats would be in a better position to counter the anticipated adoption of the convoy system in U.S. coastal waters.

On 21st April there were ten to twelve medium boats in American waters and the Caribbean, and a larger number on the way there. As it was the beginning of a full-moon period, only four were near the coast, the remainder being some 300 miles to the eastward. The U-tanker (U.459) had arrived the previous day in a position 500 miles northeast of Bermuda. The first boat (U.108) refuelled from her on the 22nd, and by 6th May the tanker had exhausted her stocks. Refuelling was handicapped by lack of experience and by bad weather, with the result that a number of boats accumulated in the vicinity. This undesirable and dangerous condition was to occur on numerous subsequent occasions, and no action by the Command ever succeeded in eliminating it entirely. Fuel was supplied to twelve medium and two large boats, which afterwards operated mainly between Cape Hatteras and the Florida Strait, where they had seldom appeared before.

188. The Enemy introduces Convoys

Early in May, with the boats refuelled by U.459, the total number in the American zone reached its peak, sixteen to eighteen being deployed between Cape Sable and Key West. We had some able commanders among them, but the anticipated high rate of sinkings did not occur. On 21st April, at the beginning of the full-moon period, the hitherto continuous stream of shipping had suddenly declined, and as the targets became fewer, so the U-boat commanders asked to be given new areas. Dönitz believed that the reduced results were only temporary:

"... As in the previous month, the decline in sinkings is due to the combination of full-moon and fine weather. The boats cannot operate near the coast where strong sea and air patrols keep them submerged, and give them no opportunity for surface movements or for recharging batteries. Yet the conditions for operations in the American zone are still very good" (264).

But the change of moon and weather brought no improvement. The reason became apparent on 9th May, when the very first convoy was reported near Cape Hatteras.

"... It is probable that shipping is being formed into convoys to avoid the Hatteras danger zone, and subsequently dispersed..." (265).

This theory was supported by reports of considerable single ship traffic in the vicinity of New York, and heavy north-south traffic off the coast of Florida. It would have been highly dangerous to operate against shipping off New York, which sailed in daylight only and in waters of less than 15 metres. The only coastal locality in which boats could still operate was east of Florida, which had been unoccupied since February. But now three boats were there, U.98, 333 and 564, the two latter commanded by very able officers, Lieutenants Cremer and Suhren. U.333, on her way out, had been rammed and seriously damaged in action with a tanker. Cremer continued doggedly to his allotted area, where he and his colleagues operating in shallow water in the face of strong air and sea patrols, achieved good results. In an attack on 6th May, U.333 was surprised by A/S forces and subjected to a prolonged depth-charge attack in 30 metres of water. Despite further serious damage, Cremer managed to evade his pursuers by working his way along the sea bed into deep water, and escaping after dark.

These three boats off Florida accounted for more than ten ships, equalling the aggregate sinkings by the fourteen other boats operating up to 500 miles from the coast. Dönitz wrote on 16th May:

"... Since 20th April the situation on the North American coast, and between Cape Fear and New York has been extremely bad. The boats situated near the principal ports having reported no traffic, it seems that it has either been temporarily suspended or so routed as to escape their observation..." (266).

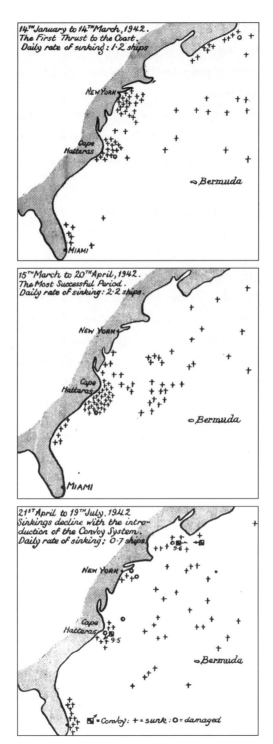

Plan 7. Sinkings claimed by U-boats in American waters, January-July, 1942

In actual fact traffic had been completely reorganised at the beginning of May with the partial introduction of the convoy system. Though he was long prepared for this development, it is perhaps curious that Dönitz failed to recognise the new situation. Favourable conditions having persisted for so long, and enemy counter-measures having made such slow progress, he believed that there would be no sudden change, and he remained confident that the situation could be restored.

189. Failure to attack a Troop Convoy

A convoy was sighted on 1st May by U.576, 80 miles southwest of Cape Sable, as it was leaving the Gulf of Maine on a northeasterly course, escorted by aircraft carriers, battleships and a strong force of destroyers. It passed over the position of the U-boat, which, having expended all torpedoes, was unable to exploit the unique opportunity. Consideration was given to sending to the attack four westbound boats which were still 600 to 1,000 miles to the eastward.

"… It seems unremunerative to concentrate from this long range, when we have no shadowing reports, particularly as the boats will have to move to the Newfoundland Bank with its fog and shallow water. But in view of the importance of the target - seven large troop transports - this will have to be done…" (267).

The four boats were ordered to assume a 120 mile north-south patrol line southward of Cape Race by 3rd May, while U.576 was told to make every effort to regain contact. She actually sighted rear units of the air escort on the 2nd, and soon located the convoy by hydrophone, but was driven off by aircraft. Available reports indicated that the convoy intended to hug the land, and our patrol line was moved northward towards the coast. But on the 4th, when there was no longer any chance of interception, the operation was abandoned and the boats were deployed between Nova Scotia and New York.

190. Renewed Operations in the Caribbean

The controversy between Raeder and Dönitz over the occupation of the Caribbean delayed the resumption of operations in that area. A month had elapsed before three large boats again appeared there. They were disposed, as before, between Trinidad and Curacao, and off the Greater Antilles. On instructions from Raeder, U.130 was ordered to bombard the oil storage tanks at Bullen Bay. Approaching Curacao during the night of 18th April, this boat arrived off the Shell Company's oil depot early the following morning. She opened fire on the oil storage tanks at 0300 (local time) at a range of 3,600 metres, but was driven off by the shore batteries after firing only twelve rounds.

With nine boats - including two refuelled by U.459 - due to arrive in the Caribbean by 10th May, it was hoped to achieve a widespread attack. The disposition was as follows: U.108 between the Bahama Channel and the Windward Passage, U.506 and 507 in the Gulf of Mexico, U.125 between Cuba and the Strait of Yucatan, U.69 and 502 off Curacao and Aruba, U.66 off Trinidad and U.162 between Trinidad and the Guiana coast. It had been intended to station U.155 and 156 at the approach to the Panama Canal, but as reports came in of heavy tanker traffic in the region of Trinidad, they were sent there as reinforcements. Operational conditions in the Caribbean were far better than off the American coast, and the boats were able to sink from six to ten ships each, results being particularly good off Trinidad, in the Strait of Yucatan and the Gulf of Mexico. As shipping in the Gulf of Mexico was neither protected nor controlled, and in fact behaved as in peace-time, it seemed that the enemy had not yet reckoned with the appearance of U-boats in those waters.

MAY, 1942
POLICY AND PROSPECTS

191. Review of Policy in U.S. Waters

After three months of successful operation by U-boats in the Western Hemisphere, the German Naval Staff decided to make a critical examination of policy (268). Dönitz was asked to state whether the overall effect of the U-boat campaign would not be increased by concentrating operations in the vicinity of the British Isles, and off Murmansk and Archangel. His war diary for 15th April, 1942, contains the answer to this question:

"… The enemy merchant navies are a collective factor. It is therefore immaterial where any one ship is sunk, for it must ultimately be replaced by new construction. What counts in the long run is the preponderance of sinkings over new construction. Shipbuilding and arms production are centred in the United States, while England is the European outpost and sally port. By attacking the supply traffic - particularly the oil - in the American zone, I am striking at the root of the evil, for here the sinking of each ship is not only a loss to the enemy, but also deals a blow at the source of his shipbuilding and war production. Without shipping the sally port cannot be used for an attack on Europe… I consider that we should continue to operate the U-boats where they can sink the greatest tonnage with the smallest losses, which at present is in American waters."

In May, however, sinkings on the east coast of America started to decline, and it was necessary to reconsider this policy. Following the established procedure, its effectiveness was gauged by listing the average sinkings per boat per sea-day. The estimated averages for all areas for the first six months of 1942 were as follows:

Average Tonnage Sunk Per Boat Per Sea-Day In 1942

	Jan.	Feb.	March	April	May	June
As first assessed (269)	209	378	409	412	-	-
After checking	281	327	354	327	361	348

These figures seemed encouraging, but in the Western Hemisphere it was becoming more difficult to find the traffic, and if this tendency increased a proportion of the U-boats would have to be moved back to the North Atlantic convoy routes.

192. Poor Results in Northern Waters

The transfer of so many U-boats to Norwegian bases for duties in

Northern Waters had deprived us of many sinkings in the Atlantic. In a lengthy memorandum to the Naval Staff on 3rd May Dönitz gave the reasons for the poor results by the Norway-based U-boats, mentioning the lack of dockyard repair facilities, the long daylight and the interference by British carrier-borne aircraft and surface escorts. He also doubted the value of these U-boats for repelling invasion:

"Owing to opposition in Northern Waters our losses are proportionately higher than in the North Atlantic... On the whole I do not consider the employment of U-boats in Northern Waters to be worth while" (270).

The attack on PQ 16, resulting in damage to five U-boats, with only one ship sunk, fortified Dönitz's argument (271). But the Naval Staff commented:

"Every ton of war material that can be denied to Russia relieves the pressure on our Eastern Front in the present fateful battle... Though conditions may be unfavourable to U-boats in Northern Waters, there will always be opportunities to attack stragglers and damaged ships. Moreover, continuous shadowing is necessary to enable the *Luftwaffe* to strike when the weather permits" (272).

At U-boat headquarters the idea of using U-boats to shadow convoys in the summer within range of our own Air Force, seemed ridiculous, and merely proved how unsuited the *Luftwaffe* was to naval operations.

193. Operational Strength in 1942

So much depended on the number of U-boats available at different stages of the war that a review of the situation as it appeared to us in July, 1942, will not be amiss, for it illustrates the gulf between anticipation and realisation.

During the second half of 1941 newly constructed U-boats had been commissioned at an average rate of 20 per month. The normal training and working-up practices for each boat occupied four months, so that all of these should have been added to our operational forces by the middle of 1942. But another severe winter had caused the freezing-up of the Southern Baltic ports, which had seriously delayed the training. While some of the new boats had been transferred to North Sea ports before the Baltic froze, no less than 45 others were ice-bound for many weeks. As a result only 39 new boats were ready to join the operational flotillas in the first quarter of 1942, and only 30 in the second quarter (273, 274). Of these 69 boats, 26 were sent to Northern Waters to meet the requirements of the Naval Staff, and two were sent to the Mediterranean.

Allowing for the 12 boats that had been lost in the first half of 1942 the net gain in operational strength for the Atlantic during this period was only 29 boats, instead of the 82 that would have accrued but for these frustrations.

The hold-up due to the ice in the Baltic was of course only temporary, and in consequence the second half of 1942 saw new boats becoming operational at the high rate of 23 per month. This would permit the resumption of large-scale convoy operations in the North Atlantic whenever conditions in American waters deteriorated, and would also enable us to provide U-boats for remote areas, where the enemy's protective measures were still weak. Yet it was the dearth of new boats in the critical early months of 1942 that constituted an irreparable handicap to the whole campaign.

194. Enemy's Shipbuilding Capacity

Since the entry of the United States into the war, reports began to pour into Germany about American shipbuilding capacity. It was difficult to sort truth from propaganda, which was intended to undermine our morale. We treated these reports with reserve, but it was obvious that by June, 1942, the Americans had embarked on a huge programme. Only a year earlier our Naval Staff had estimated that the combined Anglo-American building capacity could not exceed 1 million tons gross per annum. Now, however, a reported American target of 2,290 ships aggregating 16-8 million tons between 1939 and 1943 was regarded as feasible. Of this huge total, it was reported that 15-3 million tons would be completed in 1942 and 1943. Some German experts were sceptical, but the U-boat

Command used these figures as a basis for their calculations. The following table compares estimated and actual results in these two years (275).

	1942			
	U.S.A.	ENGLAND	CANADA	TOTAL
	(million tons)			
(a) As estimated by U-boat Command.	6.8	1.1	0.5	8.2
(b) As estimated by the Naval Intelligence Division	5.4	1.1	0.5	7.0
(c) Tonnage actually built (from British Admiralty Sources)	5.19	1.3	0.6	6.99

	1943			
	U.S.A.	ENGLAND	CANADA	TOTAL
	(million tons)			
(a) As estimated by U-boat Command.	8.7	1.1	0.5	10.3
(b) As estimated by the Naval Intelligence Division	900,000 tons a month			10.8
(c) Tonnage actually built (from British Admiralty Sources)	12.29	1.2	0.9	14.39

The estimates in lines (a) and (b) were compiled in May, 1942. They revealed that if by the end of the year any effective reduction were to be made in the aggregate tonnage of our enemies, sinkings over the whole year would have to exceed 700,000 tons per month. At this time the Naval Staff believed that the rate of global sinkings by the naval and air forces of the three Axis Powers was considerably above that figure. But our authorities had failed to make allowance for the exaggerated claims of the *Luftwaffe* and of the Japanese. On the other hand they were alive to the urgency of inflicting the utmost damage before the year had run out. By 1943 the monthly rate of sinkings would need to be at least 900,000 tons - a task that would present the greatest difficulties.[10]

195. Effect of Tanker Losses

The majority of these ships were being built on the eastern seaboard of the United States, where the shipbuilding and associated industries were adapted to oil-fuel firing.

"... Between 15th January and 10th May, 1942, 112 tankers totalling 927,000 tons were sunk, of which some 23 were carrying oil to the U.S.A. Each tanker sunk represents a direct blow at American shipbuilding. It would take a very considerable time to install an oil pipeline, so that for the next year at least the Americans will have to rely upon tankers for their oil supplies. It would not be possible to transport sufficient quantities by rail or road, nor would it be feasible for American industry to revert to coal firing. Even if the total oil consumption were reduced at the expense of private consumers, the loss of tankers should seriously affect the American shipbuilding industry on the east coast" (276).[11]

These opinions of the U-boat Command meant that operations in the Western Hemisphere would be continued as long as sinkings were maintained. But the Naval Staff was less optimistic, and believed that American industry could still have sufficient oil by the exercise of economy in other directions (277). Later, when we had analysed the names of the sunken tankers, it transpired that many of them were destined for Great Britain so that their loss affected British war industries rather than the American shipbuilding industry.

---

10 Morison (p.404) gives a diagram of Allied merchant ship losses and new construction in 1942 and 1943. The last quarter of 1942 marked the beginning of a net gain in new construction over total losses by enemy action and marine casualties.

11 F.O. U-boats was certainly not exaggerating. That the losses (especially of tankers) through U-boats off the American Atlantic seaboard and in the Caribbean "now threatened the entire Allied war effort" is shown by correspondence between General Marshall and Admiral King in June, 1942, quoted by Morison, pp. 308, 309.

MAY - JULY, 1942
EMPHASIS ON THE CARIBBEAN

196. Timely Arrival of U-Tankers

Between May and July, 1942, operations off the American coast declined and eventually ceased, while the U-boats were concentrated in the Caribbean. Of less importance were the few attacks during this period on Atlantic convoys by Groups *Hecht* and *Endrass*. But all the operations were made possible by the arrival of the first U-tankers, U.459, 460 and U.116 (a minelayer). Their availability for refuelling the operational U-boats in the Western Atlantic was of great benefit to the whole campaign, for our medium boats could not otherwise have been maintained in the Caribbean. Boats on outward passage were refuelled from these tankers so that they could start operations with a full load of torpedoes and fuel. The remote periphery of the Caribbean was 4,000 miles from the Biscay bases, and the Caribbean zone was from 500 to 1,000 miles wide, yet we were able to sustain our operations there for nearly three months. Of the 37 boats involved, 20 were refuelled at sea, comprising eight Type IXC, three Type IXB, and nine Type VIIC.

On her first operation U.459 refuelled six of these, which were later transferred from the American coast to the Caribbean. On her second she topped up six medium boats involved in the attack on HG84, and together with U.460, supplied small quantities of fuel to 10 large boats. These two U-tankers not only enabled 13 boats of otherwise insufficient range to be sent on to the Caribbean, but they themselves were able to remain in the area until their supplies of torpedoes and ammunition were exhausted.

Outward-bound U-tankers reported when clear of the danger areas in the Bay of Biscay, and boats in the operational area were then informed by radio that refuelling would be possible before returning to base, and were given the waiting position of the tanker. If they still had torpedoes they continued to operate until their remaining fuel was just enough to take them to the replenishing area. The loss of a

U-tanker would have resulted in a number of boats being unable to reach the Biscay bases. This risk had to be accepted in the early days, and it disappeared later when we had a number of tankers always available.

197. Decline of U.S. Coastal Battle

The U-boat Command believed that operational conditions off the American coast would again improve, but as the Caribbean had proved so rewarding, it was decided to send six boats slowly southwards between 5th and 18th May. These comprised four Type VIIC and two Type IXB, all refuelled by U.459. Thus of the boats operating in American waters at mid-May, 10 were disposed between Cape Hatteras and Nova Scotia, while six were heading for the Caribbean, some of the latter being already near the Bahamas and Florida Strait. The boats still off the American coast were mainly to the south of Cape Sable and in the Gulf of Maine, where fog was prevalent. The Commanding Officers were allowed considerable freedom of action and sought their targets independently. Cdr. Thurmann, in U.553, on his own initiative entered the St. Lawrence estuary, sinking two ships there on 12th May. This attack evoked such strong enemy air activity that U.553 had virtually to keep submerged in daylight for a whole fortnight, and found no further targets.

Reports from the boats showed that they were making a vigorous search of the operational area, yet extremely few ships were sighted, and as the days passed, it became evident that the traffic situation had fundamentally changed. The Press reported the suspension of all sailings to and from South America, but this seemed improbable. Single-ship traffic was scarce even in the immediate vicinity of the ports and coastal inlets. But between 14th and 20th May three convoys were sighted in the Florida Strait by the boats en route to the Caribbean.[12] Despite these observations, the U-boat Command still doubted whether the adoption of the convoy system had become general, and the U-boats were once more ordered to hard and fast

---

12 Between Hampton Roads and Key West the first southbound and northbound convoys sailed on 14th and 15th May respectively.

attack areas, such as the approaches to New York, Delaware and Chesapeake Bay. As these dispositions found no traffic routes, only two boats were left, one off Halifax and one off New York, and the remainder were assembled on 21st May to form Group *Pfadfinder*, and were moved 300 to 400 miles to the eastward. By this step it was hoped to discover whether traffic between the U.S. ports and Central and South America passed at a distance from the coast. But only occasional sightings or sinkings indicated that a few single ships were still coming from the south to Cape Sable, and from the southeast to New York. After a few days, most of these boats were once more sent close in to the coast - two to the south of Cape Sable, three to attack sectors off New York and one to Cape Hatteras - -while the remaining two were left 400 miles east of New York, where the routes from Halifax and New York met. These dispositions also were of little use, for sinkings averaged only one to three ships per boat, while torpedoes were sometimes aimed at poor targets, such as fast single vessels, or vessels located in the fog by hydrophone.

198. First Minelaying in U.S. Coastal Waters

The prospects of U-boat minelaying in American coastal waters had been examined at U-boat headquarters soon after America's entry into the war. It was decided that mines could be laid in two parallel strips of water extending along the coast from New York to Cape Canaveral. The inshore strip, varying in width between 10 to 40 miles, was suitable for laying ground mines (TMB and TMC) in depths up to 35 metres. The other strip, further to seaward, had its inner boundary parallel to the first strip, and was 50 to 200 metres deep. It would need moored mines (SMA). Separating these strips was a channel 35 to 50 metres in depth in which either type of mine could be laid ; the ground mine because the water was too deep to give full effect to the detonation, and the moored mine because its design did not permit of less than 50 metres of water. Nearly all the large ports were situated within this coastal sector, so that minelaying promised good results.

U.116 (Type XB) was the first minelaying U-boat to be built since the First World War. Displacing 1,700 tons, she was designed to carry 66 SMA (moored) mines which were carried in 22 shafts, fitted inside and outside the pressure hull. She had only two stern torpedo tubes. In the Spring of 1942 the Naval Staff had drawn up plans for employing this type on extensive mine-laying operations, but the first trials had shown a defect in the mine itself, which caused several of them to detonate prematurely. It was regrettable that during the several months that it took to rectify the fault, the ample carrying capacity of the U-minelayer could not be exploited. Meanwhile U.116 was used as a U-tanker in the Atlantic, where she could supply up to 240 tons to operational boats.

The only other mines were TMB and TMC, which could be stowed in the torpedo tubes of normal U-boats. These mines were not used by U-boats in the early months of the American campaign because targets were so numerous that the torpedo was a far more effective weapon. But as.soon as sinkings by torpedo dropped off, preparations were made for minelaying. This alternate use of torpedoes and mines was a feature of operations in fresh areas in 1942 and 1943. Once the boats started launching mines, it usually meant that the prospects with torpedoes in that area were becoming poor.

The first plan envisaged three lays during the new-moon period in July ; one at the entrance to New York, by U.87 with 10 TMCs to be laid in 20 to 30 metres, and the others at the entrances to Delaware and Chesapeake Bay, by U.373 and 701, each with 15 TMBs, in depths ranging from 12 to 20 metres. The mines were set to become inactive after 60 days, so that the same areas could be mined again at a later period, if necessary. A few days before the operation was due to commence, the Naval Staff cancelled the laying of the New York field, because of the belated departure of some neutral ships carrying the returning German and Italian diplomats. U.87 laid her mines instead off Boston. The mines originally intended for Chesapeake Bay were laid to the southeast of Cape Henry, so as not to interfere with neutral shipping in which Germany herself was interested. It was gathered from radio intercepts and from a neutral source that these mines caused the loss of four ships off Chesapeake, and three in Delaware Bay and that both bays were temporarily closed to shipping. These encouraging results led to the planning of similar operations.[13]

199. Agents landed on the U.S. Coast

During the same new-moon period secret agents were landed on the American coast. This undertaking - cover name Pastorius - was planned by OKW Amt Ausland Abwehr II, a section that specialised in the organisation of sabotage and fifth column activities (278). One party of four, and another of five Germans who had been formerly resident in, or familiar with, America, were specially trained for sabotage on the North American continent. Their objectives were the sabotaging of military installations, the undermining of American morale, and the recruiting of additional personnel for these activities. They were also to try to re-establish the interrupted radio communications with Germany, and to obtain general intelligence. The U-boat Command was averse to embarking these individuals in U-boats, for some of them were not actuated by patriotic motives, but rather by an adventurous spirit or merely by the desire to seek refuge in the United States. If arrested, they might, to save their skins, divulge all they had seen and heard on board. But the task had to be undertaken since there was no other means of transport to the United States. Care was taken that the agents, while on board, acquired no secret information.

One party was landed at Long Island by U.202 on 13th June; the other on the beach at Jacksonville by U.584 on the 17th. The boats proceeded inshore well trimmed down by the bows until they touched ground, and the disembarkation was then made by rubber dinghy. A few weeks later it appeared from Press reports that both parties were seized by American guards before they could commence their activities, and their conduct after capture confirmed the U-boat Command's distrust of certain of these men (279).

---

13 According to British records, the mines accounted for a tug in Delaware Bay, and the loss of three ships totalling 19,000 tons and damage to a tanker off Cape Henry.

200. The Boats are driven from the Coast

On completion of the minelaying and Operation Pastorius the boats involved remained near the coast between Cape Sable and Cape Hatteras. In a new effort to control operations from U-boat headquarters - which had proved so successful in the past - the boats were assigned to attack areas close in shore. U.132 was moved from south of Nova Scotia to the mouth of the St. Lawrence, where she operated for nearly three weeks. Incidentally, she possessed a detailed report of U.553's previous experience in the same area. On 6th July she sank three ships of a convoy and later, an independent vessel.

It was thought possible that coastal traffic would increase during the full-moon period, when our boats were unable to operate near the coast. If this should prove correct, it would be uneconomical to continue operations near the U.S. coast. But the situation appeared to change when, on 24th June, a number of small convoys and escorted single vessels were sighted near Cape Hatteras. U.701 and 404, commanded by experienced officers, Lt.-Commanders Degen and Biilow, managed to sink some ships in convoy off Cape Hatteras, while at the same time two fast independent vessels were sunk 200 miles to the eastward. It now became evident that the fewer sightings were attributable not to the suspension or diversion of traffic, but to the introduction of the convoy system. Because of these successful convoy attacks the boats were kept in the Hatteras area. It was thought that the sighting boat would be able to direct several others to the attack. Three convoys were subsequently sighted, but the plan failed on each occasion ; for even the sighting boat had been unable to reach an attacking position in the face of strong enemy air cover. U.701 and 404 had owed their success to their initial favourable position ahead of the convoys. Such chances would probably recur when the volume of traffic increased, and it seemed worth trying again. But from mid-July nearly all our boats were being attacked from the air, and the damage caused to U.87 and U.404 through bombs forced them to return. By mid-July we had to write off U.215,

576 and 701[14], all destroyed. These losses, representing one third of the forces engaged, were not commensurate with results. On 19th July the two boats still operating near Cape Hatteras were ordered to evacuate the coastal area. Thus the increasing ascendancy of the American A/S forces drove us from their coast, and henceforth it was our intention to send only single boats there occasionally, and perhaps to lay mines off the ports (280).

201. U-Boats overrun the Caribbean

Our primary objective in May and June was to exploit the unique opportunities in the Caribbean, where, with the U-tankers that had become available, we were able to maintain ten to twelve U-boats. With the six boats that were sent south from the American coast in the latter half of May, the Caribbean now became our main theatre of operations. These six entered the Caribbean through the Florida Strait and the Windward and Mona Passages, where they found considerable traffic. When targets there became scarce through the suspension or diversion of shipping, they continued towards their allotted areas. The larger boats which came after them were assigned to remoter areas. Proceeding slowly through the waters traversed by their predecessors, they too interrupted their passage to attack shipping wherever encountered. In May the U-boats had been on the edge of the Caribbean, in the east of the Gulf of Mexico and south of Cuba. In June they moved westward into the Gulf up to the Mexican coast and south of the Yucatan Strait. Some reached the Panama Canal on 10th June, and the Gulf of Campeche on the 15th.

In these waters the control of shipping and A/S measures developed step by step towards proficiency, as had occurred earlier off the American coast. But from the very beginning, there was lively air activity off the principal ports and in various passages, for by now the U.S. aircraft were being extensively equipped with radar. On the other hand A/S vessels were relatively scarce. Sinkings in May had occurred chiefly between the Florida Strait and the mouth of the Mississippi, and between the Windward Passage and the

---

14 U.701 was the first kill by the U.S. *Army* Air Force, on 7th July.

Yucatan Strait. Those in June were spread over the whole of the Gulf of Mexico, south of the Yucatan Strait, north of the Panama Canal, west of Aruba and south of the Mona Passage .

In the Trinidad area, the enemy's aircraft greatly preponderated over the surface forces. The former forced the boats to remain submerged throughout the day, but the latter were too few to chase them from the vicinity of the island. The heavy traffic to and from Port of Spain followed fixed inward and outward routes which were changed at intervals. If our boats could identify one such route, there

Plan 8. Sinkings claimed by U-boats in the West Indian zone,
15th April-31st August, 1942

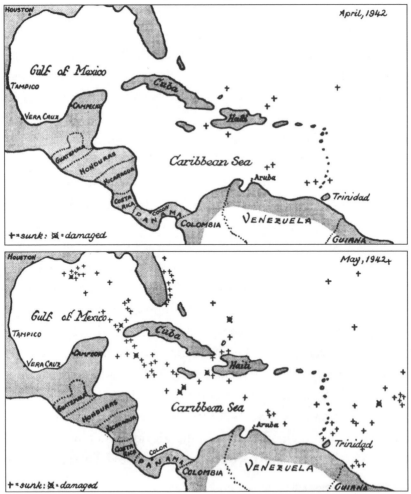

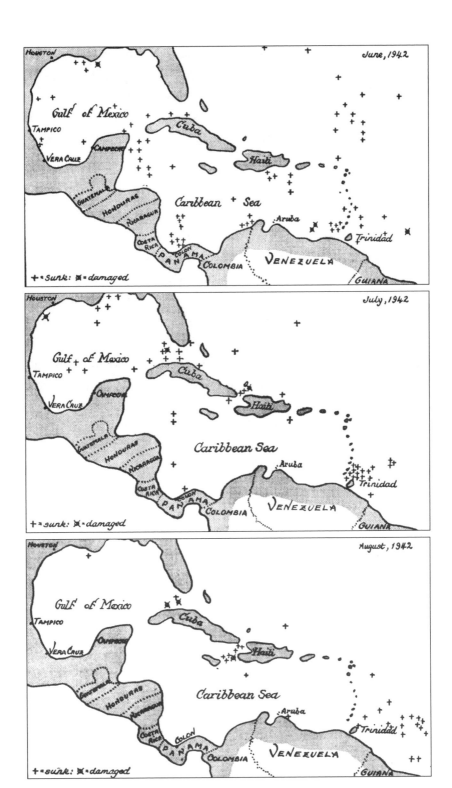

53

was every prospect of encountering a regular procession of ships. At full-moon periods air activity was so intense that the boats had to evade up to 100 or 200 miles east or west. On such occasions the freedom to use their radio transmitters proved very useful, for this allowed us to re-deploy them as soon as we had established a change of route.

202. Off Martinique

About the middle of May when it was reported that the harbour of Port de France was being watched by American light naval forces and flying boats, the Vichy government expressed fears of the seizure, by the Americans, of the French war and merchant ships lying there (281). On Naval Staff orders U.69 and 156, then operating in the Trinidad area, were sent to Port de France to attack the American warships. They had also to report on the ships in port, and to sink any French ships leaving harbour. An exception was to be made in the case of ships sailing with German authority, details of which were passed to the U-boats. U.156 arrived off the harbour on 21st May, and on the following day torpedoed an obsolete American destroyer, which, though badly damaged, managed to reach the inner harbour. A few days later the U-boat commander reported that his ship's company had reached the limit of their endurance, enemy reconnaissance during the full-moon period having compelled him to remain submerged for no less than 120 hours in one week, a terrible ordeal on account of the very high temperatures in the boat while submerged. The retention of U-boats off Port de France appeared uneconomical, and as fears of an American attack had abated, they were withdrawn at the end of May and sent back to the Trinidad area.

203. Unsuccessful Operations off Brazil

Italian U-boats operating between Belem and Fernando Noronha on the north coast of Brazil in March and April, 1942, had encountered considerable shipping proceeding from Capetown and South America to Trinidad and New York. Such information being of great value in assessing the enemy situation in the Caribbean theatre, it was decided to send three German U-boats to the area, and U.161, 126 and 128 sailed at the beginning of May. Proceeding south in company, they combed the area between the 25th and 28th meridians. This procedure, which in 1941 had sometimes led to the sighting of SL convoys, again fulfilled its purpose, for on 11th May the northbound SL 109 was encountered 220 miles northwest of Cape Verde. Its watchful escorts drove off the shadowing boat, and it took 24 hours to regain contact. In the attacks during the succeeding nights, only one boat, U.128, scored a hit. Torpedoes fired by U.126 were betrayed by the fluorescence of a " surface runner " and were avoided by the target. The attack was broken off on the 14th.

This operation had set the boats back nearly 400 miles to the northward, and cost them much fuel, but in view of the improved U-tanker situation (U.461 and 462 were to be ready in June), they were ordered to resume their route to Brazil. No traffic was sighted west of the line St. Paul's Rock-Natal. Possibly the sinkings here in April had caused the enemy to divert his routes away from the coast, north into the open sea. Reconnaissance of the Brazilian coast began on 1st June when the boats, disposed over a 400-mile front, swept northwestward, zig-zagging broadly across their mean line of advance. As there was no sighting, it was decided to incorporate the boats into the Caribbean force. U.128 was assigned to an area northwest of Trinidad, U.126 to the eastern Caribbean, and U.161 to the Panama Canal zone. By the time these boats arrived in position, they had covered over 8,000 miles.

204. Caribbean Battle Declines

Though fewer boats were in the actual operational area in June than in May, aggregate sinkings were higher. This was primarily due to the chance discovery, by boats en route to the Caribbean, of single-ship traffic, including many large modern vessels, in the waters northeast of the Lesser Antilles, and between Bermuda and the Greater Antilles. This traffic, whose volume was greater than any hitherto encountered, persisted during the June full-moon period and then suddenly stopped. Captured ships' papers subsequently revealed that our boats had chanced upon the current shipping route. By the end of June single-ship traffic seemed to diminish, while a number of small convoys had begun to appear. These were first sighted in the Trinidad area, along the Greater Antilles as far as Key West, and finally in the Yucatan Strait. The convoy system was evidently being extended inside the Caribbean and the adjacent waters.

The Secretary of the U.S. Navy announced that the convoy system had been adopted everywhere in the Caribbean except in the Gulf of Mexico.and this was confirmed by the observations of our U-boats. They were therefore re-disposed to catch the single-ship traffic in the Gulf and in the Trinidad area, while other parts of the Caribbean were left sparsely occupied, and were later evacuated.

MAY AND JUNE, 1942
NORTH ATLANTIC

205. Operations by Group *Hecht*

Since November, 1941, planned pack operations against Atlantic convoys had been suspended, and meanwhile there had been only occasional fortuitous attacks on these convoys by boats bound for the Western Atlantic, or by boats allocated to the Norwegian bases. The British must have long realised that such incidental attacks were not governed by any preconceived plan, yet we did not know whether the lull had caused them to relax their protective measures. Two reasons now encouraged us to resume Atlantic operations. Firstly we did not want to see the A/S forces transferred from the Atlantic to American waters, but, more important still, we wished to make better use of our boats during their long passage to those waters. Early in May, therefore, when eight medium boats were due to sail for the American coast, it was decided to form them into a group and operate them against the Atlantic convoys.

Enemy radio traffic during the previous three months having revealed that since the suspension of Atlantic pack operations the convoys had generally used the great circle from the North Channel to the Newfoundland Bank, these boats had only to be diverted about 300 miles northward in order to find their targets. They could then sweep southwestward in scouting formation and, if nothing were sighted, carry on to the American coast after refuelling south of the Newfoundland Bank. The eight boats - Group *Hecht* - were due to commence the sweep on 14th May, and W/T silence was enforced. On 11th May, while making for the starting position, U.569 sighted ONS 92 heading southwest, and five other favourably situated boats were concentrated for the attack on the first night, when seven ships were sunk. In the following two days contact was lost several times in bad visibility. At daybreak on the 14th six boats were in patrol line trying to regain contact. Meanwhile Headquarters had discovered from decryption that at 1600 on the 13th an HX convoy had been 300 miles further west, but the boats still tried to find the ONS convoy, which however eluded them, being sighted only by U.406, which was astern of station. Neither did they catch the HX convoy, because of heavy head seas.

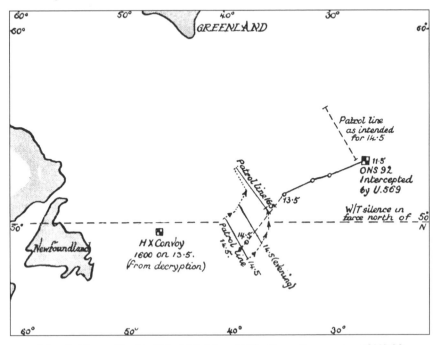

Plan 9. Group Hecht, 11th-15th May, 1942. Operation against ONS 92

Group *Hecht* remained in stationary patrol line from 16th till 18th May, and then swept southwestwards according to a predetermined plan. On 20th May ONS 94, on a westerly course, closed the formation, but when nearing the Newfoundland Bank was lost in the fog. The boats continued their search independently during the night, and daylight saw them in a shortened patrol line ahead of the convoy's anticipated track, but neither ONS 94 nor the next expected convoy was sighted.

On 25th May the U-tanker (U.116) arrived at her position 600 miles south of Cape Race. After refuelling from her, the boats of Group *Hecht* were originally intended to operate off the U.S. coast, but meanwhile the convoy system had been introduced there, and so it was decided on 30th May to send them to sweep across the transatlantic convoy routes. At first they patrolled south of the Newfoundland Bank and were then sent to a position 600 miles southeast of Cape Farewell, where according to Radio Intelligence the east- and west-bound convoys crossed.

ONS 96 was sighted on 31st May, when a strong westerly gale and bright moonlight frustrated an attack by the sighting boat. The weather was deteriorating, and as the convoy was due to reach the Newfoundland Bank next day, the attack was broken off after a few hours, and the boats resumed their sweep. Six days passed before the next convoy (ONS 100) was sighted. Again bad weather intervened. Touch was lost for nearly two days, and when regained on 11th June, errors in dead reckoning were so great that only two boats made brief contact. It was then decided to abandon the operation. The U-boats claimed to have sunk a destroyer and five ships totalling 28,000 tons.[15]

The boats continued their search northeastwards. On 16th June the left wing of the formation intercepted the outward-bound ONS 102, and was ordered to attack. This convoy - the largest encountered so far - was apparently protected by two remote A/S screens. Two U-boats were damaged in an eight-hour depth-charge attack, and

---

15 British records confirm the sinking of the corvette *Mimosa* and four ships aggregating 19,500 tons.

were unfit for further operations. When contact was lost, the group was ordered to break off and start for home. On the morning of 18th June U.124 again sighted the same convoy, which had been delayed, and sank one ship. Two of the boats had to refuel before reaching their base.

206. Convoy Attacks by Group *Endrass*

The order prohibiting attacks on convoys westward of the Bay of Biscay had been in force for two months. Several convoys had been sighted and reported here during this period, but not attacked. It was probable that in this area too, the enemy, feeling himself safe from attack, had cut down his escort forces, and our agents in Southern Spain had confirmed that the escorts of HG convoys were weak. It was therefore decided to attack these convoys.

The new undertaking differed in one respect from that of Group *Hecht* the previous month, in that it envisaged the tying down of the enemy forces. This was now essential since the situation in the American theatre had deteriorated considerably in the course of the month. We wanted to stop A/S vessels from hurrying to the aid of the U.S. coastal shipping, and attention to the Gibraltar convoys might persuade the British to keep their escorts nearer home. If our attacks against HG convoys failed, the boats could still be employed either against North Atlantic convoys or in the Western Atlantic, for they would be able to refuel from one of two U-tankers - U.459 and 460.

On 9th June German Intelligence in Spain reported the departure of HG 84 from Gibraltar. The first sighting was made on the 11th by FW 200s. On the 14th, Group *Endrass* was formed of five boats then available, which were drawn up ahead of the convoy's presumed course. Four more boats which sailed later were ordered to be in a position 60 miles north of this patrol line by the night of the 16th. At 1330 on the 14th the convoy was located by air reconnaissance 50 miles south of the group. A fix on the aircrafts' beacon signals placed it about 35 miles further north - another example of inaccurate aerial navigation. The beacon signals enabled the boats to intercept the convoy, from which five ships were torpedoed during the night by U.552. Further attacks were prevented by the escorts which were stronger than expected. The enemy's air cover in the form of land-based bombers which arrived the next day, forced the boats so far away from the convoy that contact was not regained until late on the night of the 15th, but one by one they were frustrated by the A/S screen. In the calm sea the boats stood no chance against the strong air opposition, so the attack was abandoned on the morning of the 16th. All the boats but U.552 remained at sea, two refuelling from U.460 near the Azores before going on to the U.S. coast, and the rest from U.459. Altogether five ships were sunk in this operation, which was satisfactory.

207. Lessons of Convoy Attacks

Large-scale attacks on the North Atlantic convoys would have to be resumed shortly, and in this connection the recent experiences of Groups *Hecht* and *Endrass* were valuable. These were summarised and distributed to all concerned. Briefly, they confirmed that the prospects of attacking convoys remained unaltered, and that the A/S situation had undergone no radical change during the past nine months (282). Subsequent operations bore out the first part of this statement, but as regards the second, F.O. U-boats did not sufficiently appreciate that *Hecht* and *Endrass*, having caught the enemy unawares, the opposition to their attacks was probably less than could normally be expected. The attacks occurred in May and June, just as the existence of A.S.V. radar had been confirmed. The evidence of radar in surface ships was also carefully analysed, but it was mainly negative.

The following signals were exchanged on 17th June between F.O. U-boats and the Commanding Officer of U.124, Lt.-Commander Mohr, the most experienced of the group:

"From F.O. U-boats. 'What are your personal experiences of enemy surface radar?' From U.124. 'Altogether seven times yesterday I had to use full speed to dodge destroyers, which, according to the plot, came over the horizon almost straight towards me. Apart from two occasions on which I had to dive, and the destroyers disappeared after dropping deterrent depth-charges, I do not think I was sighted. In my opinion all these vessels were merely following normal zig-zag procedure, for when I took evasive action they held to their courses...'" (283).

So we still thought that:

"... There is still no conclusive evidence of enemy surface radar. That boats were sighted and driven off was due, in many instances, to lack of caution on the part of inexperienced boats, as a result of which the more experienced boats were also forced to submerge..." (284).

208. Danger of U-Boat Beacon Signals

The above mentioned convoy operations had shown that the enemy was able to pick up and D/F the U-boat beacon signals. The following instance is quoted from the log of U.94 for 9th June, 1942:

"... 1645 to 1715, transmitted beacon signals. Shortly afterwards a corvette is sighted steering straight towards us. She cannot have seen us by any visual means. (On two previous occasions of transmitting beacon signals I was approached by enemy escort vessels, which I was able to avoid in time. I suspect that our beacon signals were being intercepted by the enemy.) I proceed northward followed by the corvette, which gains on me but slowly. A destroyer is sighted heading for me at high speed. 1806, crash dive ! - attacked with depth-charges... 12th June, 0245, convoy in sight right ahead. Transmit sighting report and beacon signals. 0320, a corvette and a destroyer come straight towards me. I at once stop transmission, and 15 minutes later the enemy ships sheer off and return to the convoy. I do not suspect radar, for I would have detected this while shadowing and attacking during the past few days..." (285).

The transmission of beacon signals was evidently attended with danger, and often resulted in loss of touch or a depth-charge attack. The Naval Communications Specialists had however been unable to devise any better method of U-boat control and the inaccuracy of the boats' reckoning made beacon signals essential. But as an additional safeguard greater and more frequent changes of frequencies were introduced.[16]

THE BAY OF BISCAY

209. British Airborne Radar

From the Spring of 1942 the enemy, using fast aircraft, intensified and extended his activity over the whole Biscay area. Suspicion was aroused by numerous surprise attacks, when the aircraft appeared out of the clouds or down-sun so suddenly that there was barely time to submerge. These aircraft must have started their attacks while outside visibility range. In June, 1942, the first dark night attack was made in the Bay of Biscay when a U-boat was caught in the beam of a searchlight which switched on suddenly 1,000 to 2,000 metres away. Before fire could be opened, an aircraft, with a powerful light in its nose, roared over the conning tower at low level, dropped bombs, and turned to renew the attack.[17]

210. Tardy Appraisal of Enemy Radar

We now know that British aircraft were first equipped with ASV Mark I early in 1941. How was it then that we were so late in detecting it ? In the year 1941 most experienced U-boat commanders believed that their lookouts had sighted the aircraft before the latter had sighted them. If occasionally the boat were taken by surprise, it was thought that the lookout had been lax, or that the commander had misguidedly remained surfaced during unreliable conditions of visibility. Many were the cases in which surfaced U-boats managed to avoid British aircraft. For example, the author himself while in command of U.107 off Freetown on 5th October, 1941, sighted two Sunderlands and four or five of Eagle's aircraft simultaneously. These were flying about

---

16 The first accepted use of H.F./D.F. in a convoy escort occurred in July, 1941. By the end of 1942 H.F./D.F. was accepted as an essential part of the equipment of escort craft.

17 This is a reference to Leigh Light, which came into operational use in May, 1942. The aircraft switched on the light as soon as the radar faded out in the "sea returns" - about 1,000 to 2,000 yards from the U-boat.

on the horizon, but nothing in their behaviour indicated the use of radar. Of the numerous bombing attacks in 1941, two by night in the Strait of Gibraltar in December had been significant. But even these could be accounted for by the prevailing bright moonlight and strong surface fluorescence. That nothing suspicious had been observed in the behaviour of British aircraft was attributable to limitations of the first ASV equipment, or - and this the author considers to be more likely - to the relatively low speed of the aircraft then in use. When attacked by slow aircraft, the U-boat could nearly always dive in good time; whereas fast aircraft could take full tactical advantage of their radar. Between 1939 and 1942 the German Navy's knowledge of the possibilities of radar was definitely scanty. The U-boats had no radar, and at the U-boat Command headquarters we heard little of the developments that were taking place in the fleet and experimental establishments, and we relied almost entirely on clues from the U-boat commanders' reports. The Naval Communications Division and the Technical Communications Development Section of the German Admiralty scrutinised all ships' and U-boats' logs, and these were the organisations that should have discovered the facts. That they failed is evident.

The first surprise attacks early in 1942 caused the U-boat Command Communications Officer to consult the experts in Berlin as to whether it were possible to home aircraft on to a U-boat by radar. These gentlemen were sceptical; they thought that the U-boat was probably too small to be located from the air, particularly in a seaway - and so on. It was not until Rear-Admiral Stummel, Head of the Naval Communications Division, paid an official visit to U-boat headquarters in Paris in June, 1942, that the question was clarified. His investigations had convinced him that U-boats were being located by airborne radar. This, incidentally, was the first positive information that F.O. U-boats had received from the experts. Rear-Admiral Stummel suggested as counter-measures either a radar interception or a radar warning set, with the possibility, later, of devising some form of camouflage against radar. F.O. U-boats decided on the radar interception set, and urged that the development of other counter-measures should be given high priority.

211. German Counter-measures

Bombing attacks in the Bay in the first quarter of 1942 had caused no casualties; in June three U-boats were so severely damaged that they had to return to base. Should this rate of casualties continue, the consequence would be most serious, and it was decided to equip the boats with radar search receivers at the earliest possible moment. A suitable receiving instrument which had been produced for a different purpose by the French firm *Metox* happened to be available, and it required only slight modification and the addition of an auxiliary aerial. Production was hastened so that delivery could commence within six weeks.

Meanwhile the only thing to do was to deny the enemy aircraft the chance of attacking, so on 24th June all boats were ordered to remain submerged day and night when traversing the Bay of Biscay, surfacing only to recharge batteries.[18]

It was also essential to strengthen the U-boats' A.A. armament. But as the necessary structural alterations would require some months, the boats were meanwhile supplied with four 8 mm. machine guns (MG/C 34), in improvised mountings on the conning tower rail, which could be taken below before diving. At best these had a certain moral value, for their low penetrating power afforded little protection to any boat incapable of diving. In such cases heavy-fighter cover had to be provided by Fltegerfiihrer Atlantic. But his aircraft were neither sufficient in numbers nor of the right type, as was proved during the return of the three boats damaged in June. Though close personal contact between F.O. U-boats and Fliegerfiihrer Atlantic ensured that every available aircraft was used, there was only one FW 200 available on 5th June for

---

18 For a survey of Allied A/S operations in the Bay of Biscay in 1942 and 1943, see Naval Staff History of the Second World War, *The Defeat of the Enemy Attack on Shipping*, 1939-1945, Volume I - *A Study of Policy and Operations*, C.B. 3304 (1), Chapters IV, XIII and XIV. In future references to this work the C.B. number only will be quoted.

U.71, severely damaged 120 miles west of Bordeaux, and none on the 11th for the badly damaged U.105, 130 miles west of Cape Finisterre.

"... That there should be no air protection for a damaged and defenceless U-boat is deplorable, and must have a depressing effect on the crews. Even a few heavy fighters or modern bombers would suffice to keep off enemy aircraft. At least they could escort a a damaged U-boat until she came under the protection of our minesweepers and patrol vessels... There being no defence in the Bay of Biscay against Sunderland aircraft and heavy bombers, the R.A.F. can do as it pleases..." (286).

As the Fliegerfiihrer's requests for reinforcements had gone unheeded, he asked F.O. U-boats to intercede with the Air Staff. With the approval of the Naval Staff Dönitz visited *Luftwaffe* headquarters in East Prussia on 2nd July, 1942, and after putting his case to Goring, he obtained a promise to allocate 24 Ju 88 C6 aircraft to Fliegerfiihrer, Atlantic - there being no other aircraft available at the time (287).

ABORTIVE PLANS

212. Intentions against Brazil

On 27th January, 1942, Brazil broke off diplomatic relations with Germany (288). Until then we had avoided any attack on Brazilian shipping, and in the Pan-American safety zone our boats had kept north of the 20th Parallel. Between February and April we torpedoed seven Brazilian ships, which carried no distinguishing marks and could not be identified as neutrals. In two cases only, s.s. Arabutan on 7th March, and s.s. Parnahyba on 1st May, was it possible subsequently to establish their Brazilian nationality. When attacked these armed ships were exhibiting neither ensign nor distinguishing marks (289). When we learned that Brazil and other South American states were arming their merchant ships, our U-boats were given permission on 16th May to attack all such ships, except those belonging to the Argentine and Chile.

At the end of May Brazil announced that her air force had attacked and would continue to attack Axis U-boats encountered off the Brazilian coast, and on the 29th the German Naval Staff sought permission to attack all Brazilian ships. At the same time F.O. U-boats was ordered to examine the prospects of a co-ordinated surprise attack in the event of war with Brazil. The effectiveness of such an attack would depend on having an adequate number of boats in Brazilian waters at the right moment, but if war did not develop, they would be wasting their time (290). The Führer, to whom these points were referred for decision, preferred to open hostilities on Brazil with a sudden overwhelming attack by a strong force of U-boats: "If we are to act, we must go the whole hog" (291). Plans were accordingly made for a simultaneous attack on Brazilian waters by 10 to 15 U-boats (292). This new commitment came at an awkward time, for the re-disposition of U-boats and tankers would certainly weaken our operations in the Caribbean.

Ten boats, due to leave the Atlantic bases at the end of June, were to refuel off the northeast coast of Brazil from U.460, and would be ready to start operations in the first week in August, off Santos, Rio de Janeiro, Bahia and Pernambuco, and attempts would also be made to attack shipping inside these ports, or to lay mines at the entrances. These proposals were submitted to the Führer on 16th June, and approved. The first of the ten boats had already sailed when on 29th June the German Foreign Office suggested to Hitler that such an attack would have serious political repercussions in the Argentine and Chile. Consequently the operation was cancelled, and the boats already on passage were re-routed to the Caribbean, where they achieved better results than would have been possible in Brazilian waters.

213. The Azores and Madeira

It was realised that the Azores and Madeira might be valuable to the Allies as naval and air bases in the Battle of the Atlantic, and possibly in the preliminary phase of the invasion of Europe. Hitler, ruthless himself in the pursuit of his political aims, anticipated that the Allies would have no respect for Portuguese neutrality. He therefore demanded that a group of U-boats be held in immediate readiness in the event of Allied negotiations for the occupation of these islands (293). Dönitz, who as always, was averse to weakening his forces in the vital area - which was now the Western Atlantic - doubted the efficacy of such measures for preventing an Allied occupation of the islands (294). This time the Naval Staff came to the same conclusion, and the proposal was dropped. Dönitz used the occasion of these discussions to suggest various measures for accelerating the repair and construction of U-boats, which were approved.

CHAPTER 5

JULY-DECEMBER, 1942

214. Review of First Half of 1942

In looking back on the first six months of the year, the Naval Staff could be well satisfied with the course of the U-boat war. The expectation of big successes in the American and Caribbean zones had been more than fulfilled. In this period we had lost an average of 3-9 per cent, per month of U-boats at sea. In the very first month of operations off the American coast we had sunk 362,000 tons of shipping, and in March the figure had risen to 511,000 tons. In April the rate of sinkings fell owing to improved A/S measures in these waters, but thanks to the appearance of the U-tankers we were able to maintain the pressure there and in the even more rewarding Caribbean waters. With more U-boats operating, our successes mounted, so that in May we sank 684,000 tons and in June 778,000 tons.[19]

The following table, compiled from post-war data of the antagonists, gives for each month the true average number of tons of shipping sunk per U-boat per day in the whole Atlantic and Caribbean area:

Month (1942)	Jan.	Feb.	March	April	May	June
Average tonnage sunk per U-boat per day	209	278	327	255	311	325

The overall figures for February and March do not reflect the great and sudden successes off the American coast and the Caribbean. This is because they include the very poor results by the boats which Hitler had mistakenly ordered to be stationed between Iceland and the North Channel for the protection of Norway. In February, these

19 These German estimates were used by F.O. U-boats in currently assessing the situation. Allied records however give the sinkings in May as 559,000 tons and in June 577,000 tons. The German estimates and the true figures can be seen in Plan 60.

sank only 11,000 tons for 203 U-boat days, and in March only 1,700 tons for 206 U-boat days. If the poor results from these boats were excluded the figures in the table for February and March would read 352 tons and 382 tons respectively. In other words, it can be calculated that if these boats had been sent to the West Atlantic, a further 300,000 tons of shipping would have been sunk there in these two months.

Our great successes off the U.S. coast in these early months also reflect the failure of the U.S. Navy to profit from Britain's war experience. The Americans had devoted insufficient resources to the U-boat menace in their own waters, an omission which proved most costly to Allied shipping in general.[20]

215. Plans for Large-scale Convoy Battles in the North Atlantic

By May, 1942, the general situation seemed to demand a resumption of convoy battles as well as the continuation of operations in remoter areas. More U-boats would soon be available. By June the German shipyards had been able to make good the delays caused by earlier shortage of labour and by the severe weather of the previous winter. The port of Kiel became a hive of activity, as a stream of new boats left on their first operation. We were able to increase our forces by 15 boats in June, 32 in July, 31 in August, and 32 in September, and this permitted us to keep enough medium boats in the Atlantic to maintain two or more packs against the convoys while using the larger boats in the more distant areas.

The experiences of Group *Hecht* against ON convoys in May and June had indicated prospects of further operations against North Atlantic convoys. On the other hand, unsatisfactory results in the previous year against the Gibraltar convoys seemed to discourage further attacks on these, despite our accurate knowledge of their movements.

The locality of our pack operations was in fact determined by the

---

20 Yet the situation was undergoing a rapid change, for according to Morison (p. 346) "By and large, sailing along the east coast (of America) in convoy after 1st August, 1942, was no longer dangerous."

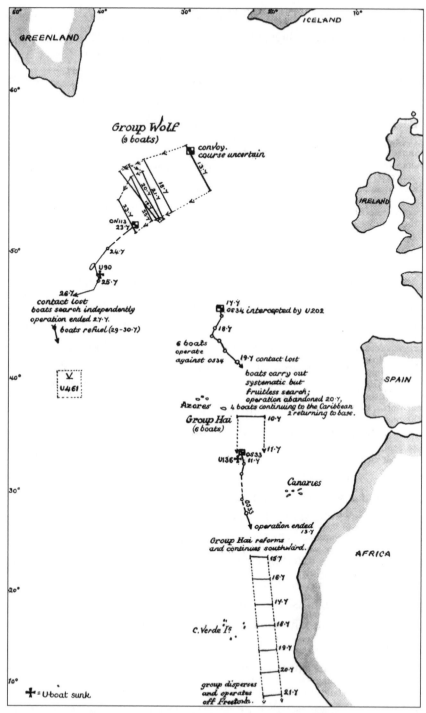

Plan 10. Groups Wolf and Hai, 13th-26th July, 1942.
Operations against ONS 113, OS 33 and OS 34.

70

extent of Allied air protection for the convoys. Assuming protection could be provided up to 500 miles from Allied shore bases, a Gibraltar convoy could be air protected along its entire route, provided it kept inside the 12th Meridian. Should the convoy move out to 16 degrees W., there would be a gap of 300 miles which no land-based aircraft could cover. But not until it reached 20 degrees to 25 degrees W. was the unprotected gap sufficient to allow our boats time to harass the convoy for several days. Here, however, the convoys were beyond the range of German air reconnaissance, and the U-boats would need an extended patrol line to locate them.[21] The ships in the Gibraltar convoys were usually smaller and less valuable than in the Atlantic, and the interval between convoys was about ten days. The same interval marked the sailing of the SL convoys, which were even more difficult to locate. Moreover, as our U-boats seldom contacted them, the volume of their radio traffic, and hence the opportunities for decrypting their signals, were small. The only favourable feature about these convoys was the invariability of their route between 20 degrees and 25 degrees W. ; and it was this alone which in 1941 had enabled us to attack them on several occasions. In the future we intended to harass them only with boats that happened to be on passage to Freetown, Guinea or Brazil, and then only if several such boats were in company.

216. Plans for the Central and South Atlantic

In April, 1942, U.68 and U.505 had reported that shipping from Capetown to Freetown or the United States seemed to be giving up the former Pan-American safety zone in favour of the eastern part of the Atlantic. This meant that Freetown, where the sudden appearance of our boats in 1941 had brought success, would again become important. When in July, 1942, the Naval Staff gave permission to operate boats in the South Atlantic Zone A, which had previously been reserved for our raiders and blockade-runners, this meant that all the waters between Freetown and Natal could be exploited. We

---

21 In June, 1942, refuelling of escorts from tankers in the transatlantic convoys was started, and better evasive routeing became possible (C.B. 3304 (1), Section 30).

wished also to attack the refrigerator-ship traffic off the River Plate, but this was refused because of the probable effect on our relations with the Argentine. Freetown and the Gulf of Guinea therefore came into consideration. In the latter area the raider Ship 28 had sunk three ships in July, and had reported by radio that further operations in the northern part of the Gulf appeared worth while. On 25th July, F.O. U-boats decided to re-occupy the Capetown area. Several Type IXC boats, supported by a U-tanker, all with experienced commanders, were to leave on this mission in August. Freetown, Guinea, the Brazilian coast and Capetown all came into the picture. At that time we were still occupying the Caribbean, and our problem was to exploit the various possibilities of all these areas to the best of our available resources.

JULY - SEPTEMBER, 1942
NORTH ATLANTIC OPERATIONS

217. Operations against OS 33 and 34

The resumption of convoy battles began earlier than originally intended. At the beginning of July the U-boats of the Hai group had assembled southeast of the Azores, whence they were to make a southerly sweep between the meridians 20 degrees and 25 degrees W. as far as latitude 10 degrees N. and then refuel from U.116 before operating off Freetown.

Our expectation of constancy in the habits of the SL convoys was realised when on 11th July the convoy from England to West Africa - OS 33 - penetrated the Hai patrol line from the north. During the first night of the operation the ships destined for South America were evidently detached, and this caused a splitting up of the attackers, for one boat operated against the eastern section, while three attacked the western section. After an initial success during the night, when five ships, totalling 32,000 tons, were sunk, our boats failed to re-penetrate the screens, and one was lost. The patrol line continued southward until it had passed Dakar, when the boats were dispersed for independent operations off Freetown.

The action against OS 33 was followed within a few days by another convoy battle. On 17th July U.202, returning from the U.S. coast, came upon the southbound OS 34 about 450 miles north of the Azores, and succeeded in shadowing it until the following day when four others, bound for the Caribbean, were brought into the attack. Of the latter U.564, commanded by Suhren, obtained hits by night on four ships. One of these, carrying munitions, exploded so violently that the bridge personnel of the U-boat had to take cover from the flying wreckage. U.108 also heard five detonations as a result of six torpedoes fired, but these had apparently exploded at the end of their run without hitting the target. Further attempts to attack we^re repulsed when daylight came, and the boats continued their passage to the Caribbean. They claimed to have sunk four ships, and damaged five more, which we regarded as a distinct success. But post-war records show that only two were sunk. A feature of this operation, the significance of which escaped us at the time, was that the aircraft round the convoy were 800 miles from their land bases. They had apparently achieved this radius of action by sacrificing bomb loads to extra fuel tanks.[22]

218. Further Convoy Battles

At the beginning of July F.O. U-boats was anxious to continue exploiting the favourable situation in the Western Atlantic, where our losses remained small in relation to the results. Moreover, in these American coastal waters, now heavily patrolled by aircraft but still inadequately protected, new U-boat commanders were getting experience which would be invaluable whenever Atlantic convoy battles were resumed. It was therefore decided to assemble the Wolf group 600 miles west of the North Channel for a sweep along the great circle towards the Newfoundland Bank, and then southward.

---

22 By September, 1941, R.A.F. Coastal Command had scraped together a squadron of American *Liberators* capable of operating up to 750 miles from thier base. Not until the spring of 1943 were there any more V.L.R. aircraft available to fill the Atlantic gap.

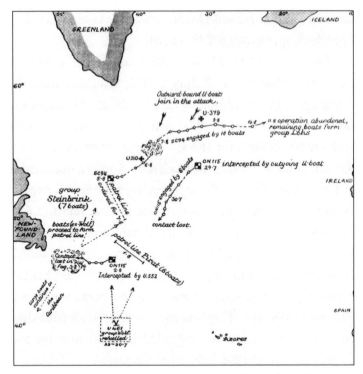

Plan 11. Group Steinbrink and various U-boats, 29th July-11th August, 1942.
Operations against SC 94 and ON 115

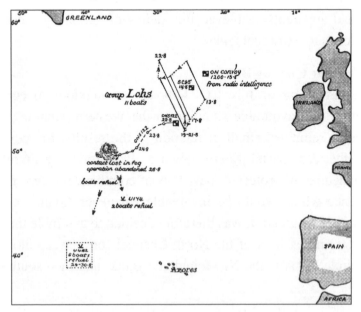

Plan 12. Group Lohs, 13the-30th August, 1942.
Operations against SC 95 and ONS 122

Depending on the situation off the U.S. coast, this group would either remain there or go on to the Caribbean.

On 13th July the nine boats of the group were in scouting formation and about to start the westward sweep when a convoy was sighted at its northern wing. Believing this to be an HX or SC convoy, several boats set a northeasterly course for some hours before the shadower reported that the target was moving west. The loss of time proved fatal, and the boats resumed their scouting formation, hoping that our Radio Intelligence would give them further data. When by 19th July there was no further indication, it was decided to send the boats south across the convoy routes. On the 22nd, when they were about to make for the replenishment area, our Radio Intelligence discovered the position of the westbound convoy, and consequently a patrol line was formed which led to the sighting of ON 113. In bad visibility contact was lost several times and the movements of the strongly escorted convoy prevented us from sinking more than two ships, while one U-boat was lost. The group was then dispersed, and headed south to refuel from U.461.

Meanwhile a considerable number of fresh Type IX and Type VII boats had arrived in mid-Atlantic, and it was decided to send them on to the Caribbean, while the reinforced group Wolf would remain in the Atlantic for further convoy battles. This resumption of North Atlantic operations without previous approval by the Naval Staff later caused some feeling among the latter (295).

219. Attacks on ON 115 and SG 94

While the Wolf boats were refuelling, another boat (U.164, bound for the Caribbean) chanced upon ON 115, 480 miles southeast of Cape Farewell. The nearest boats, though 400 miles to the southwest, were ordered to close the target, which they contacted on 30th July. The convoy's screen drove them off one after another, and one boat was lost. On the morning of 1st August the boats were formed into the patrol line Pirat ahead of the presumed track of the convoy, but failing to locate it by the evening, they were sent north and south to search. On the following day U.552 sighted the convoy which had evidently made large alterations of course and speed, and other boats were ordered to close. By now we had sunk or damaged three ships out of the convoy, and when it reached the fog belt of the Newfoundland Bank, the attack was broken off.

While the large boats that had fortuitously taken part in this operation continued their passage to the Caribbean, the old group Wolf was heading for a new position 400 miles northeast of Newfoundland, where it was to form a patrol line Steinbrink. Two days before reaching this position, U.593 at the northern end of the line, sighted SC 94. The remaining boats, 200 to 300 miles astern of her, were ordered to close the convoy. It was hoped that some other boats, approaching the convoy from the northeast, would be able to maintain contact until the whole of Steinbrink arrived. For several days there was almost continuous contact, "although in the periodic bad visibility the boats were repeatedly pursued by the screen, and exposed to depth-charge attacks. On 9th August the convoy received air protection, yet we inflicted the loss of eleven ships, totalling 53,000 tons, while three boats, including U.335[23], were lost, and four damaged. All except one of the U-boat commanders involved were inexperienced, and the fact that they succeeded against heavy opposition seemed to give promise for future operations.

220. Attack on ONS 122

Fresh boats joined with the Steinbrink group in a new patrol line (Lohs) 600 miles west of the North Channel, where they expected to sight an ON convoy, whose noon position of 13th August had been decrypted. To avoid making contact during darkness, the boats were ordered slightly west, but while doing this, and before daylight, they sighted a convoy (SC 95) escorted by destroyers, heading north. The manoeuvres of the screen prevented our boats from determining the line of advance of the convoy. Hence only three boats attacked, scoring one hit. Now contact was lost, and on 16th August another target group, consisting of destroyers and two steamships, was

23 U.335 was destroyed by H.M. S/M *Saracen* west of Norway on the 3rd August.

sighted. Their unusual behaviour led two of the U-boat commanders to believe that this was a special hunter-killer group. The pursuit was broken off and a new patrol line formed.

During the preceding weeks our Radio Intelligence had succeeded in obtaining a whole series of positions of ON and SC convoys, from which F.O. U-boats deduced that the enemy was beginning to move his transatlantic routes to the north. Consequently on 21st August the Lohs group was moved northward. Yet the next ON convoy ran somewhat to the south of the normal route, passing the southern end of the patrol line on 22nd August. It was sighted by chance by U.135, who having incorrectly decoded her radio instructions, was 100 miles south of the position ordered. At midnight on 22nd August all boats were ordered to close the convoy, now identified as ONS 122. In poor visibility the shadower lost contact, which was not re-established until daylight on the 24th. By 0300 on the 25th nine boats were in contact, and prospects looked good, when a sudden fog prevented further attacks. We had sunk four ships (17,000 tons) and two U-boats had to return because of damage from depth-charges. Most of the remainder headed south to refuel west of the Azores from U.462 and U.174.

221. Operations against SL 118 and 119

From the beginning of August single boats from the former Hai group began their homeward passage from the Freetown area, and replacements had to be found for these. The situation in this respect was satisfactory, for in September we had three U-tankers at sea, while a number of medium boats was setting out from the Biscay ports. The first of these began to assemble southeast of the Azores from 13th August. On the next day, and before the whole group (Blilcher), consisting of six boats, had assembled, SL 118 entered their waiting area from the south. Shadowing was successful and although the convoy's remote screen kept the attackers off at night, several underwater attacks were made on the 17th, 18th and 19th. From the evening of the 18th the convoy had air protection which made the regaining of attacking positions so difficult that by the morning of the 20th the attack was abandoned. We had sunk four ships totalling 28,000 tons, and torpedoed H.M.S. Cheshire.

U.653, damaged by aircraft bombs, had to return to base, after transferring her surplus fuel to two other boats. The remainder of the group were reassembled southeast of the Azores, and sent southward. The anticipated meeting with SL 119 occurred on 26th August. In addition to the Blucher group the four boats of Eisbar, proceeding towards Capetown, were ordered to join in the attack. They managed to attain a favourable position, but a bold alteration of course by the convoy frustrated the attempt, and in view of the urgency of their mission they continued southward.

Meanwhile the four Blucher boats pursued the convoy until the evening of 28th August, and in several attacks sank two ships and one straggler. U.566 was rammed while attacking ; after using welding gear to burn off the damaged parts of the bridge, she returned home safely.

U.107 and U.214 remained off Lisbon to await the formation of a new group for operations off Freetown. U.107 torpedoed two British ships out of a number leaving Lisbon. This was one of the few cases in this war when we scored results off that port.

222. Attacks on SC 97 and ON 127

For the first time at the end of August we had two groups simultaneously in the operational zone of the North Atlantic convoys. Lohs 500 miles west of the Azores was refuelling from U.462, while *Vorwärts* was making a sweep to the southwest. At the northern end of this group U.609 on 31st August sighted SC 97, and in a surprise underwater attack sank two ships. Further boats approaching from the south during the night were repelled by the escorts. On the following morning, when six boats were in contact, the first Sunderland appeared, after which there was continuous air protection, evidently from Iceland. This forced the boats to remain submerged and consequently drop astern. In the moonless nights and with evasive convoy tactics, they lost contact, and by the morning of 2nd September the operation was broken off.

To the south of *Vorwärts* the new group Stier, assembled on
31st August, made a brief but unsuccessful effort on 1st and 2nd

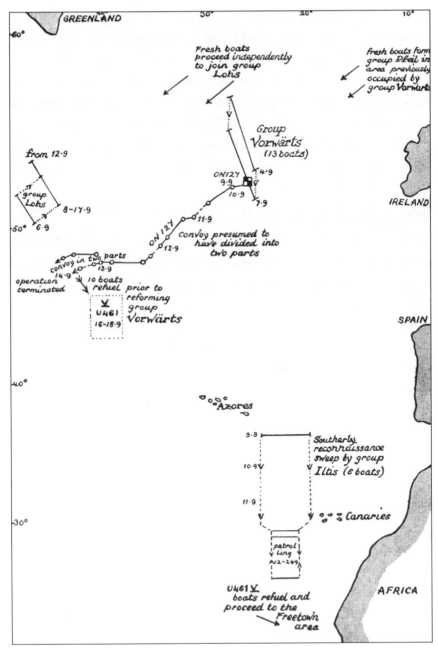

Plan 13. Group lohs, Vorwärts, and Lltis, 4th-24th September, 1942.
Operation against ON 127

September against an ONS convoy. On the 4th Stier was combined with *Vorwärts* to form a long patrol line. The expected ON 127 passed the south end of the formation on the evening of 9th September. Contact was lost in the night, but regained at daylight on the 10th. A number of successful attacks that evening evidently decided the Commodore of the convoy to divide it into two parts. The many radio reports confused the U-boat Command, for all differed as to the position of the convoy. By 13th September it was within range of air protection from Newfoundland, and in the deteriorating visibility the operation was terminated. Our boats claimed nineteen ships sunk or damaged, but in fact only seven and the destroyer Ottawa were sunk, and four damaged.

223. Attacks on SG 99 and ON 129

While the Vorwdrts group was heading southwest with ON 127, some fresh boats were moving towards the area previously occupied by it. On 13th September U.216, while on her way to reinforce Lohs off Newfoundland sighted SC 99, but was immediately forced to submerge and lost the convoy. On the following day U.440, one of the fresh boats, having made contact, was pursued with Asdics and damaged by depth-charges. After the screen had disappeared, she lay on the surface, having to receive assistance from other boats. On the evening of the 14th the pursuit was abandoned. Fresh boats arriving were formed into Group *Pfeil*, and on the 15th one of these sighted and shadowed ON 129, while the others tried to concentrate. Once again the shadower was frustrated by fog. On the following day two boats sighted the screen, and were lured away from the convoy, which took bold avoiding action. The search was given up on 18th September, when *Pfeil* was moved slightly eastward to intercept the next ON convoy.

The disappointing results against these two convoys show the difficulty of continuous shadowing when - as happened in both cases - the convoy is first sighted at one extremity of an extended patrol line.

224. Attack on SC 100

Having completed with fuel from U.462, the Lohs group waited from 6th September 400 miles northeast of Cape Race for eastbound convoys (Plan 14). The patrol line was lengthened by the arrival of fresh boats, but nothing was sighted for ten days. On 17th September we decrypted the noon position on the previous day of SC 100 - 150 miles southeast of Cape Race. A slight southward movement would suffice to put the group on the anticipated path of the convoy by 18th September. It was not until the following day that one or two boats made contact, but the weather prevented any night attacks. On 20th September F.O. U-boats ordered the *Pfeil* boats, then 300 miles southeast, also to close SC 100. But now with a westerly gale reaching hurricane force, and the depression moving eastwards, we thought that most of the pursuers had been left far behind the

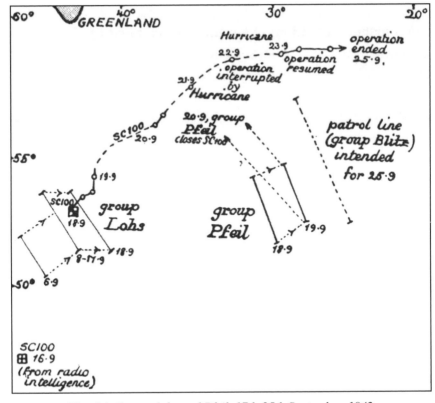

Plan 14. Groups lohs and Pfeil, 17th-25th September, 1942.
Operation against SC 100

convoy, and on 22nd September the operation was stopped. While a new patrol line (Blitz) was being formed, however, U.617 sighted and successfully attacked the convoy, which had also been much retarded by the storm.

On 23rd September Vorwdrts, east of Newfoundland, had sighted an unidentified convoy heading northeast, and the Blitz boats were sent southwest towards the new target. One of them, U.258, while carrying out this instruction, again sighted SC 100, which had apparently been hove to for a long time. This sighting occasioned still new orders, and four boats renewed the pursuit until 25th September. But the strong air protection was too much for them. The final score against SC 100 was three ships and three stragglers sunk. The U-boat Command lamented that this promising operation, at one time involving twenty U-boats, was frustrated by the exceptional weather.

225. Further Operations of Groups *Vorwärts* and *Pfeil*

Between 16th and 18th September Vorwdrts had replenished from U.461 and by 22nd September had taken up a line east of Newfoundland. On the following day an unscheduled eastbound convoy (RB 1) passed through the centre of the formation. The convoy, including eight two-funnel ships, proceeding at 11 or 12 knots, was believed to be carrying troops. It was therefore decided to concentrate all available boats on the target. The *Pfeil* boats, then 400 to 600 miles southeast of Cape Farewell, were ordered southwest at high speed towards the approaching convoy, and succeeded in shadowing it from 23rd to 26th September.

Having once attacked, U-boats found it impossible to regain a forward position for further attacks, since they had only 2 knots advantage in speed. They claimed to have sunk three large U.S. transports - a claim that was thereupon broadcast by the German radio. But the claim was grossly exaggerated, for it was based on mistaken identification. The U-boat commanders in a hurried look through their periscopes had imagined that the silhouettes were those of some big liners shown in " Jane's Merchant Ships." Actually they

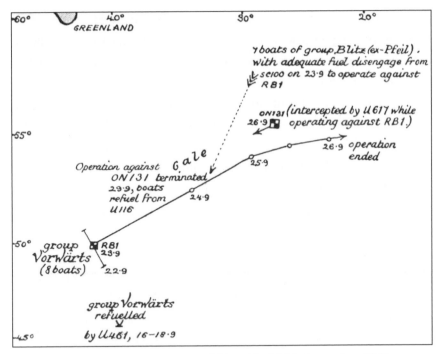

Plan 15. Groups Vorwärts and Blitz, 22nd-29th September, 1942.
Operations against ON 131 and RB I

had sunk three two-funnelled river steamers which had no troops on board - the New York and Boston, each of 5,000 tons, and the Yorktown, of 1,500 tons, and H.M.S. Veteran. During the pursuit of this fast convoy, the boats had become very scattered, and before they could be reformed U.617 sighted ON 131. All boats still ahead of this new target were ordered to operate against it. But the original shadower, having attacked, lost contact, and the prevailing bad weather prevented further search. On 29th September the boats were ordered to refuel northwest of the Azores from U.116 and U.118.

THE WESTERN ATLANTIC

226. Gulf of St. Lawrence and Newfoundland

By 19th July the growing efficiency of American A/S measures forced us to withdraw the boats from the U.S. coast. Not that the prospects further to seaward were much better, and indeed F.O. U-boats actually considered recalling all boats that were still north of Cape Hatteras. But on further reflection it was decided to continue operations south of Nova Scotia while fuel stocks lasted. In these waters there was hope of encountering not only the regular North Atlantic convoys, but also the feeder convoys from Boston and New York to Halifax and St. Johns. On 28th July ON 113 (previously attacked by the Wolf group) was sighted and one ship sunk. Fog prevented the other boats from finding the target, and when U.754 was lost, it was decided to evacuate even this area, and the last remaining boat, U.458 was sent towards Newfoundland.

By the middle of August a number of fresh Type IX boats had reached a position south of Iceland. As the Caribbean and Freetown areas were already sufficiently occupied it was decided to send three of these large boats into the Gulf of St. Lawrence. According to agents' reports convoys and also independent ships issued from the Strait of Belle Isle bound for the Greenland Coast and Great Britain via Iceland. Such traffic had so far been immune from our organised packs, and it was clear of our normal U-boat transit routes. On 23rd August the three boats occupied both sides of the Strait of Belle Isle. In the first few days they sighted only a small convoy east of the island, from which two ships were sunk. They then proceeded up the Gulf of St. Lawrence where another small outward-bound convoy was sighted. U.165 chose an area 100 miles southwest of Anticosti. where the St. Lawrence narrows, and U.517 took up a position between this island and the New Brunswick coast. These boats independently made contact with the same two convoys, one outward-bound on 6th and 7th September and one inward-bound on 15th and 16th September, and between them sank seven ships and torpedoed two others.

This encouraging experience seemed to promise better results than off the U.S. coast or south of Nova Scotia. In the Gulf of St. Lawrence the persistent air patrols had forced the boats to remain submerged during daylight, yet the surface escorts did not press home their attacks. Moreover, the pronounced stratification in the waters of the Gulf much affected the A/S vessels' use of Asdics. But the U-boats also got into difficulties from this cause, for they found that full submerged speed and rapid blowing or flooding of diving tanks were needed while crossing the strata that existed at 60 to 80 metres.

U.513 remained to the southeast of Newfoundland and on 4th September was ordered to make a night attack on ships loading ore at Wabana in Conception Bay. She sank two ore ships, but was rammed during the attack and temporarily withdrew from the coast for repairs. Later she returned to St. Johns where she made two more successful attacks against small convoys, and then headed for Conception Bay and Cape Race.

227. Further Decline in Caribbean Operations

From the beginning of July the volume of sinkings within the Caribbean had fallen and our boats had begun to move to the perimeter of this area. By mid-July we had only two boats between Panama and Trinidad, but six around the Greater Antilles and one southeast of Trinidad. Four boats operated in the Gulf of Mexico where the introduction of convoys had been slow. By the end of July independent ship traffic in this area had become so scarce that U.509 and U.134 were ordered to move through the Yucatan Channel to the Western Caribbean.

Two minelaying operations took place in the latter part of July. The first was on the 20th when six T.M.B. mines were laid at the entrance to Port Castries (St. Lucia). The second occurred four days later, when nine T.M.B. mines were dropped 600 metres off the passes of the Mississippi. At the time F.O. U-boats could not know whether these efforts achieved any results. Later it was learnt that at Port Castries one U.S. Coastguard cutter had been sunk and one British M.T.B. had been damaged.

In the last half of July only one ship was sunk in the Caribbean zone, whereas several were destroyed north and southeast of Trinidad. Consequently at the beginning of August we concentrated six boats

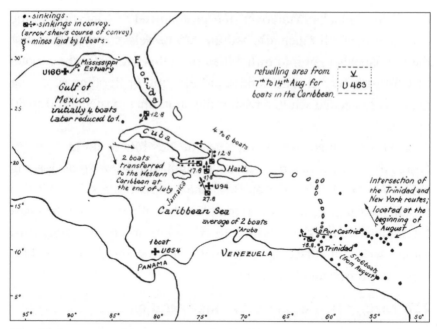

Plan 16. Last successful operations in the Caribbean, 20th July-31st August, 1942

here. Shipping from Gibraltar or Britain to Trinidad followed set routes, which were altered from time to time. Direct traffic from the South Atlantic to the U.S. coast also followed set routes, which passed close eastward of the Antilles. The U-boat Command, using the U-boat reports from this area, worked out the nodal points of the shipping to Trinidad and the U.S. coast. Early in August one such point was established 360 miles east of Trinidad, whence traffic for this island proceeded on a course between 230 degrees and 250 degrees and traffic for the U.S.A. on a course between 310 degrees and 330 degrees. Here within a few days we sank ten ships, and we continued to occupy these waters in force, in the hope of spotting any changes in the routes.

228. Last Important Concentration in the Caribbean

Once they had left their home or Biscay bases, it took the boats from two to four weeks to reach the various operational areas. Thus when planning operations in remote areas, we had often to anticipate the situation a month ahead. The most difficult periods were those immediately after we had decided to occupy a new area or to abandon an old one, for it frequently happened while boats were in transit that conditions in their destined operational areas had undergone a sudden change.

Such a situation arose during July. Quite a number of new U-boats became available early in the month and some of these were ordered to a position southeast of Bermuda for refuelling from U.463, on completion of which they would move to the most promising part of the Caribbean. But by the time the U-tanker had arrived, the situation in the Caribbean had greatly deteriorated due to the formation of convoys. There was no point in sending these boats back to the North Atlantic hunting-ground, or even to Trinidad, for these areas were already receiving attention, and so it was decided to adhere to the original plan. But in view of the now extensive Caribbean air patrols[24], the boats were told to operate independently while seizing any chance of co-ordinated attacks.

Accordingly the Greater Antilles area was occupied by one large and four medium boats , while three boats were placed off Curacao and Aruba and two boats northwest of Trinidad. One boat (U.654), was sent to the Panama Zone. Thus the month of August, 1942, saw the last concentration of any considerable U-boat force in the Caribbean battle area.

229. Successes near Trinidad and the Windward Passage

The narrow waters of the Greater Antilles - the Windward Passage, the waters north and south of Cuba, the Bahama and Nicholas Channels, the Florida Strait - could be easily watched by the enemy, for in these areas his co-ordinated air and surface ship patrols were extensive, forcing the boats to remain submerged for long periods. The tropical heat made conditions on board the U-boats almost unbearable. During August our several attacks on convoys occurred more by chance than due to planning. Thus, on the night of 12th August, U.658

---

24 Allied air coverage in the Gulf and Caribbean in July, 1942, will be found in the Chart in Samuel Eliot Morison's The Battle of the Atlantic, Vol. I. On p. 348 he states that during August, 1942, the approaches to the Windward Passage were as dangerous for shipping as any part of the ocean.

met a convoy apparently assembling in the Windward Passage, and pursued it northward.[25] Further boats joined in the pursuit which did not end until the quarry reached the Nicholas Channel, by which time we had sunk five ships and damaged another. On 17th August U.658, when 90 miles south of Santiago de Cuba, contacted the northbound PG 6, sinking two ships and torpedoing a third. U.553 picked up the sighting report and headed for the Windward Passage in order to join in the attack, but while doing so encountered another convoy, steering west (TAW 13) from which she succeeded in sinking three ships, totalling 17,000 tons. This convoy was also pursued by U. 163 up to the Yucatan Channel, but suffered no further casualties.

On 27th and 28th August, two U-boats about 120 miles southeast of Jamaica attacked TAW 15, sinking two ships and damaging a third. Near Trinidad there was one attack on TAW, from which three ships were sunk between 18th and 21st August, west of Grenada.

In the above cases the participation of further U-boats in the attack was facilitated by the navigational restriction on convoy courses due to the islands and channels. In numbers and efficiency the surface escorts of these convoys were weak. The enemy appeared to rely mainly on strong air patrols, which operated day and night. The aircraft were presumably helped by radar, yet in darkness they appeared to have difficulty in distinguishing between U-boats and surface escorts. When approached by aircraft at night, our boats were in the habit of turning at once to the convoy's course and speed, so as to confuse the air escorts.[26] In this connection Suhren and Thurmann, both experienced commanders, believed that the aircraft did not possess radar, but identified their target by sight.[27] The log of U.564 states:

"The aircraft will always have to drop a flare first, for when

---

25 British records show that at this time the northbound convoy, TAW 12, and a southbound convoy, WAT 13, were in the Windward Passage.

26 With regard to the author's use, here and elsewhere, of the terms "air patrols" and "air escorts", it must be realised that the U-boats were not always able to distinguish between these two forms of air activity.

27 According to Morison, radar had been fitted to most of the U.S. aircraft by the summer of 1942.

the wake of a ship is sighted at night, there is no other way of distinguishing between friend and foe."

230. End of the Caribbean Operations

It was known that, while attacking TAW 15, U.94 had been lost, and U.654 had suffered a similar fate through an air attack north of Panama.

We believed that in these Caribbean operations we had lost two U-boats as the price of sinking 19 ships.[28] The profit and loss account was not much better than the contemporary results in the North Atlantic. But a comparison between results in the two areas would have to allow for the wasteful transit distances to the Caribbean, and the unfavourable climate. During August we had sunk only two independently routed ships in the Caribbean, and September found us planning the eventual evacuation of the whole Central American zone. In future only an occasional U-boat would appear in these waters, so as to dissuade the enemy from reducing his local A/S effort.

The boats were withdrawn to the Trinidad area at the beginning of September. In the first half of the month an average of eight operated successfully between Trinidad and Barbados, and later off the Orinoco. Off Trinidad alone they sank 29 ships totalling 143,000 tons, which constituted a peak of achievement in these waters.[29]

THE CENTRAL ATLANTIC

231. Situation near Freetown

Between March and May, 1942, our Radio Intelligence Service had successfully decrypted a number of routing instructions for shipping in the South and Central Atlantic (296). If such data were applicable

---

28 Actually 15 ships had been sunk during the period under review.

29 In the five months between May and September, 1942, U-boats in the Caribbean and adjacent waters sank an average of 1.5 ships per day, and destroyed over one million gross tons of shipping. By September however a complete interlocking system of coastal convoys came into force, and immediately proved its worth. (Morison, p. 258)

to the conditions in July, it seemed that ships leaving Freetown for Trinidad or New York headed southwest for about 500 miles before turning for their destination. As the volume of shipping was adequate, we decided to send one boat to the area between Fernando Noronha and Natal, and another about 500 miles from the coast between Sierra Leone and Liberia, while the Hai group on 21st July occupied the waters southwest of Freetown. Results off Freetown were disappointing, for by the end of the month only one patrol trawler and two merchant ships had been sunk. But conditions 500 miles west of Freetown were better. Here two boats on their way to refuel from U.116 sank five independent ships between 22nd and 30th July.

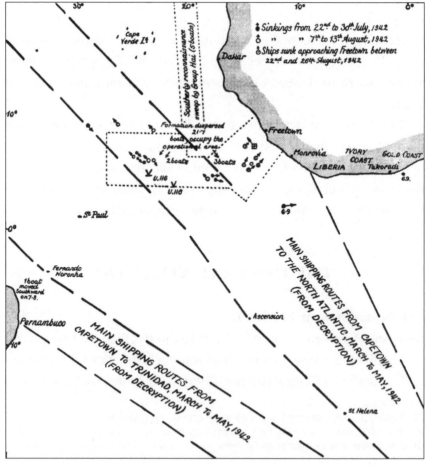

Plan 17. The central Atlantic, July and August, 1942

All were steering either northwest or southeast, about 400 miles off the Sierra Leone-Liberia coast. U.752, 572 and 109 were ordered to operate in this zone, where between 7th and 13th August they sank six further ships. It was then decided to shift the main activity back to the sector southwest of Freetown. This move occurred just in time to sink four ships out of a number that happened to be heading for the port between 22nd and 26th August.

The *Blücher* group, originally intended as relief for the Hai group, was delayed by attacks on SL 118 and 119. Thus no reinforcements arrived in the Central African zone during September, where we had not more than two to four boats to the south and southeast of Liberia. These attacks on the SL convoys between 20 degrees and 24 degrees W. longitude were perhaps more economical than operations off Freetown, for the attackers were much nearer their bases.

232. Attack on Brazilian Coastal Traffic

When by 7th August U.507 had failed to find any traffic between St. Paul's Rock and Natal, she suggested proceeding south along the Brazilian coast. This was approved, and on 16th and 17th August she torpedoed five Brazilian coastal vessels off Bahia, outside territorial waters. A Supreme Command directive dated 4th July had authorized attack without warning on all Brazilian merchant ships, as retaliation for the activities of the Brazilian Air Force and the arming of Brazilian merchant ships. The sinking of these five ships caused Brazil to declare war on Germany on 22nd August.

The German Foreign Office had been informed of the Supreme Command's directive regarding Brazilian ships, and had raised no objection. But now the Foreign Office requested the Naval Staff to desist from further attacks on Brazilian coastal traffic, fearing the possible effect on Chile and the Argentine (297). U.507 was therefore ordered to discontinue these attacks and was advised to proceed to a promising shipping zone 500 miles east of Natal. Her Commanding Officer preferred to wait well off the Brazilian coast until the end of the month, but finding no traffic, he started his return journey via Freetown where he hoped to expend his torpedoes.

Brazil's entry into the war made no difference to our U-boats, which had regarded Brazilian aircraft as hostile ever since the declaration by the Brazilian Air Minister in the previous May.[30] Brazil's surface forces were not expected to embarrass our operations.

233. Views on Capetown Operations

The earliest operation against shipping at the Cape was similar to the original attack on the U.S. coastal shipping, in that both would have to show good results to justify the very long transit routes of the U-boats. While on passage to these remote areas the boats were told to seize every opportunity of attacking targets. The U-boat Command therefore requested the Naval Staff to remove operational restrictions in Zone A between the Equator and 15 degrees South for the boats on their way to Capetown. But the Naval Staff felt that attacks south of the Equator would prematurely disclose our intention to operate in the Cape area, and thereby precipitate the strengthening of A/S measures and the diversion of traffic (298, 299, 300). A surprise appearance off Capetown however would cause confusion to the whole of South African shipping, whose strategic effect would far outweigh any fortuitous successes by U-boats while on passage. F.O. U-boats was not impressed, as his diary shows:

"Strategic pressure alone is hardly sufficient justification for a long-range operation. But if that is all that the Naval Staff requires, it can be achieved as well between the Equator and 15 degrees South. What point is there then in sending the boats on to Capetown?" (301).

This opinion evoked outspoken comments from members of the Naval Staff, whose attitude remained unchanged.

234. The Sinking of the Laconia

Four U-boats with experienced commanders and the tanker U.459, forming the Eisbar group, left Lorient in mid-August, and when west of Spain operated temporarily against SL 119, which had been pursued by the Blucher group. The boats then headed south in formation, sweeping as far as the Cape Verde Islands, after which

---

30 The airport at Natal had been used by a U.S. Naval Air Squadron since 11th December, 1941. See Morison, Chapter XV, for details of U.S. Naval Air bases in Brazil.

they continued independently. When nearing the Equator they were ordered to complete refuelling by 20th September. The Naval Staff now modified their earlier attitude by permitting attacks up to 5 degrees South latitude. While on this parallel on 12th September U.156 torpedoed the British liner Laconia.

As well as normal passengers and crew, this vessel carried about 1,800 Italian prisoners of war. The radio report by her Captain led to a decision which must be unique in the naval history of the war. In order to help the survivors, F.O. U-boats ordered all the boats of Eisbar, together with U.506 and 507 and the Italian U-boat Cagellini, to hurry to the scene of the sinking. To embark all the survivors in U-boats was out of the question, so an attempt had to be made to tow the life-boats towards the Ivory coast. The German Naval Staff proposed to the Vichy Government that French ships should leave Bingerville and Dakar to pick up the survivors. Meanwhile Hitler had informed F.O. U-boats that he did not wish the operations of the Eisbar group to be hampered, or the U-boats to be endangered by any rescue measures.

While negotiations with the Vichy Government were proceeding, U.156 alone started the rescue work in darkness, embarking 193 survivors, including 21 British. At 0600 she broadcast her position in plain language on 600 metres announcing that she would not attack any ship assisting the Laconia survivors. After daylight on 13th September another 200 survivors were picked up and distributed among the crowded life-boats.

The Vichy Government agreed to the German Naval Staff's suggestion and promised to send a French cruiser to the place of sinking. Consequently on 14th September the Eisbar group was instructed to continue its southward journey, provided they carried no survivors. U.504, 159, 172 and 68, who had not yet arrived at the scene of the sinking, therefore continued south. U.156 was to turn over her survivors to the U-boats coming from Freetown and then proceed according to previous instructions. U.506 and 507 arrived on the scene on the night of 14th/15th September, and assisted in towing the life-boats and rafts, and shepherding the scattered boats. U.156 remained on the scene in order to transfer her 260 survivors. On the morning of the 16th a U.S. four-engined aircraft sighted this U-boat and circled several times. An hour later another aircraft of the same type flew past, very low, dropping two bombs, although the U-boat was flying a large square Red-Cross flag. One of two further bombs fell into a life-boat, which capsized. Another exploded very close to the U-boat, causing some damage, and all survivors were ordered out of her. Resulting from all this, instructions were received during the night of the 16th to discontinue all rescue operations. Despite these further instructions the Commanding Officers continued their work.

On 17th September the French ships Annamite and Gloire arrived to take over survivors from U-boats and life-boats. A further air attack was made on U.506, which managed to escape by diving with 142 survivors on board.

The U-boats engaged in these rescue operations had been greatly imperilled by the efforts of the enemy aircraft to sink them. The situation required immediate clarification, for whereas the conduct of the enemy under the harsh conditions of war was understandable, Dönitz's rescue directive had gravely endangered his boats. On the evening of the 17th therefore the following radio message (referred to in the post-war Niirnberg proceedings as the Laconia Order) was sent to all U-boat commander:

"1924/17.9

1. All attempts at rescuing members of ships that have been sunk, including attempts to pick up persons swimming, or to place them in life-boats, or attempts to upright capsized boats, or to supply provisions or water, are to cease. The rescue of survivors contradicts the elementary necessity of war for the destruction of enemy ships and crews.

2. The order for the seizure of Commanding Officers and Chief Engineers remains in force.

3. Survivors are only to be picked up in cases when their interrogation would be of value to the U-boat.

4. Be severe. Remember that in his bombing attacks on German cities the enemy has no regard for women and children."

F.O. U-boats"

In the major trials at Niirnberg the prosecution failed to prove that this directive by F.O. U-boats constituted a clear order to U-boat commanders to kill survivors from torpedoed ships. Neither was there any condemnation of Dönitz as regards his conduct of the U-boat war or of the naval war in general. Moreover, the thousands of U-boat actions in the Second World War produced only one case (*Kapitanleutnant* Eck in U.852) where a commander shot up survivors.

Statements by the prosecution at Niirnberg were much publicised at the time, yet the fact that these allegations were not upheld by the Court received no corresponding publicity, so that false ideas as to the conduct of U-boat personnel still persist today.[31] The German U-boat service claims to have fought hard but decently and chivalrously until the end.

ENEMY A/S DEVELOPMENTS

235. Use of *Metox*

The period between July and September, 1942, marks a transition to a new conception of U-boat operations, with emphasis on attacking, rather than finding, targets. It will be recalled that in commenting

---

31 The author's conclusions cannot pass unchallenged. In pronouncing judgement, the Tribunal considered that although the evidence (which included the *Laconia* Order) did not establish with the certainty required that Dönitz deliberately ordered the killing of survivors, the orders were undoubtedly ambiguous, and deserved the strongest censure. Moreover, the rescue provisions of the Protocol of 1936 had not been carried out, and Dönitz had ordered that they should not be carried out. The Defence argued that the security of the submarine was paramount to rescue, and that the development of aircraft made rescue impossible. But the Tribunal maintained that the Protocol was explicit. If the commander (of a submarine) could not rescue, then under its terms he could not sink a merchant vessel. The orders therefore proved Dönitz guilty of a violation of the Protocol. (See Command Paper 6964 "Judgement of the International Military Tribunal for the Trail of German Major War Criminals - Nuremberg", p. 109.)

on the attacks in May and June, 1942, on the ON convoys by the *Hecht* group, the U-boat Command considered that the enemy's A/S methods had developed little since the previous Autumn (Section 207). This reassuring estimate was valid only in the open Atlantic, for in the Bay of Biscay the enemy's airborne radar had already become an alarming factor. The first counter-measures began in June with the fitting of a radar search receiver and of anti-aircraft machine guns. Increased German fighter protection was provided in the Bay of Biscay, where the boats were ordered to remain submerged. But these measures hardly sufficed to meet the new crisis, for within five weeks in July and August three experienced commanders (U.502, U.578 and U.751) fell victim to the Biscay patrol of the R.A.F. Coastal Command. As far as we then knew, these were the first enemy air successes in those waters.

The first delivery of the anxiously awaited radar search receiver (*Metox*) was made early in August. This equipment was deliberately kept simple in order to hasten its production. It took the form of an ordinary receiver in the radio room, connected by a flexible cable to an aerial mounted on a wooden cross. Every time the boat broke surface, this contraption was rushed up to the fore end of the conning tower and mounted in a socket. It had to be turned through 90 degrees at frequent intervals in order to eliminate the dead sectors characteristic of this instrument. The equipment in this primitive form was not popular, for in heavy seas or when having to dive suddenly the wooden cross would suffer damage and the cable would get in the way when closing the conning tower hatch.

A Radio Petty Officer - later a Warrant Officer - was assigned to each U-boat for *Metox* duties. Searching on all probable frequencies, his function was to report to the conning tower as soon as he heard any radar impulses. This equipment, though primitive, produced results. On 2nd August U.107 reported that while in the Bay she had several times been caught in a radar sweep on 169 cm, and had escaped attack by promptly diving. Other U-boats had similar experiences. But the supply of the *Metox* equipment did not keep pace with requirements, and we lost some boats between Iceland and the Shetlands, including the valuable tanker U.464. It was therefore just as important to equip U-boats from Kiel and Bergen with *Metox* before they started for the North Atlantic, and by September it was possible to do this.

Boats already at sea which had not got the equipment were told that when returning and within operational range of the R.A.F. Coastal Command, they were to form convoys, the leader keeping *Metox* guard. This procedure was not easy at night or in bad visibility, when the warning signals had to be passed rapidly to the U-boats, but it worked fairly well.

Before long the supply of *Metox* was sufficient for spares to be carried by outward-bound boats so that exchange or replacement of the equipment could be made at sea. Often this occurred northeast of the Azores, which ensured that returning U-boats would have their *Metox* in good order before entering the Bay.

236. Westward Extension of Atlantic Air Patrols

With the resumption of convoy battles in July, 1942, F.O. U-boats soon realised that the enemy's air power had grown sufficiently to provide several daily patrols of the Bay of Biscay and also additional aircraft for convoys being pursued by our boats. Our operations against OS 33, SL 118, SC 97 and SC 99 all had to be stopped prematurely owing to the arrival of continuous air cover. Whereas in 1941 the effective radius of action of these aircraft was about 500 miles, it had now apparently risen to 800 miles, so that when starting from Icelandic bases, they could be seen west of a line joining Cape Farewell and Gibraltar. The Sunderland flying boats and four-engined bombers used for this purpose were all fitted with radar and carried an adequate bomb-load. The handicap to the U-boats would be correspondingly greater as soon as air cover could be extended across the whole North Atlantic (302).

237. Increased Efficiency of Surface A/S Forces

Our attacks on SC 94 and SL 118 in September, 1942, proved beyond doubt that the surface screens were using an efficient location device against U-boats, and the observations on the *Metox* showed that the radar used by remote screens was becoming a menace.

We also established the presence of convoy support groups which were acting in support of the normal screens for particular convoys. Such groups, consisting of destroyers, frigates, corvettes or even trawlers, were sometimes found in a waiting area, and at other times they seemed to be closing on some convoy which was under attack by our boats. They were also in evidence on the transit routes of U-boats in the Bay of Biscay and south of Iceland. We concluded therefore that their purpose was not merely to rush to the support of convoys in difficulties, but also for general patrol and independent hunting of the U-boats.[32] We noted how well these support groups worked with aircraft. If a U-boat were sighted by an aircraft, it was frequently not long before a hunter group or a single destroyer arrived at the position where the boat had dived. Both aircraft and surface vessels searched the area so thoroughly that it was no easy matter to escape the hunters.

The various noises heard by our U-boats when being pursued led to the conclusion that the enemy used several types of locating devices working on the asdic principle. At short ranges they appeared to be more accurate than before, and the U-boats were now forced to dive to 140 metres or more, because of the better aim and deeper settings of the depth-charges.

238. New A/S Technique

On 29th July, a U-boat commander had reported that on the northern transit route to the Atlantic he had observed British aircraft dropping buoys which emitted asdic noises for several hours. At that stage of the war German technicians did not consider that such a floating body could contain asdic equipment and transmitter, and that the dropping of these buoys could only be intended to simulate the presence of

---

32 There were no surface hunting forces in these areas at that time. The forces encountered must therefore have been convoy escorts proceeding to or from rendezvous with convoys in the course of relieving escorts.

destroyers with asdics, particularly at night, in the hope of forcing the U-boat to remain submerged. F.O. U-boats inferred that this new device was intended to discourage the U-boat from surfacing. Our successes in the past had been largely due to the ability of the U-boats to 'proceed at high surface speed towards the attacking position. This movement occurred either out of visual range of the enemy or under cover of darkness. If this ability were lost the whole future of the U-boat campaign would be in jeopardy.

GERMAN COUNTER-MEASURES

239. Development of *Walter* Boats

F.O. U-boats realised that German counter-measures were not keeping pace with developments in the enemy's A/S technique. In Germany the bureaucratic methods of peacetime still obstructed collaboration between the users of weapons and their manufacturers. On several occasions Dönitz had complained to the C.-in-C. of the Navy about dilatory methods in the departments of the German Admiralty responsible for torpedo developments, and construction and repair of the U-boats. No great improvement resulted, but when events in the Bay of Biscay imperilled the U-boat campaign, Dönitz sent a memorandum to the Commander-in-Chief, dated 24th June, 1942, proposing the most rapid development and large-scale construction of the *Walter* type U-boats. He also suggested that a U-boat officer, experienced in torpedo and location problems, be appointed to co-ordinate operational requirements with experimental developments. This officer would be directly subordinate to the C.-in-C. of the Navy and have priority with all Admiralty departments. Raeder, while approving the appointment, did not agree that the post should be subordinated to him personally, and Dönitz regretted this decision, for it limited the authority of the officer in question (303).

In June, F.O. U-boats learned by chance that the *Luftwaffe*, having made a detailed study of the enemy's radar equipment, had produced an apparatus of its own design, called Lichtenstein. Moreover the development of a remote control rocket for use by big ships against torpedo bombers was being considered.

Dönitz had received no official intimation of either development, and this prompted him on 4th September to write to the Commander-in-Chief:

"F.O. U-boats learned by a mere chance of certain weapon developments which might be vitally important to the U-boat war. This shows the lack of co-operation between operational interests and experimental establishments. The whole issue of the war depends on applying the latest technical developments to help U-boats to overcome the ever-growing menace of the enemy's A/S devices" (304).

Consequently a meeting was called on 28th September, between Raeder and the heads of all departments of the Admiralty, at which the fundamental requirements in weapon development were defined (305). One of these was the fast submerged U-boat, known as the *Walter* boat. Although in the Second World War this boat never became operational, its potentialities greatly influenced the ideas and even the policy of the U-boat Command during 1943 and 1944, and it merits a brief description here.

240. The *Walter* Boat

The restrictions imposed on U-boats by the improved enemy A/S measures could only be effectively countered by using high submerged speed. Such a boat would not have to struggle on the surface against heavy odds to attain a good attacking position, but once having sighted, heard or located a convoy, would be able to proceed underwater to a suitable position for attack. The enemy would find himself confronted by a new and surprising type of submarine, against which the existing A/S devices would be largely ineffective.

As early as 1937 Dönitz had made contact with the engineer, Professor Walter. Thereafter he made vain efforts to interest the Naval Staff in the possibilities of the Ingolin-driven turbine as invented by

Walter, which might be equally suitable for surface or submerged propulsion. Walter was eventually allowed to produce his first boat. This was a small experimental version of the real thing, and by the Spring of 1940 it was undergoing preliminary trials in the Bay of Danzig. V.80, as it was called, had a displacement of 80 tons, and actually attained a submerged speed of over 23 knots.

In January, 1940, the Naval Staff had authorised Walter to proceed with a prototype (the V.300) of an Atlantic U-boat. This experimental 550-ton boat was to resemble the existing standard Atlantic types, but with the Walter propulsion and a streamlined superstructure with Plexiglass covering it was hoped to achieve a maximum submerged speed of 19 knots. Meanwhile, the trials of V.80 in 1940-41, and the latest experience with operational U-boats had convinced F.O. U-boats that an entirely new design of hull was needed. At the beginning of 1942 he sought the approval of the Naval Staff to scrap V.300 and start again, but this was not granted, and in February the Germania Yard was ordered to proceed with the original design. At this time designs were also being produced for a smaller (250 ton) boat, to embody the lessons of the V.80 experiments. In July, 1942, Dönitz's proposal to scrap V.300 was eventually accepted in the light of further research, and an entirely new design known as V.301, was started. Contracts for two smaller *Walter* boats, of 250 tons each, were given to Blohm and Voss, and to Germania, both yards being allowed considerable latitude in their designs. These smaller boats were intended to procure data before embarking on mass production of the larger *Walter* boats.

While it is true that progress with such a revolutionary type of propulsion was bound to involve checks and delays, the author nevertheless believes that the eagerness and energy of Dönitz in pressing for the development of the " true submarine " as represented by these prototypes was in marked contrast to the hesitant attitude of the Naval Staff, which lost us many months of irreplaceable time (306).

241. Radar Counter-measures

Our experts considered various counter-measures, such as jamming and radar decoys to frustrate the enemy's increasing use of radar. They referred the problem to the scientific departments of our Universities, hoping that these would offer some solution, but preliminary replies indicated that the academic scientists had no new suggestions. In August the *Metox* search receiver was showing good results, within a limited range of frequencies. But before a more comprehensive apparatus could be designed, it was essential to organise a radar observation service to discover the methods used by the enemy (307).

F.O. U-boats now suggested a jamming transmitter to interfere with A.S.V. in the Bay of Biscay (308). Its use in a U-boat or an aircraft might involve dangers, yet it was essential to try out all possibilities. Another suggestion was to absorb the radar impulses by covering the exposed surfaces of the U-boat with a special material. We had to investigate whether the enemy was using infra-red equipment for locating. Yet another line of enquiry produced an apparatus known as the *Seehund* 3, for registering the heat radiations from the exhaust gases of enemy aircraft at night. This experimental apparatus had insufficient range, and would be quite useless against aircraft with screened exhaust flames.

242. German Radar Unsatisfactory

A German radar set, known as Bete, had been developed before the outbreak of war, but its aerial equipment was too large and its performance inadequate for use in U-boats. The criticism that U-boat officers made of the apparatus in these early days seems to have deterred the Naval Staff from further experiments, for it was not until the end of 1941 that radar equipment for U-boats was again seriously considered. The new instrument then produced - known as the Fu.M.G. - had a poor performance, and in U-boats its arc of search was limited to 30 degrees each side of right ahead, so that the boat had to be manoeuvred while searching. But as nothing else was available, it was decided to instal the equipment in U-boats in preference to hydrophone gear. The Fu.M.G. was first used in June, 1942, when 30 sets were installed in new boats. The preliminary results showed that under favourable conditions the set would register ship targets up to 8,000 metres. That the Naval Staff currently believed this instrument to be as good as that of any foreign power is an indication of our lack of reliable technical intelligence concerning the enemy's radar.

The Fu.M.G. was originally intended to locate ships only, but experience of aircraft in the Bay of Biscay, and of the surface escorts of ON 122 in particular, had shown the need for a combined air and surface radar and interception set - known as the Fu.M.G.\M.B. With this new equipment it was hoped to be able to shadow convoys by radar alone. In September it was arranged to provide such an instrument with a frame aerial which could be raised from the U-boat, and turned through the full arc. We were still experimenting with *Metox* and with the Lichstentein equipment that had been built by the firm of Telefunken. This much smaller model that the firm had built for the *Luftwaffe* was adaptable for U-boats.

243. A.A. Armament of U-boats

In the past the surest protection against aircraft had been a good lookout, so as to dive before being attacked (309). But greater air speeds had so changed the situation, that even if detected by the U-boats, the attacking aircraft could not always be eluded. If the U-boat were bombed while in the process of diving, she was most vulnerable. Therefore, the rule was not to dive unless a depth of 60 to 80 metres could be reached before the bombs began to fall. It was always a grave decision to remain on the surface and face up to an approaching enemy aircraft, for the U-boats' only weapon was a 2 cm. machine gun, which was liable to fail at the critical moment, after being exposed to sea-water for perhaps weeks on end.[33]

The gunnery experts decided that if a surfaced U-boat were

---

33 After mid-1942 British Coastal Command aircraft were being equipped with Torpex-filled depth-charges having effective shallow-depth pistols for use against U-boats (C.B. 3304 (1), Section 21).

effectively to repel an air attack, it would need either four 3-7 cm. or eight 2 cm. A.A. guns, but this was too much, and a compromise had to be sought (310). By mid-1942 a new and effective twin 3-7 cm. mounting and also a twin 2 cm. (Type C.38) had been evolved, and experiments were being made with an A.A. rocket against low-flying aircraft.

On 28th September F.O. U-boats discussed the state of anti-aircraft development in U-boats with the C.-in-C. of the Navy in the presence of the Führer. Hitler proposed the use of 3-7 cm. guns with Hexogem filling m the A.A. shells. Earlier that month U.256 had returned with extensive damage from bombing attacks, and it was decided not to repair her for further torpedo operations, but to equip her specially as an A.A. U-boat, with the latest radar and guns. The intention was to use her in the Bay of Biscay to escort returning lame ducks, which could not dive (311). This experimental boat could dispense with its normal 8-8 cm. gun and with torpedoes, the weight and space being taken up with anti-aircraft guns and ammunition.

244. Long-range Aircraft demanded by the Naval Staff

Another means of countering the enemy air menace in the Atlantic was to use our own long-range bombers as fighters (312). F.O. U-boats' visit to General Jeschonneck - Chief of Staff of the *Luftwaffe* - on 2nd July resulted in the allocation to the *Fliegerführer*Atlantic of 24 Ju 88 C VI, to be used as heavy fighters in the coastal areas. But they could not operate beyond 8 degrees West. In July and August several U-boat operations against convoys were abandoned because of the appearance of air escorts. Consequently, F.O. U-boats officially requested the Naval Staff to ask the *Luftwaffe* for He 177 aircraft to be used as long-range fighter-bombers. This multi-purpose 4-engined machine was reputed to be superior in speed, maneuverability and armament to all known enemy types of A/S aircraft. The He 177 had a designed radius of action of 2,200 kilometres, enabling it to reach the very areas where we had been forced to break off our attacks. The employment of such aircraft in support of convoy operations was expected to favour the U-boat by causing scattering of ships owing to bombing attacks and by drawing off the enemy's air patrols. A good example of what could be achieved was the attack on PQ 17 in northern waters, when our U-boats scored successes, but only after the *Luftwaffe* on 4th and 7th July had caused the ships of the convoys to scatter.[34] Commenting on that operation, F.O. U-boats had stated:

"Even a slight dispersion of ships of the convoy produces weak spots where our U-boats can penetrate and attack. Alternating attacks by aircraft and U-boats provide the best possibilities for both methods."

F.O. U-boats had been promised one Staffel of He 177. Unfortunately, however, Hitler had decided to use the first formation of this new type for reconnaissance work on the Eastern front. In spite of Raeder's personal appeal, this decision remained in force. The Commander-in-Chief of the *Luftwaffe* had himself promised the aircraft to the Navy, but the transfer was postponed from month to month.

But even the He 177 had insufficient range for operation in mid-Atlantic or for support of blockade-runners, whose safe passage was vital to our war economy. The Naval Staff therefore appealed to the *Luftwaffe* High Command on 15th August and again on 26th September to produce an entirely new design of aircraft for naval requirements. The reply from the C.-in-C. *Luftwaffe* on 3rd October stated that the naval requirements were too exacting and beyond technical realisation. It should be noted that an identical excuse had been made by the *Luftwaffe* in 1940, when the requirement of long-range reconnaissance aircraft for naval purposes was first raised (313).[35]

---

34 The scattering of PQ 17 was *not* caused by the *Luftwaffe*, but was ordered by the Admiralty, on 4th July, because of the threat from enemy surface ships. (See revised Battle Summary No. 22 *Convoys to North Russia, 1942*.)

35 The differences between Raeder and Göring over the role of the *Luftwaffe* in naval warfare have a counterpart in the acute controversy between the United States Army and Navy about the organisation of land-based A/S aircraft, which reached its climax in 1943. But whereas the German Navy failed to solve its air problem, General Marshall decided on 1st September, 1943, to order the disbandment of the Army A/S Air Command, and thereafter the U.S. Navy acquired complete control of the aerial aspects of A/S warfare in all'areas not covered by the Coastal Command or the Royal Canadian Force.

245. New Weapons against Enemy Escorts

In the First World War the U-boats' principal enemy had been the destroyer. Before the Second World War we had devoted much time to the problem of providing an antidote. When war came, the development of radar and other locating devices gave the destroyer still greater advantages and the problem became acute (314). Among the possibilities which had been considered since 1937 were a target-seeking acoustic torpedo, also a torpedo controlled by a radio beam, and a small rocket-propelled torpedo (315). Of these the acoustic torpedo, known as the G7s, had been in the experimental stage for some years. Some speed had to be sacrificed in order to accommodate the necessary acoustic steering and control mechanism. The control mechanism functioned when the inclination of the target was between 60 degrees and 180 degrees. There was some risk that the firing U-boat or another U-boat in the vicinity might be hit by the torpedo, yet the advantage of being able to attack a destroyer coming straight towards one is so considerable that this risk had to be accepted (316). There were patents in Great Britain and the United States for a steering mechanism on the acoustic principle ; hence if we began to use the weapon, it would probably evoke an antidote such as a noise-making body towed by the target ship to deflect the torpedo.

The first hundred G7s torpedoes were to be issued in the Autumn of 1941 (317), but difficulties in development much retarded delivery. For instance, the impact pistol of our torpedoes could not be relied upon to function when the track angle was less than 50 degrees, whereas the magnetic pistol was still not reliable. All this occasioned F.O. U-boats to remark on 12th October:

"The utmost priority must be applied to the development of an effective anti-destroyer torpedo, for without such a weapon the future of U-boat operations is in jeopardy" (318).

At *Peenemünde* in August, 1942, the technicians working on rocket development considered that a remote-controlled rocket would have distinct possibilities against destroyers. They pointed out that the Navy had already placed a contract for the development of a remote-controlled rocket, for use in big ships to repel torpedo-bomber attacks (319), but that the project would require several years to develop. F.O. U-boats stressed the much greater importance of providing U-boats with such a weapon. He was ready to sacrifice some of the attacking power of his boats provided they had some means of defence against destroyers. Thereupon the Commander-in-Chief ordered personnel to be made available for the necessary research work.

The possibility was even explored of firing rockets from submerged U-boats against attacking destroyers. In the summer of 1942 preliminary experiments were made in co-operation with the *Peenemünde* establishment. At that time the object was to provide a submerged U-boat with a weapon against the shore, for example, to attack the Russian railway lines along the Black Sea coast. The possibility of using this weapon against destroyers depended on whether an adequate target-seeking control mechanism could be devised.

246. Defence against Asdic Pursuit

Before the war it was customary in the Press of several foreign countries, including Great Britain, to decry the submarine as somewhat antiquated because of vastly improved methods of location.[36] Dönitz thought that this might be a propaganda device by the British to dissuade foreign Navies from building submarines. Before the war we had tried rubber and plastic materials as coatings for the hull of the U-boat, which were intended to absorb the asdic impulses. Trials with U.11 showed that such devices would definitely decrease the effective range of asdics. But it was difficult to get the sheet rubber to stick to the hull. For example, U.67, while on passage from Norway to a French base in 1941, lost 60 per cent, of the covering. By 1943 a satisfactory material had been found, but as the fitting to boats was costly and lengthy, the plan was dropped,

---

36 It is true that before the war there was a misplaced optimism in British naval circles as to the effectiveness of asdics in countering U-boats.

although our scientists could suggest no other method of countering asdics.

In 1941 Dönitz had told Admiral Mertens, the Director of the Signal Division, that some form of asdic decoy was needed and by the autumn of that year a device had been produced. It consisted of a cylinder about 15 cm. in diameter containing a substance which on contact with sea water decomposed into large quantities of gas. On being pursued with asdics the U-boat would discharge three such cylinders from a specially fitted tube in the stern. The gasses produced would cover a sufficient area to provide false echoes in the enemy's asdics, and so mislead him as to the U-boat's position. Some U-boat commanders reported that this method, if used with skill, would mislead the pursuing destroyers. But although the supply of this decoy had some beneficial effect on the morale of the crews, most Commanding Officers realised its limitations. Other applications of the principle were now investigated, such as explosive decoys and buoys which would reproduce the characteristic noises of a U-boat.

In addition to asdics the enemy escort vessels sometimes carried hydrophones. During working up training our crews were taught the importance of travelling under water with a minimum of noise. Before proceeding on operations, all boats were tested for undue submerged noises from the electric machinery. Beginning in 1942 all engine and machinery were mounted on vibration-absorbing bearers, which also served to mitigate the strain or damage from exploding depth-charges.

Always the best protection against depth-charges was to dive deeply. In the early stages of the war we discovered many leaks at these bigger depths, but by 1940 these weaknesses had been remedied so that all boats could dive to 160 or 180 metres without danger. But now the deeper settings of depth-charges sometimes forced the boats to go even deeper ; and the specifications for the new boats of Type VIIC included standard resistance at 200 metres, which in practice meant that in an emergency they could go down to 300 metres without harm. The pressure hull of these boats had to be strengthened so much that the displacement increased by nearly 250 tons. It should be mentioned here that some U-boats of Type VIIC (1941) were still being commissioned for operations in 1945. Eighty boats of Type VIIC (1942) had been contracted for and were partly on the stocks when it was decided on 13th August, 1943, to concentrate on the construction of Type XXI, and all older contracts were cancelled (320).[37]

247. Improvements in Torpedo Design

The following extract from F.O. U-boats' diary, dated 24th June, 1942, reveals continuing difficulties with our torpedoes:

"Compared with the First World War, we now have two main improvements - the bubble-free discharge and the trackless run, which, however, has reduced the speed of the torpedo to 30 knots. Yet the depth-keeping and detonation qualities of the torpedo have not even reached the level attained in 1918, although we have now had 1\ years of trials and strenuous efforts. The destructive effect of the warhead when used with an impact pistol is insufficient, as is shown by the many cases of ordinary freighters needing more than one torpedo to sink them."

The most important requirement was a usable magnetic pistol. As explained in Volume I, Section 48, it had been decided in June, 1940, to give up using the magnetic pistol. An analysis of the results of hits with the impact pistol for the first six months of 1942 is given by the following tables: (321)

Sunk by:	
1 hit	210 ships or 40.3 %
2 hits	149 ships or 29.9 %
3 hits	39 ships or 7.4 %
4 hits	6 ships or 1.0 %
Total	404 ships or 77.6 %

Damaged by:	
1 hit	83 ships or 15.9 %
2 hits	29 ships or 5.7 %
3 hits	4 ships or 0.6 %
4 hits	1 ships or 0.2 %
Total	117 ships or 22.4 %

In order to sink 404 ships the boats had needed 806 torpedo hits. Had we been able to use a magnetic pistol, which requires only

---

37 For details of U-boat construction policy see Volume I of this work, Appendix I.

one torpedo to sink a ship, this would have virtually doubled the opportunities for destruction of shipping. The sinkings in the first half of 1942 would certainly have been much bigger. It will be recalled that most U-boats operating off the American coast or in the Caribbean had to begin their homeward passage prematurely because of empty torpedo tubes.

The Italian Navy had developed a magnetic pistol which worked on the principle that interference with the magnetic field of the torpedo would be achieved by the magnetic influence of a target ship. The German Torpedo Experimental Department having tried out this Italian device, was ready to take it over for the U-boats if it should prove more reliable than the existing German Pi.2.[38]

The development of enemy A/S technique forced us to consider using only long-range torpedoes for attacking convoys. In that case special devices would have to guide the torpedo to its target. The G7s, an acoustic torpedo, originally intended for attacking enemy destroyers, might be suitable. But by mid-1942 another torpedo had passed successful trials, namely the F.A.T. It was designed to run on a straight course for a controlled distance, and thereafter in a series of loops either to the right or the left of its original line of advance depending on the course of the target. This was a compressed air torpedo, with a range of 12,500 metres at 30 knots.

We were anxious to conceal this new device from the enemy. At first, therefore, it was to be used only at night, because of its conspicuous bubble track. When using it, an accurate range of the target was essential so that after the requisite straight run, the loop run would cover the water on both sides of the target. In fact radar ranging (Fu.M.G.) was necessary when using this torpedo, and the manufacture of the electronic equipment was expedited. Meanwhile it was planned to carry out final trials of the G7a F.A.T. torpedoes

---

38 The German Navy was not the only one to suffer from ineffective magnetic pistols. In U.S. *Submarine Operations in World War II* by T. Roscoe, published by the U.S. Naval Institute at Annapolis, it is revealed that the U.S. Navy had been at war for nearly two years before their submarine torpedoes had a reliable magnetic pistol, and the author comments that "the cost of this deficiency to the U.S. war effort in lives, dollars and time remains incalculable."

in October in the presence of F.O. U-boats. A similar torpedo with electric propulsion (G7a F.A.T.) was expected to be ready a few months later.

For attacks on fast targets construction was started of the G5ut, with an Ingolin piston engine, and the G7ut, Ingolin-turbine driven. Both types were intended eventually for *Walter* boats, and although preliminary trials had shown them to be capable of running 3,000 to 4,000 metres at 47 knots, many difficulties had arisen, and no definite completion date could be given.

248. Other Improvements to U-Boats

In the course of the war the U-boats had gradually increased their loads of fuel, torpedoes, A.A. ammunition and stores, and the resulting increased draft affected their maximum surface speed. The loss of even one knot is a serious matter when trying to gain a forward position against a convoy. One method of increasing the surface speed was to super-charge the diesel engines, and in some cases an increase of 1£ knots was achieved by using *Buchi* or *Kapsel* blowers. The engineering firm of Deutz was developing an efficient two-stroke Diesel.

It was most important that our long-range U-boats of Type IXD should have adequate speed to attack the numerous fast independently sailed vessels carrying valuable war material. Two of these U-boats, U.180 and U.195, were fitted with six 12 cylinder motor torpedo boat engines, manufactured by *Daimler-Benz*. F.O. U-boats was never in favour of such engines, because of their unreliability, but the Naval Staff considered that they were "more practical than Dönitz's 'Utopian' idea of the *Walter* boat" (322). Once again F.O. U-boats' objections proved valid, for these two U-boats had continuous engine trouble and required eight months' trials before proceeding on their first operation. On their return the Daimler engines had to be replaced by M.A.N., diesels, which taxed the resources of the dockyard at Bordeaux.

In order to increase the range of vision of U-boats, a Helicopter type of kite was designed, to be towed by the U-boat. It was known as the F.A. 330, and was given the cover name of "Water-wagtail." When not in use this kite had to be stowed in two water-tight boxes, nearly two metres high, which were secured on the after side of the conning tower. When assembled, the kite rested on a small platform on the after side of the conning tower. When the boat steamed at high speed into the wind, the rotating blades lifted the kite and the observer into the air up to a height of 150 metres. The observer could communicate with the conning tower by telephone. Should an enemy aircraft attack, or the boat have to crash dive, the tow rope was slipped, and if the observer were lucky, he descended undamaged on the water and was later picked up by the U-boat. It can be seen that this apparatus was only suitable for use in remote areas where there were no enemy air patrols.

Another type of Helicopter known as the Kolibri, was a small version of the Helicopter designed for ships and A/S vessels, known as the FL 282. The rotor blades were propelled by an electric motor, driven by power supplied from the U-boat along the electric cable incorporated in the tow rope. In September, 1942, the prototype of this Helicopter had undergone trials, but difficulties in stability caused delays in equipping operational boats.

249. Prospects in October, 1942

Numbers of U-boats alone would no longer provide a solution, for the survival of these boats depended absolutely on improvement in weapons and technique. Yet F.O. U-boats, though aware of the dangerous trend of the enemy's A/S technique, did not at this period regard the continuance of operations as seriously threatened. His policy would be to apply all technical advances towards reducing U-boat losses, while awaiting the entirely new methods that the *Walter* propulsion foreshadowed.

The introduction of *Metox* had at once alleviated the threat from airborne radar.[39] Why therefore should not further improvement result

---

39 *Metox* had reduced the efficiency of our day air patrols in the Bay of Biscay, and defeated the night patrols altogether. The only solution was to fit aircraft with 10 centimetre A.S.V. and on 26th November, 1942, the C.A.S. appealed to General Arnold to accelerate the fitting of this equipment to the British allocation of Liberators and any further American

from the new Flak, the new acoustic torpedo, the magnetic pistol, and the Fu.M.G./M.B. After the sudden heavy losses during July, amounting to 15 per cent, of U-boats at sea, the figure had dropped to 9·3 per cent, for August, and 6 per cent, for September. This was considered acceptable, as compared with the overall average for 1941 of 11·4 per cent. Moreover, sinkings had mounted since July. In that month they were 504,000 tons, and in each of the two following months about 650,000 tons. This result had been achieved despite a reduction in the number of boats in the remote areas, where opportunities were better than nearer home.

We were now getting 18 to 20 new boats every month, and with the growing operational strength, it would soon be possible to employ three or four groups simultaneously against North Atlantic convoys. In September also some new boats with experienced commanders had started for the remote areas, so that here too we could hope for good results. Four were on their way to the St. Lawrence, four to Freetown, three to the Guinea coast, and two to the mouth of the Congo.

250. Effect of Weather on Location of Attacks
In September bad weather had robbed us of success against SC 100 and ON 131, and early in October the C.-in-C. of the Navy suggested that " with the advent of seasonal bad weather in the North Atlantic it might be worth while to shift the boats to the Central Atlantic, where prospects of targets are equally good" (323).

This problem of weather constantly occupied the U-boat Command, at whose instigation trained meteorologists had been drafted to some of the boats in 1942. But weather forecasts were not sufficiently accurate or timely to justify extensive transfer of boats to remoter areas, for the main object was to sink all possible shipping between U.S.A. and Britain.

---

units destined for work in the Atlantic. Difficulties in supply of centimetre A.S.V. are described in The R.A.F. in Maritime War, Volume III, Chapter XII.

OCTOBER, 1942
NORTH ATLANTIC CONVOY BATTLES

251. Cause of Exaggerated Claims by U-Boats

British records, available since the war, show that only seven ships were sunk and four damaged out of convoy ON 127, in September, 1942, whereas the U-boats involved had claimed no less than 19 sunk. Such exaggerated claims seemed largely unavoidable, for as the enemy's locating devices improved, the U-boat commanders, once having fired their torpedoes, were naturally reluctant to hang about to observe the ultimate result of their shots. At U-boat headquarters it was impossible to sort out all these reports and reduce them to their true value. The discrepancies between the reported and the true sinkings in all convoys between January, 1942, and May, 1943, are shown in Plan 60. In most cases of attacks by single U-boats the claims were accurate, but whenever a number of boats participated in large convoy battles the claims greatly exceed the true result. It must be frankly admitted that the extent of these discrepancies was not realised at the time by the U-boat Command, who therefore overestimated the possibilities of large-scale attacks on convoys. It should be added that the excessive claims by the U-boat Command were made in good faith, and not - as some suggest - to boost German morale.

252. Great Value of German Radio Intelligence

During 1942 our Radio Intelligence Service succeeded at times in penetrating deeply into the enemy's code and cypher systems, which provided us with vital information not only about the actual convoys, but also on the positions of single ships and stragglers. In this cryptographic work our experts were helped by the enemy's habit of consistency in the form of his messages. For example, signals from C.-in-C. Western Approaches contained times of starting and stopping the sea and air escorts for inward and outbound convoys, and stereotyped orders to stragglers and other shipping. The external appearance of such cypher messages being familiar to our experts, it was often possible to deduce changes in cyphering tables and in the basic British signal book, which could thus be kept up to date.

The decryptions confirmed or refuted the picture derived from the other sources of intelligence. Above all, they provided the most precise data on times of leaving ports, speeds, and periodicity of convoys. Two officers in the U-boat Command were constantly engaged in plotting the tracks of convoys, and recording all possible alternative routes. The convoys concerned were HX, SC, ON, ONS, OS, SL, HG, and OG, and the key points were New York, Sydney, Gibraltar, Freetown, North Channel and Halifax.

The extent of our penetration into British and American cypher procedure varied considerably in the different phases of the war. Sometimes weeks or months elapsed without any valuable decryption ; yet there were periods, as in May, 1943, when we currently discovered the evasive courses of the very convoys we were seeking. Sometimes only a few hours elapsed between the time of transmission of the enemy signal and the arrival of the decrypted message in F.O. U-boats' office. Such reports usually occasioned immediate transfer of our patrol lines, and often led to contact with the convoy. Decryptions of obsolete messages also provided an insight into the habits and routes of convoys.

In addition to the decryption of British naval radio messages, we unravelled British aircraft signals quickly and extensively. Although these were usually of minor importance, their value was occasionally very great. The mere fact that an aircraft was in radio communication with a convoy often sufficed to confirm the suspected presence of that convoy. D/F bearings of these aircraft sometimes gave us a clue to the position of the convoy.

253. Unchanging Enemy Methods

The following is an extract from the War Diary of F.O. U-boats, dated 9th September, 1942:

"It is amazing how in the last few months the British convoys have been consistently using tracks only a little to the north or south of the great circle routes, despite the several large-scale attacks by U-boats. For some weeks now westbound convoys have been repeatedly intercepted in the same area."

It seemed to us that those responsible for the routeing of the British convoys had shown more ingenuity in 1941, when the routes were being considerably altered without any discernible system. In those days HX and SC convoys sometimes followed the Greenland coast. Now, however, they seemed to remain within 300 miles north or south of the great circle between the Newfoundland Bank and the North Channel. On 28th September F.O. U-boats, in reporting this peculiarity to Hitler, suggested that owing to shortage of shipping the enemy could no longer afford to send his ships on wide detours (324). Whatever the validity of this view, it is certain that the lack of variety in the convoy tracks was most welcome to us.[40]

254. Value of U-tankers

In 1941 between August and October there had been eleven convoy operations of which seven were against Gibraltar convoys, and the average number of boats had been eight for each attack. In 1942 between July and September (an equal period of time) there had been fifteen convoy operations, averaging 13 U-boats in each. The total number of boats involved in the 1941 period had been 97, whereas in 1942, the number had been 106. In 1942 the much greater number of operations and boats per operation was due entirely to the availability of one or more U-tankers. Considerations of health and strain on the personnel restricted the number of convoy operations per boat per sortie to two or three. Under pressure of later events this number was raised to four or five.

The organisation of replenishment was an intricate matter, for the aim was to send the boats to the tanker only when their fuel was nearly exhausted. Sometimes the tanker followed 50 to 100 miles astern of the convoy, ready to refuel boats that had completed their attack. No doubt the enemy made every effort to discover our

---

40 "In the winter of 1941 and spring of 1942 the fuelling problem of the convoy escorts was acute. It prevented the transatlantic routes from being shifted further to the south... and was often the cause of escorts having to leave the convoy." (C.B. 3304 (1), Section 30).

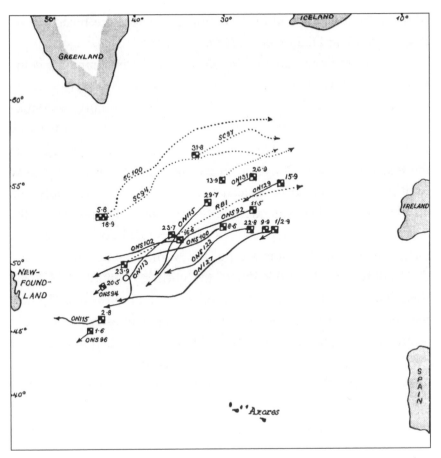

Plan 18. Routes of ON, ONS and SC convoys intercepted between May and September, 1942

replenishment areas, yet in 1942 at least he seemed unaware of the decisive role of the U-tankers, since he made no particular effort to eliminate them.

255. Methods of operating the U-boats

It must not be imagined that the great assistance provided by our Radio Intelligence, together with the consistency in the North Atlantic convoy tracks, were in themselves sufficient to remove all difficulties from our planning. Even when U-tankers were being used, we never had sufficient operational boats to pick up every convoy, and therefore our dispositions had to be selective. The views of the U-boat Command on how best to operate the boats are set down in the War Diary dated 2nd October, 1942:

"Our counter-measures to the enemy's A/S developments being relatively backward, we have to use a large number of boats in order to disperse the surface escorts and to ensure continuity of contact with the convoy. In view of the wide areas involved, and the lack of depth in our U-boat patrol lines, it may take days to concentrate the boats for attack. Convoys should therefore be picked up early to allow the attack to be spaced over several days. Secondly, the attacks should whenever possible be launched in areas where the convoys have no air escorts. Thus ON and ONS convoys must be picked up 300 to 500 miles west of the North Channel, and HX and SC convoys 300 to 500 miles to the north or southwest of Cape Race. These conditions govern the disposition of our boats. The best method of using fresh outward-bound boats is to assemble them in a formation against an ON convoy. They will pursue the convoy to the southwest, and on terminating the operation in the area of the Newfoundland Bank, they should refuel east of Cape Race. They should then form a patrol line northeast of the Newfoundland Bank, the distance out depending on the state of fog, and attempt to pick up an SC or HX convoy."

If, after a reasonable interval, the group should fail to pick up an ON or ONS convoy near the North Channel, then the boats would start a sweep to the southwest on the chance of picking up an HX or SC convoy.

The Naval Staff enquired whether we could not concentrate on special HX and SC convoys known to be carrying important war material to Great Britain. But this method was turned down as being uneconomical. Our dispositions in the North Atlantic were arranged so that, if possible, the boats in the patrol line would sight a convoy in daylight hours. The normal distance between boats might be 10 to 20 miles, but in bad weather the cumulative errors of dead-reckoning soon caused gaps up to 40 or 80 miles. If an expected ON convoy had not been sighted by the evening of the intended day of attack, the

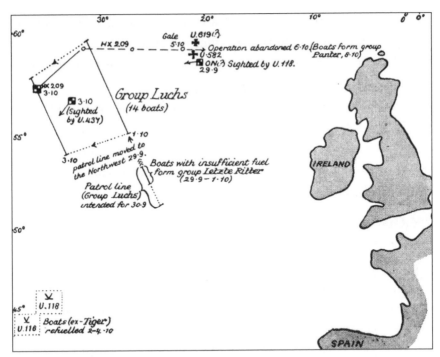

Plan 19. Group Luchs, 30th September-6th October, 1942.
Operation against HX 209.

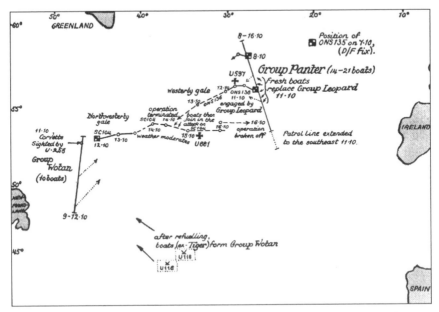

Plan 20. Groups Leopard, Panter and Wotan, 8th-16th October, 1942.
Operations against ONS 136 and SC 104.

119

patrol line would move westward at night at 9 knots. At dawn on the following day it would turn east again, so as not to lose the necessary " battle space." This procedure was reversed by the U-boat groups waiting for HX and SC convoys.

If a sweep were being made from east to west, the line of boats would remain stationary on those nights on which contact was expected with an HX or SC convoy. But the individual boats would patrol on each side of their allotted positions, and would frequently dive to make an all-round hydrophone search.

256. Operations against HX 209

On 28th September the disposition of U-boats in the North Atlantic was as follows:

Fifteen boats of the Tiger group were 500 to 600 miles southeast of Cape Farewell, where in stormy weather they were searching for the elusive ON 131, which had been sighted only once on the 26th. Several fresh boats were endeavouring to join the patrol line *Luchs* west of Ireland, where the next ON convoy was expected on 30th September. The tanker U.118 was hurrying to the Azores, where she was to refuel the Tiger group. On 29th September, when 250 miles south of Iceland this tanker sighted a westbound convoy, which drew the following comment from the U-boat headquarters:

"If this should prove to be an ON convoy, it means that the British have for the first time in six months chosen a new and much more northerly route."

The *Luchs* patrol line was immediately moved about 250 miles northwest. One or two boats, having insufficient fuel for this move, remained in the old area. As by the evening of 2nd October the convoy sighted by U.118 had not been contacted, the *Luchs* group began to sweep southwest. On the following day HX 209 was sighted at the northern end of the line, that is, in a relatively unfavourable position. Bad weather with a northwesterly wind up to force 8, delayed the concentration of the boats, and bad radio conditions held up an important radio message from U.437 which on the night of 3rd October had sighted another convoy steering southwest, being 120 miles southeast of HX 209. It would have paid to concentrate on this westbound convoy, which was much nearer to the majority of the *Luchs* boats. But ten hours elapsed before U.437 could deliver her message, and by then it was too late to act. Meanwhile, the pursuit of the eastbound convoy continued, but on the following day it received air escort, apparently from an air base in Greenland, F.O. U-boats' diary states:

"We can only hope that the progressive freezing of the Greenland coast as winter sets in will prevent the take-off of the flying boats, and thereby extend the area eastwards in which U-boats may attack convoys having no air escort."

The combination of bad weather and air escort prevented our boats from approaching HX 209 and the pursuit was broken off on the morning of 6th October. We had lost two boats through air attack, and had sunk only one large drifting tanker, which had apparently been abandoned.

257. Attacks on ONS 136 and SC 104

On 8th October two long patrol lines were in position, one on each side of the Atlantic. The *Wotan* group, consisting of the former Tiger boats, which had refuelled at sea, was 300 miles northeast of Newfoundland, while the larger *Panter* group, was spread over a considerable area 700 to 800 miles west of the North Channel. It was considered from observations on 29th September and 4th October that convoys were no longer following the great circle but were probably using a much more northerly route. Other evidence indicated that the ON route had certainly been moved somewhat north, though a general change of routes was not evident for SC and HX convoys. On 7th October we intercepted signals from a British aircraft apparently escorting ON 135, rather northward of the usual route. On the night of the 8th at the northern wing of the *Panter* line two ships were pursued, of which one was sunk. On the evening of the 11th a small westbound convoy was sighted in the centre of the line, which we supposed to consist of stragglers from ON 135. Actually this was part of ONS 136, and the eight U-boats in the

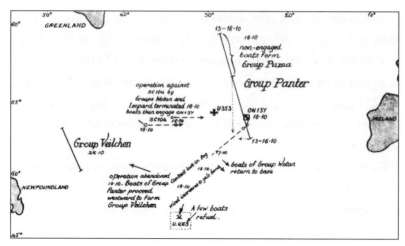

Plan 21. Groups Leopard, Panter and Wotan, 16th-19th October, 1942.
Operation against ON 137.

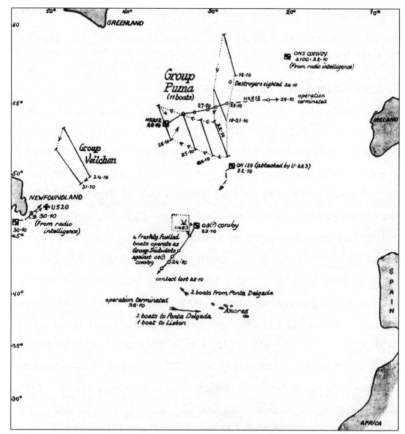

Plan 22. Groups Puma Sudwarts and Veilchen, 16th-31st October, 1942.
Operations against HX 212, ON 139 and an OS convoy..

centre of the line were formed into group *Leopard*, and ordered to attack the ships. The gap in the *Panter* line was immediately filled by fresh boats. In the heavy weather the attempts of the *Leopard* boats to attack this portion of a convoy failed, and they continued the westward search for SC 104.

This convoy had been expected by the *Wotan* group since 11th October. On the afternoon of that day U.258 at the northern end of the group had temporarily sighted an escort vessel heading northeast, but her sighting report was delayed 12 hours. The remaining boats were then ordered northeast at high speed, and eventually SC 104 was sighted on the night of the 12th. In the following two nights U.221, commanded by Lt.-Commander Trojer, skilfully eluded the radar activities of the screen, and sank seven ships, including the tanker Southern Express (12,000 tons), which was intended for refuelling the escorts.

On 14th October the convoy had reached the zone where the *Leopard* group was looking for ONS 136, and these boats were now ordered to join in the attack of SC 104. The enemy too had transferred his escort forces from the westbound to the eastbound convoy, which may also have had protection from an independent support group. In any case the SC convoy, now divided into two groups, was so heavily protected that in the calmer weather no results were achieved. Once again failure was due to the boats being forced under water for long periods so that they could not keep up with the target.

When on the evening of 15th October an air escort was provided, the convoy then being 800 miles from Iceland and 480 miles from Greenland, it was decided that further attempts would be useless, and the opportunity was taken to move the boats eastward towards a new target that had just been sighted, namely ON 137.

In the attacks on SC. 104 we had claimed 11 ships sunk, but actual losses were eight. One U-boat was lost and one heavily damaged. The comment by F.O. U-boats on 16th October reads:

"Although the enemy must regard his losses as serious, since out of 19 ships seen, 11 were lost, the attack was also disappointing to the U-boats."[41]

258. Operations against ON 137

As anticipated, this convoy appeared in the forenoon of 16th October in the southern part of our long patrol line, on the eastern side of the Atlantic. Twelve boats of the *Panter* group and the 15 boats of *Wotan* were ordered to attack, but soon after the original sighting the weather deteriorated so much that the shadower had great difficulty in holding on to the convoy. At one time this U-boat was within 2,000 metres of a corvette[42] and attempted to fire torpedoes by hydrophone bearings, but was attacked with depth-charges which forced her to dive to 80 and later to 170 metres, with considerable damage.

The remaining boats searched on an arc between 200 degrees and 250 degrees but although they sighted several escorts and sank a straggler, the convoy was not found. By 17th October a gale had set in, and on the 19th the operation was abandoned, when the *Panter* boats proceeded westward to occupy a new patrol line 400 miles east of Newfoundland, called group *Veilchen*. Other boats turned southward to refuel from U.463.

259. Attacks on ON 139 and an OS Convoy

The northern boats of the *Panter* line which had not taken part in the operation against ON 137, were formed into the Puma group on 16th October. The U-boat Command believed that the ON convoy following upon ON 137 would use the same southerly track, and hence these boats were ordered to move 200 miles and later another 180 miles south. On 22nd October U.443 sighted ON 139 as anticipated. Although the Puma boats were rather far astern, they were ordered to pursue, but it was soon discovered that the convoy's speed was 10 to 12 knots so that only the original shadower was able to attack, sinking two ships. The remainder, with the exception of U.301, were now ordered northward to a new patrol line.

ON 139 was heading for the replenishment area 300 miles further

41 Actually SC 104 contained 47 ships in all.
42 H.M.S. *Celandine*

south, where U.463 was busy refuelling boats. This was expedited, and the boats turned to meet the approaching convoy. On 23rd October U.706 sighted some ships steering southwest at 15 knots. This could not be the main body of ON 139, but was probably a detached group which after the attack of U.443 had separated from the main convoy. At Headquarters it was believed that these ships were an OS convoy. U.301 and four U-boats that had just finished refuelling operated against these ships, and three further large boats, 600 miles further south were ordered to close. Attempts on 23rd and 24th October to attack were repelled by the escorts before the large boats could join in, and contact was lost on the 25th. Search courses between 180 degrees and 200 degrees failed to locate the convoy. Two of the boats were now ordered to patrol off the harbour of Ponta Delgada (Azores), and one boat off Lisbon. Their reports from these observation points did not confirm our agents' reports of Allied shipping activities.

260. Operation against HX 212

On 24th October the Puma group had re-occupied its patrol line and was moving westward. On the 25th we decrypted the exact position of an ONS convoy for the 22nd at 2100, namely 500 miles west of North Channel, and steering 240 degrees. On 24th October U.606 had sighted two destroyers 280 miles southwest of this position, probably the screen of an ONS convoy. The Puma boats were sent northwest at high speed. In the middle of their line on 26th October instead of the ONS convoy they contacted HX 212. This looked promising and for the next two days the boats succeeded in shadowing this convoy in a moderately heavy sea, regarded as difficult for the enemy's surface and submerged location devices, and favourable to our boats. On 28th October the convoy received air escort, but by then we had sunk six ships and damaged another.

261. Attack on SC 107

After the failure of the operation against ON 137 the *Panter* boats had formed a new patrol line northeast of Newfoundland, named

Veilchen. Their first contact with the enemy was on 29th October, when an ON convoy was sighted by the southernmost boat. No attacks followed this sighting report, and the whole line was moved slightly southwest.

South of Newfoundland at this time were three boats bound for Halifax and the Gulf of St. Lawrence. On 30th October one of them, U.522, sighted an eastbound convoy near the coast of Cape Race, which was SC 107. Simultaneously, F.O. U-boats received a decryption of a British radio message containing a reference position for this convoy east of Cape Race. Its course of 045 degrees would have led the convoy towards our patrol line, but in the meantime the U-boats bound for Halifax were ordered to shadow, which they failed to do in the prevailing fog.

Since the position of the convoy was accurately known, F.O. U-boats took the risk of narrowing the *Veilchen* patrol line and

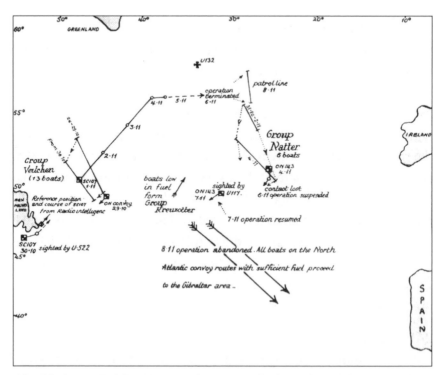

Plan 23. Groups Veilchen, Natter and Kreuzotter, 24th October-7th November, 1942. Operations against SC 107 and ON 143

moving it up to the limit of the fog belt, in readiness for a concentrated attack. The convoy passed through the centre of the line, and within a few hours six U-boats were in contact. The screen appeared weaker than usual, and the convoy kept a northeast course until 4th November, when it headed east, presumably to obtain air cover at the earliest moment. The weather conditions being favourable, our attack developed in a most successful manner. Before the air escorts arrived on 5th November most of our boats had broken off the engagement due to lack of fuel or torpedoes. By the morning of 6th November they had reported 23 ships, aggregating 136,000 tons, sunk and one destroyer and one corvette torpedoed.[43] During the pursuit of the convoy we had lost two boats, U.520 through air attacks in the fog off Newfoundland, and U.132 on 4th November due to damage through the explosion of an ammunition ship.

262. News of North African Landing interrupts Convoy Operations

At the end of October the only U-boats on the eastern side of the Atlantic were the six boats of the Natter group. By 5th November this reinforced group was to form a long patrol line further south. While the boats were moving to the new position, our Radio Intelligence indicated that ON 143 had already passed the area, and the consequent re-disposition of the boats enabled U.92 to sight the target on 4th November. But the remaining boats of the group had hardly reached their new positions, when U.92, receiving no support in shadowing, lost contact, and in spite of a wide search by the other boats, contact was not regained by 6th November, when the operation was broken off. Meanwhile U.117, a U-tanker on her way to the replenishment area, sighted ON 143 on 7th November further to the west. Only four boats succeeded in reaching it. But now news arrived of the invasion of North Africa, and F.O. U-boats immediately ordered all boats with sufficient fuel to hurry towards Gibraltar and the Moroccan coast.

---

43 British records show only 15 ships, totalling 88,000 tons, sunk and no damage to escorts.

ACTIVITY IN OTHER AREAS

263. Tardy Reinforcements in the Canadian zone

The activities of U.517 and 165 in the Gulf of St. Lawrence in September had shown excellent results as regards tonnage sunk per day per boat, and we intended to follow up this success. At the end of the month our two minelayers (U.69 and U.455), having completed their laying off the U.S. coast, arrived in the Gulf of St. Lawrence. Further boats leaving home bases for this area were ordered while on passage to report on shipping along their route, which was north of the normal U.S.-Britain convoy tracks. In two waves, each of three boats, they passed from the south coast of Iceland via Cape Farewell to Belle Isle Strait. Neither on passage, nor while waiting off the Greenland coast and in the Strait, did these U-boats find any traffic.

In October we had an average of four to six boats at the focal points in the Gulf of St. Lawrence and near Newfoundland. They spent several weeks waiting in these areas, which were heavily patrolled from the air, but they had difficulty in finding worthwhile targets. By the time the second wave, consisting of U.520, 521 and 522, had reached the Strait, conditions within the Gulf of St. Lawrence had deteriorated and they were ordered towards Halifax. On 30th October U.522, while south of Cape Pine, ran into SC 107, and with the two other boats operated against this and other convoys.

On 2nd November U.518 succeeded in sinking two iron-ore ships in the harbour of Wabana. Shortly afterwards the U-boats were given freedom to attack anywhere between Conception Bay and Halifax, for the U-boat Command had no precise knowledge of the shipping lanes. This marked the end of activity in the Newfoundland area, and by the middle of November the boats had begun their homeward journey. U.608 laid 10 T.M.A. mines off New York on 10th November, before returning home.

264. Further Successes near Trinidad and the Lesser Antilles

After the termination of the operations within the Caribbean, F.O. U-boats anticipated that the waters round Trinidad would also become unproductive. His reasoning was that the enemy had first driven the U-boats from the coast between New York and Chesapeake Bay, then from Hatteras and the Florida and Yucatan Straits, and then from the Gulf of Mexico and the rest of the Caribbean. Now he would surely make the greatest efforts to protect the focal point at Trinidad, where his losses had been so heavy. But events took a different course, for the Trinidad area continued to give excellent results throughout October and November (Plan 24 overleaf).

To the U-boat Command it seemed remarkable, indeed unintelligible, that the enemy failed to extend his A/S measures to this vital area and that he kept his shipping routes unchanged, although it was obvious from the SOS calls from torpedoed ships that their routes were well known to us. In the first days of October we had spotted another focal point for shipping off the delta of the Orinoco, and at once concentrated boats there to score further successes. Consequent upon this activity we observed that shipping was moved further east and became more scattered. This was confirmed by the chance decryption of sailing orders for a steamer. We accordingly moved the U-boats away from the coast up to 300 miles north, where five ships were sunk.

Most of the ships sighted were sailing independently and making for Trinidad. Only very few were seen heading east, so that the U-boat Command doubted whether outward traffic for the South Atlantic and Freetown was still being routed via Trinidad. During October we realised that this eastbound shipping was being collected into convoys in Port of Spain. Two such convoys were sighted. One of them was attacked on 16th October, with poor results, for the full moon and the enemy's air activity prevented us from sending further boats in to attack.

In the second half of October we noticed a reduction in shipping activity east of Trinidad, and consequently we sent single U-boats to

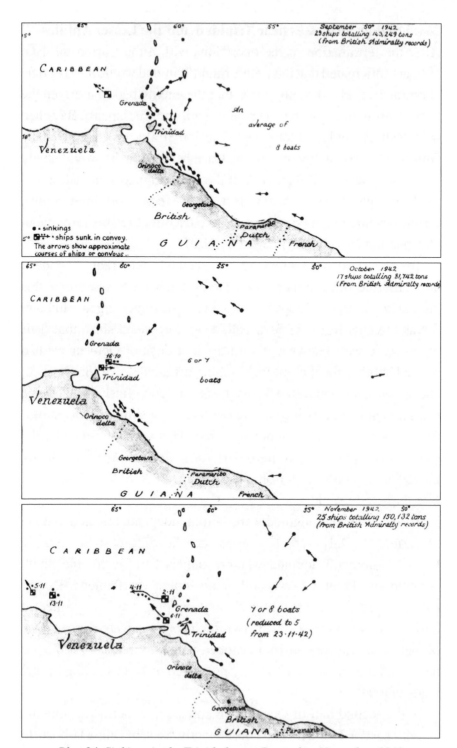

Plan 24. Sinkings in the Trinidad area, September-November, 1942

the west of the island as far as Aruba. In the first week in November these boats came into contact with several convoys leaving Port of Spain and Aruba for the northwest, and out of them 10 ships were sunk. Our total score in this area between 1st October and 7th November was 25 ships, with the loss of only one U-boat. It had become the most rewarding zone of all. But it was wrong to conclude from our own small losses that the enemy would remain so weakly protected. He was ever increasing the number and range of his air patrols, and in the coastal zones he was using twin-engined bombers. Many of the night air attacks on U-boats were ineffective because the pilots lacked experience, yet several boats were slightly and one seriously damaged. On 10th November U.505 was lucky to escape destruction, when a fast aircraft made a low-level attack on her, and a bomb hit the loaded after 3-7 cm. gun, whose explosion brought the attacking aircraft down. The seriously damaged U-boat, unable to dive, proceeded northwards and after making temporary repairs, managed to return home.

265. Ineffectiveness off Freetown

On 9th September the six boats of the Iltis group had left the Azores area heading for Freetown, and looking for SL convoys on the way. But they saw nothing, and on 24th September they were ordered to take up various sectors off Freetown. On 6th October U.333, while 70 miles west of this port, was pursued in bad visibility by a corvette, whose guns obtained several hits on her. The U-boat narrowly escaped destruction by lying on the bottom in 100 metres, and eventually returned safely. We had six to eight boats off Freetown in the first three weeks of October - the highest number since the beginning of the war. But results here were disappointing, and F.O. U-boats commented:

"This is all the more remarkable, since agents' reports indicate particularly heavy movements of troops and stores to Freetown and also to Liberia consequent upon the United States' landing. We must assume that the British have now at last included this harbour in their convoy system, which was to be expected after the heavy sinkings of

July, 1942. Attacks on convoys off Freetown have therefore become very difficult because of the sea and air escorts, and because of the shallow depths and prevailing calm sea."[44]

The *Streitaxt* group, originally intended as reliefs for the Freetown boats, did not get so far south, for while on passage it contacted SL 125 (Section 271). This was just as well, for conditions off Freetown had deteriorated so much by 7th November that the last two boats, U.128 and 552, were moved to a new attack area south and southwest of the Cape Verde Islands. It was not until April, 1943, when the situation in the North Atlantic had greatly deteriorated, that the Freetown area again came into prominence.

266. Failure off the Mouth of the Congo

In July, 1942, the Commanding Officer of Ship 28 had reported by radio that U-boat operations in the Gulf of Guinea seemed to offer prospects, and we also possessed a number of agents' reports concerning activities in Central African harbours, particularly near the mouth of the Congo. According to these, troops and stores for the Allied front in North Africa were to be disembarked at Cabinda, Banana, Point Noire and Loango. The Naval Staff considered that interference with supplies and traffic in these places would eventually relieve pressure on the German troops in North Africa, and should therefore be attempted. If, however, the intelligence should prove incorrect, it would still be worth concentrating on the inner Gulf of Guinea and particularly the harbours of Lagos and Tacoradi.

Two U-boats, U.161 and 126, with experienced commanders were selected for this task. While on the outward journey off the Liberian coast U.126 on 12th October contacted a small westbound convoy in a position 80 miles south of Cape Palmas. In the ensuing submerged attack, the U-boat was located by the asdics of the screen at six to seven thousand metres, and the depth-charge attack so damaged her upper-deck torpedo containers that in spite of immediate blowing

---

44 From July, 1941, end-to-end A/S surface escorts had been established for HG and SL convoys. In 1942 a West African coastal convoy system linked up the ports between Takoradi and Freetown.

of tanks, she was forced down to 240 metres, without however suffering harm at this great depth. Several hours later, after dark, the boat managed to surface and escaped the screen, whose radar was apparently not so good as their asdics.

From 20th to 29th October the boats maintained their position off the mouth of the Congo, but saw very little shipping. There was constructional work in the harbour of Cabinda and the patrol activity in the Congo Delta seemed to indicate preparations to receive shipping. Our only success was the torpedoing of the cruiser *Phoebe* by U.161 on 23rd October off Loango. Early in November the boats were moved to the more promising waters off Lagos and Tacoradi.

267. Good Results off Capetown

U.156 had been damaged during the rescue oiLaconia survivors, and U.159, originally intended for the Congo Delta, was ordered to take the place of the damaged U-boat in the Eisbar group. While the boats of this group were moving south, they sighted a few independent ships, but were not allowed to attack them. Their orders had stated that no single ships were to be attacked unless they were battleships, aircraft carriers or large troop transports. When 600 miles south of St. Helena they refuelled from U.459.

It was intended to launch a surprise attack by two U-boats in the anchorage at Capetown, where agents had reported as many as 50 ships sometimes assembled. If the first attempt should fail, a further one would be made 24 hours later. But on arrival off Capetown in the early hours of 8th October, the boats found the anchorage empty and protected by powerful searchlights. This they reported to the U-boat Command, who considered that the appearance of Japanese U-boats off Madagascar in June and July, 1942, had precipitated these precautions.

The appearance of our U-boat off Capetown apparently surprised the enemy, for in the first three days we sank 13 ships, after which the traffic appeared to cease. From the middle of October there were heavy storms and bad visibility, so that sinkings declined rapidly, and U.68 and U.172 had to start their return journey before expending all torpedoes. On the other hand U.504 and U.159, who had gone south and east as far as Durban, met with some success.

On the same day as the Eisbar group, U.179, the first of the new U-cruisers (Type IXD 2) arrived off Capetown. This type displaced about 1,600 tons and carried 24 torpedoes. The radius of action was over 30,000 miles though the gun armament was no greater than that of the Type IXC. U.179 had a short career, for on the very first day, after sinking one ship, she was destroyed by H.M.S. Active, being the only U-boat lost in the Cape area up to the summer of 1943. The succeeding boats of this type arrived in the area in the latter half of October, so that the return of the Eisbar group did not ease the pressure on =hipping off the southeast coast of Africa.

EFFECT OF OPERATION "TORCH"

268. Failure of German Intelligence

Operation " Torch " involved the use of a vast quantity of shipping, yet the event took the German Supreme Command so much by surprise that it was incapable of mustering even the few military means at its disposal for repelling the invasion. The function of the German Naval Staff was to keep an eye on all the seas, and it may be asked why it also was caught unawares. How was it possible to be ignorant of the huge preparations, the embarkation of troops and stores in the American and European ports, and the assembly and passage of nearly 800 ships ? The answer is revealed by an appreciation by the German Naval Staff dated 20th October, 1942, which can be summarised as follows (325):

At that time it was thought that the formation of a second front was still militarily impossible,although Allied propaganda and an occasional raid by the British had made the threat appear greater than it really was. Hitler had considered it necessary to send considerable forces to Norway and France, thereby weakening the eastern front. Briefly, the threat on the Western European flank was not then taken seriously, though it was realised that later we should have to face a major landing. The situation on the southwest flank, however, seemed more threatening, since the Allies could land on the Iberian Peninsula without undue risk. Moreover, several sources in contact with the Allies had indicated that an Anglo-American landing in Spain was imminent - a belief that was shared by the Spanish General Staff. The occupation of Spain would not constitute a second front, since the German forces in the Pyrenees would resist the advance into Europe, yet it would constitute a major threat to the Axis position in the Mediterranean, and have a great political effect on France and Italy. In addition, the U-boat bases in the Bay of Biscay would be seriously threatened.

To sum up, although the danger existed of an Allied landing in Spain, it was not regarded as acute, and the Spaniards were expected to resist any such attempt. Even if it should succeed, the immediate effect on the German conduct of the war would not be regarded as serious. There was no mention of a possible landing in French North Africa.

269. Naval Staff's View in October, 1942

At the beginning of October we noticed increased activity by British Naval forces and shipping at Gibraltar, but although this aroused some suspicion, we believed that it was connected with a major convoy operation for the relief of Malta, and that it did not imply a landing in North Africa.

In the French North African Colonial territory the coastal fortifications and local air and sea defences were considerable though somewhat antiquated, and their stocks of ammunition and stores were known to be small. Should Algeria and Tunis be invaded, supplies would have to be brought from Metropolitan France in order to keep the garrisons going, and this would require the use of the French Naval forces. In the view of the German Naval Staff the risks run by an invasion fleet would be so great that a landing on the Algerian or Tunisian coast was considered improbable.

Similarly owing to the weather conditions and the prevailing swell on the French Moroccar coast during the winter, a landing here was considered unlikely (326), and moreover the French forces were expected to offer resistance. The German Naval Staff at the beginning of Octobei urged the Supreme Command - contrary to its previous policy - to obtain the extensive co-operation of the French Fleet. Any attack on the French possessions by the Allies would, it was thought cause a final break between them and France and should help the *rapprochement* between the Vichj Government and Germany. No doubt the German Naval Staff over-estimated the fighting capacity of the French Navy and the political effect in France of action by the Allies. When the test came, the French naval personnel was divided by the inconsistency between their orders and their inclination. The Naval Staff also greatly underrated the power of their enemies, who by the autumn of 1942 were quite capable of carrying out a major landing in North Africa without undue risk.

As regards a landing at Dakar, this was not regarded as a serious menace, since the great desert areas between it and the North African front formed an impassable barrier. At the most a landing here would stop the flow of tropical produce from West Africa through France to Germany

270. U-boat Dispositions Unaffected by Preparations for "Torch"

The German Navy's only means of combating the North African landings would have beer to send a sufficient number of U-boats to the landing points, and even then their role could never be decisive. The withdrawal of numerous boats from Atlantic operations for the defence of Africa could only be justified if we possessed precise evidence of the imminence of landings, and this was not the case.

Up to the time of " Torch " we had received numerous reports from agents of the enemy's intentions in North Africa, but the true evaluation of such reports was a very difficult matter, since Allied methods of spreading large numbers of different rumours served to confuse the minds of our Intelligence officers. It must be admitted that our enemies showed themselves to be masters of propaganda and deception. Under such circumstances the German Naval Staff could hardly be expected to order entirely new dispositions for U-boats, which might merely play into the enemy's hands.

Only once, at the beginning of October, did the Naval Staff act on intelligence about the impending attack on Dakar, when F.O. U-boats was informed that:

"In the event of an operation against Dakar all U-boats within reach are to be concentrated for attacks against supply ships. F.O. U-boats is not to change present operational orders, but should report what numbers of boats are expected to be available for this task if required or 15th and on 30th October" (327).

F.O. U-boats intended to send a new group (*Streitaxt* of 500-ton boats to relieve those a Freetown at the end of October. This group, could, if necessary, b(diverted immediately for the defence of Dakar. During the weeks preceding "Torch" no German U-boat was diverted from its normal disposition in the Atlantic.

271. Attack on SL 125

The landing units and the first wave of supplies for the North African landings were seen across the Atlantic in large and small convoys to Gibraltar. In order to understand why this huge concentration of shipping reached its objectives unobserved, it is necessary to explain briefly the movement of German U-boats near Spain and North Africa in the weeks preceding 8th November 1942.

The strategic situation of the Axis in the Mediterranean had been deteriorating since the summer, and in September the German Naval Staff decided to send six U-boats there to make good the losses suffered during the previous nine months. This transfer was carried out with the utmost secrecy, and without informing the Italian Naval Staff in Rome. Experience had shown the necessity for these measures, and we were anxious not to alert the British A/S defences in theStrait of Gibraltar. Early in October, therefore, the *Tümmler* group left home ports, four boats passing the Strait between the 10th and 11th without difficulty, while two others turned back because of defects.

As already explained, the waters round Freetown, Capetown and the Guinea coast had beer strongly occupied by U-boats since the beginning of the month, and reliefs for these boats would not be required for some time. Thus it happened that in the weeks before "Torch" very few boats passed west of Spain and North Africa. The *Streitaxt* group consisting of eight boats, start on 23rd October from a position east of the Azores on its way to Freetown . Two days later in the latitude of the Canaries, a tanker escorted by two destroyers, steering east, was sighted and pursued without success. In spite of the sighting reports by radio from the U-boats.convoy SL 125, coming from the south, maintained its course and on 27th October passed through the centre of the *Streitaxt* patrol line. The ensuing convoy battle, lasting seven days in favourable weather against not too powerful A/S screens, resulted in the sinking of 12 ships, totalling 80,000 tons and damage to one other.[45]

During the period that *Streitaxt* was heading south and also while it was pursuing this convoy northwards the waters on each side of them were quite free from U-boats, and convoys and warships proceeded unobserved, and unmolested towards Gibraltar.

On 31st October German long-range reconnaissance aircraft, on their way to escort a returning blockade-runner, sighted two British aircraft carriers and a cruiser heading south in a position 280 miles west of Cape Finisterre. At this time *Streitaxt*, in its pursuit of SL 125, had reached the latitude of Cape St. Vincent, and seemed favourably placed for attacking these warships. But F.O. U-boats commented that the attack would not be worth while unless we could provide continuous shadowing of the warships from the air. The FW 200 aircraft were unsuited to this task, being easily dealt with by the enemy's fighter protection. Therefore it was decided to keep the U-boats busy with the SL convoy ; but on the morning of 1st November the appearance of air escorts and destroyers to reinforce the convoy compelled us to break off the operation and four of the *Streitaxt* boats were then sent south in a vain attempt to contact the aircraft carriers before they should reach Gibraltar. The

---

45 These are official British figures. At the time the U-boats claimed 18 ships sunk.

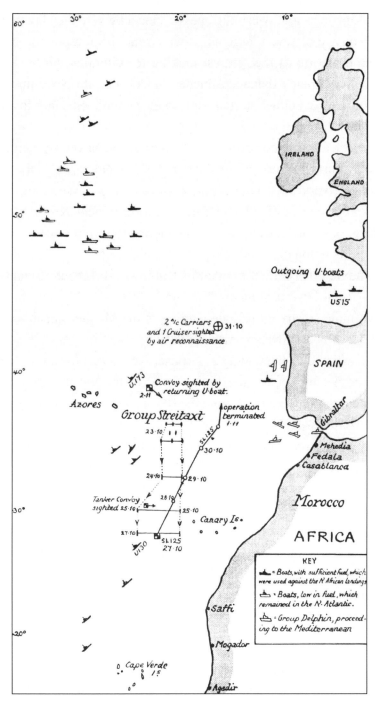

Plan 25. (i) Approximate positions of the U-boats in the Atlantic on 8th November, 1942 (ii) Group Streitaxt, 23rd October-1st November, 1942. Operation against SL 125

boats remained southwest of Cape St. Vincent where they lay in wait for a convoy of seven large ships which had been reported on 2nd November north of the Azores, making for Gibraltar. Only U.440, which was already damaged, made contact. On 4th November the remaining boats either started for home or continued south towards Freetown.

The convoy sighted north of the Azores on 2nd November certainly did not fit into the known schedule, and on 4th November our agents reported a very large concentration of shipping at Gibraltar. Even now our Naval Staff did not deduce the imminent North African landing, but still believed this was a major supply convoy for Malta. The appreciation dated 4th November continued:

"The relatively small number of landing craft (about 50) and the fact that only two passenger ships are in this assembly at Gibraltar, do not indicate any immediate landing in the Mediterranean area or on the northwest African coast" (328).

Irrespective of the enemy's purpose, we needed to reinforce our Mediterranean U-boats, and on the same day the Naval Staff ordered seven boats to be sent there from the Biscay bases. They were formed into Group *Delphin*.

On the day preceding Operation " Torch " the Naval Staff ordered all U-boats that were ready in the Biscay bases to be supplied with special cypher keys and charts for the Mediterranean. At this time 22 U-boats were on the North Atlantic convoy routes between 600 and 800 miles west of Ireland, eight boats were heading south between the Azores and Cape Verde, three were leaving the Biscay ports, while seven of the *Delphin* group were off Portugal bound for the Mediterranean. Except for the latter, the dispositions could be regarded as normal for the Atlantic.

272. Atlantic U-boats arrive too late for " Torch"
The U-boat Command received information by telephone of the North African landings at 0630 on 8th November, and F.O. U-boats immediately ordered those boats which were between the Bay of Biscay and Cape Verde and some other large boats west of England,

totalling 15, to proceed at high speed towards the Moroccan coast. Later all boats on convoy operations west of Ireland that had sufficient fuel were ordered to head for Gibraltar. The War Diary of F.O. U-boats for 8th November states:

"Evidently the landings on the Algerian and Moroccan coasts constitute a large-scale invasion, for which the enemy will require continuous supplies by sea. The U-boats, none of which can arrive at the critical area before tomorrow, will be too late to interfere with the landings but should be able to interrupt further disembarkation of supplies, and attack shipping bound for the Mediterranean. The prospects must not be overrated in the calm waters of the Mediterranean where the attacker runs big risks, which must however, be accepted."

The decisive battle for the Mediterranean having started, every Allied ship sunk meant not only the loss of tonnage but reduction in the enemy's powers of resistance on shore. The new loop torpedo (G 7a F.A.T.) was just being supplied to boats in Kiel, but it was now decided to send these torpedoes with technicians to Pola and Spezia, so that our boats in the Mediterranean could use the latest weapon. The first batch of the new-type magnetic pistol (Pi 39 H) was also sent to these bases.

The first U-boat to arrive off the Moroccan coast on 9th November was U.572. Her excessively cautious Commanding Officer (Lt.-Commander Hirsacker) failed to penetrate the outer A/S defences. In the previous January he had failed to penetrate the Strait of Gibraltar. Incidentally he was the only German U-boat commander in the whole war to be tried for cowardice. The next U-boats did not appear off the coast until 11th November by which time the enemy, having completed the first phase of the disembarkation, had had time to organise the local air and radar defences for A/S purposes. The disembarkations at Fedala and Casablanca were protected in all directions by a ring of patrol vessels and destroyers, all fitted with radar, so that within 20 or 30 miles of the coast, where depths were under 100 metres, our boats were exposed to considerable danger.

The first boat to break through the screen on the evening of 11th November was U.173, which made a surface attack on a convoy in the anchorage at Fedala, and scored three torpedo hits, which sank one transport and damaged a tanker and the U.S. destroyer Hambleton. On the same day U.130 appeared off the beach north of Fedala but could not reach the anchorage because of radar. On 12th November she approached the anchorage from the northeast while submerged and at 1600 through her periscope spotted 20 vessels, including an aircraft carrier, a cruiser and two tankers. Advancing with extreme caution owing to the flat sea, she fired four single shots from the bow tubes and one from the stern, sinking three American naval transports. By hugging the 25-metre line, she escaped northward along the coast.

Other U-boats which later approached Casablanca from northwest and south had less fo rtune U.509 was damaged by a mine, and had to return to base. When U.108 arrived at the anchorage the ships had already left. After the successful attacks by U.173 and U.130 the enemy had decided to complete the disembarkations inside the other harbours that he had meanwhile captured. At all events the commanders of our U-boats made several attempts in the following days to find shipping at Casablanca, Fedala, San and even at Mogador, Akaba and Mehdia, but no ships were seen outside the harbours. After 13th November the prospects of doing serious damage to enemy shipping on the Moroccan coast were slight. From then onwards we usually had seven or eight boats near the landing places, and in view of the difficult conditions, and the lack of knowledge of the situation at U-boat headquarters, the boats were free to attack wherever they thought fit. The little information available from agents and Radio Intelligence was passed on to the U-boats.

273. Attack on H.M. Ships *Hecla* and *Avenger*
We will now consider events in the vicinity of Gibraltar. Between 7th and 11th November the boats of the *Delphin* group had passed into the Mediterranean without encountering any difficulty in the Strait, no doubt because the British escort forces were fully occupied

with the North African landings. This group of U-boats now came under our Senior Officer in the Mediterranean for operations against shipping off Algiers and Tunis.

The first three of five further U-boats arrived west of Gibraltar on 12th November. That evening one of them, U.515, sighted a British cruiser force 150 miles south of Cape St. Vincent. Her log says:

"1915. While on the surface I sighted two cruisers of the Birmingham class and three destroyers steering east at 15 knots. I set course at high speed for five hours to attain a forward attacking position, but am forced away several times by the destroyers. Observe periodical enemy radar on 139 cm. 0015. I approach the rear cruiser and fire four torpedoes, of which two are surface runs and one a gyro failure. The fourth torpedo, after a 70-second run, hits the cruiser in the engine room, and she stops, with three destroyers round her. The second cruiser disappears to the east at high speed.

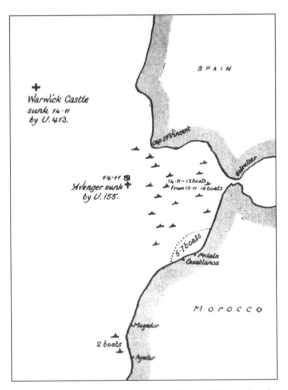

Plan 26. Dispositions against the North African landing,
14th-18th November, 1942

143

After an hour I succeed in penetrating through this destroyer screen and at 0128 a torpedo is fired, followed by another after 20 minutes. The first torpedo hits, and the cruiser lists heavily to starboard. A further shot at 0201 hits the destroyer which is going alongside the cruiser, and results in a huge column of water and depth-charge explosions under her stern. Five minutes later I score another hit on the cruiser but am forced to dive because of star shells from destroyers. Am attacked with depth-charges while at 120-160 metres depth. Reloaded torpedoes. At 0431 I surface and approach the cruiser which is lying low in the water being towed stern first by the destroyer. I am suddenly fired on by one of the screen and from the fore turret of the cruiser, and dive. Numerous depth-charges and asdic noises. 0613 I surface. As I approach the cruiser, I am fired at by a destroyer. At 0650 fire two torpedoes from bow tubes at the cruiser and hear one explosion. Then I dive deep, while depth-charges are exploding. Successfully use asdic decoy. In the course of the day I hear hundreds of depth-charges and while at periscope depth observe aircraft and A/S flotillas."

The persistence of Henke, the Commanding Officer of U.515, in the face of strong opposition was most creditable. He was uncertain of the depth-keeping capacity of his torpedoes, and fired all of them at the 2-metre setting. Five hits were necessary to sink the warship, which was H.M.S. *Hecla* and not a cruiser as the Commanding Officer believed. The damaged destroyer was H.M.S. *Marne*.

After 13th November the number of U-boats west of Gibraltar increased rapidly, and they were disposed as shown in Plan 26. Once before, in December, 1941, our boats had been driven from the Gibraltar area by the local defences, but now the patrols - fast aircraft and submarine chasers, all fitted with radar - made it impossible to move about on the surface in daylight, and very difficult at night. Even the 15 U-boats that covered the western approaches to Gibraltar were insufficient to catch any convoys that might be about. On the night of 14th November U.155, while close west of Gibraltar, sighted a westbound convoy of transports, but when about to fire, the Commanding Officer saw the ships turn away. In spite of the opening range which was now 2,500 metres, he decided to fire all six torpedoes at the centre of the convoy, and reported hits on three large transports. Actually he had hit the escort carrier *Avenger* with one torpedo and the transport Ettrick (11,000 tons) with another. Both ships sank ; a third torpedo damaged a further transport. The British kept the loss of the *Avenger* so secret that we had no confirmation until after the war. On 14th November U.413 chanced to meet a northbound convoy west of Lisbon, and succeeded in sinking the Warwick Castle (20,000 tons).

274. Enemy A/S Defences near Gibraltar

In spite of a considerable volume of convoy traffic the number of our attacks west of Gibraltar remained small, for all these formations enjoyed the radar protection of their aircraft and surface escorts, which gave our attackers very few chances of getting within firing range. Moreover, our boats had to remain submerged - sometimes up to 20 hours - while being hunted, so that it became a problem to recharge batteries. Between 15th and 18th November we lost two boats, and four others had to turn home because of heavy damage. Under these circumstances we had no choice but to move the rest further to the west, where A/S patrols were weaker, and on 18th November it was decided to dispose them and the boats from the Moroccan coast on an arc between Cape St. Vincent and Safi, as shown in Plan 27.

On the night of 19th November of two convoys sighted making for Gibraltar, one could be attacked, and two ships were sunk. But in the course of this attack we received no less than ten reports by radio from other U-boats which were being heavily pursued with depth-charges and harassed by air attacks. Hence it was decided on 21st November to move the boats still further west, mainly to give the crews some rest and fresh air. The new position was too remote to intercept the convoys coming from England, which passed not far off Cape St. Vincent. After two days of comparative rest, when no targets were sighted, the boats were again formed into an east-west

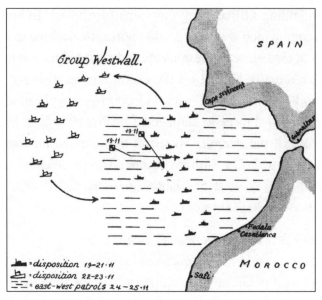

*Plan 27. Dispositions against the north African landing,
19th-25th November, 1942*

patrol line for a sweep between Cape St. Vincent and Casablanca.
The new disposition brought no results, despite frequent reports of
traffic from our agent at Tarifa. In the U-boat Command we therefore
concluded that the A/S defences had succeeded in keeping the boats
submerged so that they were unable to close the convoys. Two of our
best commanders reported that A/S measures were being intensified
from day to day.

275. Decision to Search for UGS Convoys
West of Gibraltar the boats were wasting their time while exposed
to great danger, whereas every other part of the Atlantic, and S.E.
Africa, still offered very good prospects. In November, 1942, we had
reached the peak with overall sinkings estimated at 901,000 tons.[46]
Yet west of Gibraltar since 13th November we had sunk only three
supply ships and torpedoed one, at the cost of three boats lost and six
seriously damaged.

When on 16th November the German Naval Staff suggested that

---

46 British records show that 603,000 tons were sunk during this month, as well as three
transports aggregating 21,000 tons.

the heavy U-boat losses inside the Mediterranean should be made good by sending further Atlantic boats there, and that 20 boats should be maintained west of Gibraltar, F.O. U-boats commented that this would only involve further heavy losses with no decisive effect on the enemy's Mediterranean policy. On 21st November a compromise was reached when the Naval Staff agreed that only 12 boats should be left west of Gibraltar, and only four sent to the Mediterranean.

It was the aim of F.O. U-boats to concentrate his forces entirely against Atlantic shipping, but this was not possible because of the precarious situation in the Mediterranean. On 26th November, having regard to the danger of further losses near Gibraltar, he proposed to the Naval Staff that the U-boats should be moved west of the Azores for attacks on the UGS convoys. Unless these convoys were intercepted well to the west and beyond the range of land-based aircraft, there would not be time to deal with them. On the other hand knowledge of the routes and rhythm of the UGS convoys was scanty, since radio intelligence was not available. The Naval Staff agreed that the U-boats should search the area north of the Azores between 39 degrees and 42 degrees North, which contained great circles from all the American ports (Norfolk to Boston) to Gibraltar. Even if one such convoy were successfully attacked, the result would be much greater than anything achieved within the past week or two. Accordingly all boats of the Westwall group which had sufficient fuel were formed into a north-south reconnaissance line on 27th November and headed towards the Azores. The others filled up from U.118, and joined up on 3rd December just west of the Azores, the whole forming a 260-mile wide scouting formation. Meanwhile, in order to conceal from the enemy that we had suddenly given up the Gibraltar concentration, two fresh boats were sent there, but these achieved nothing and provided no new information. The Westwall group remained in about longitude 40 degrees West, where it was assumed that the UGS convoys would cross the tracks of ships detached from ON, HX and SC convoys. On 6th December four ships steering southeast passed through the line and were sunk. One of

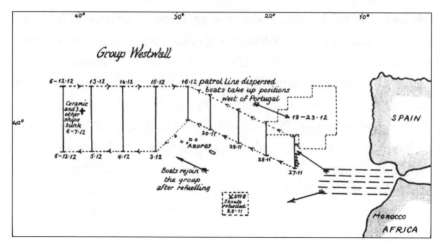

Plan 28. Group Westwall disposed against UGS convoys,
27th November-23rd December, 1942

these was the Ceramic, a troopship bound for the Mediterranean. But no convoys were found, and we discovered from new decryptions that their routes lay further to the south, beyond the range of these U-boats, whose fuel was getting low. It was decided, therefore, to move them back towards the Spanish coast from 12th December. In their new positions between 200 and 300 miles west of the coast, they searched in vain between 19th and 23rd December. F.O. U-boats never hoped for results here, but had to comply with the Naval Staff's order that twelve boats from the Atlantic were to be detailed to intercept Mediterranean-bound convoys. To him it was therefore a relief when on 23rd December this order was cancelled, and he could once more concentrate on North Atlantic convoys.[47]

NOVEMBER AND DECEMBER, 1942
NORTH ATLANTIC CONVOY BATTLES

276. Attack on ONS 144

Reverting to 7th November, when F.O. U-boats had to report to the

---

47 From the end of October, 1942, there was a stream of troop convoys from Hampton Roads to Casablanca and the Mediterranean, which had the pick of the U.S. surface escorts. None was damaged. (See Morison, p. 352.)

Naval Staff how many boats could be made available for action against Mediterranean-bound shipping, his statement included this comment:

"The effect of Operation ' Torch ' on the North Atlantic convoy escorts is most noticeable, for in the last few convoys attacked the escorts were much weaker, while many more ships seemed to be sailing independently. This is presumably due to convoy escorts being required in the Mediterranean... I believe that our recent successes in the North Atlantic were due to this weakness, and it is here that our prospects are particularly favourable at the moment."[48]

After the African landings, most of the available Atlantic boats took up a position off the Moroccan coast, so that the following weeks saw a sharp decline in North Atlantic sinkings. Only nine U-boats remained for attacking the U.S.-British convoy traffic, and most of these were short of either fuel or torpedoes. Several fresh boats leaving home bases and five boats that had been under the Admiral, Northern Waters, were now sent to a position 600 miles west of Ireland to join up with the nine boats mentioned, forming the Kreuzotter Group . They were given attack areas across the great circle joining Newfoundland with the North Channel.

On 15th November ONS 144 crossed this patrol line and during the next five days the U-boats, handicapped by intermittent fog, succeeded in sinking five ships and the corvette Montbretia. In this attack the boats claimed no less than 15 ships, two destroyers and one corvette sunk. U.521 in particular made excessive claims, later shown to be quite unjustified F.O. U-boats commented as follows on the log of this boat:

"All the attacks were made from too great a range, and it seems that the torpedoes did not hit, but exploded at the end of their runs. In all cases, due to the excessive firing range and rather poor visibility, no ships were observed to sink. Future attacks must be delivered at closer range."

---

48 But "this weakness" was only temporary. In October, 1942, the average number of escorts per North Atlantic convoy was 4.5, and by January, 1943, it was 5.5, excluding A/S trawlers. As regards air cover for the convoys during "Torch", see *The R.A.F. in Maritime War*, Volume III, Chapter XII.

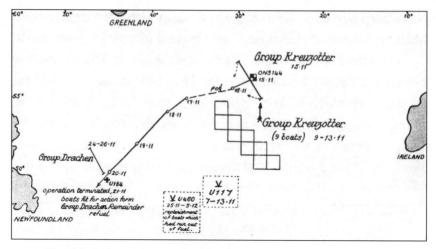

Plan 29. Groups Kreuzotter and Drachen, 8th-26th November, 1942.
Operation against ONS 144

At the conclusion of this operation the few boats still fit for action formed a patrol line (*Drachen*) northeast of the Newfoundland Bank. They were told to search independently east of Newfoundland for single ships, and several of these were found and destroyed.

277. Difficulties of Refuelling

At the start of the operation against ONS 144 some of the Kreuzotter boats were already short of fuel, but had to risk running out, because of the unique chance. After the attack, the first boats were due to refuel on 21st November from U.460 who was then about 500 miles northwest of the Azores. But a protracted storm caused much delay, so that within a few days nine boats were waiting near the U-tanker to replenish, some being by then practically empty. These were forced to ride out the storm without using engines, and in some cases" without even lighting or cooking. There was the added danger of discovery and pursuit by the enemy. During this waiting period several fast single ships and one convoy passed through the area, which normally contained very little shipping. The U-boats became widely separated in the bad weather, which prevented them from accurately fixing their positions. A considerable volume of radio traffic resulted, for the U-boat Command had to arrange for emergency supplies from other operational boats in the vicinity. In spite of beacon signals and D/F bearings it was often difficult to effect contact between the boats. Sometimes the only workable method of transferring fuel in rough weather was to float over five-gallon drums on a line. It was all very unpleasant.

278. Attack on HX 217

After 23rd November further boats leaving bases could be thrown into the Battle of the Atlantic. By 29th November the first group of these, known as *Panzer*, had reached a position 800 miles west of the North Channel, where it lay in wait for an ONS convoy. Further boats, known as Draufganger, were heading for the southern wing of this group. One of these, after being forced underwater by a flying boat, heard propellor noises, as of a convoy. The plot in the U-boat Command showed this might be ON 151. The boats were disposed ahead of the presumed track of the convoy. When on 30th November U.603 sighted several silhouettes on the horizon, she reported a convoy in sight, but lost it in bad visibility. It may have been a hunter-killer group. Draufganger was then moved northward to be ready to intercept the next ONS convoy.

Meanwhile on 29th November two boats in the *Panzer* group had

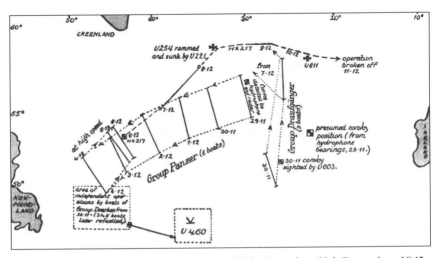

Plan 30. Groups Draufganger and Pnzer, 29th November-11th December, 1942. Operatiopn against HX 217

evidence, through hydrophone noises and through radar observations, of the presence of a convoy, and the group searched to the southwest in order not to lose bearing on the suspected ONS 151. But again nothing was located and the group continued southwestward until it reached the meridian of 45 degrees West, where it lay in wait for an expected SC convoy.

U.524 was fitted with a special receiver for recording British activities on V.H.F., and on the evening of 4th December she listened in to R/T conversations on 124.5 metres, which, while employing many code words, indicated the proximity of the expected convoy. The group was moved northeastward at high speed, and two days later a convoy appeared, which proved to be not an SC but HX 217. The report by U.524 stated that the screen's R/T traffic could be heard at ranges from 20 to 30 miles at strength 3 to 4. At 10 miles the strength was 5. At 25 to 30 miles the volume was very slight and suddenly faded out. From this it was concluded that in future it would repay the boats to listen carefully to the enemy's R/T traffic.

The *Panzer* boats pursued the convoy to the northwest, but were frustrated by poor visibility on the first two nights, when normally the best results would be obtained. The *Draufgänger* boats were ordered on 7th December to close the convoy, and made contact the next day. In spite of the numerous boats now in pursuit, results were only moderate. From 10th December the convoy enjoyed powerful air protection, and on the following day the boats were told to break off. Of the twenty-two that had taken part in the pursuit, two were lost. We claimed six ships sunk and three and one escort damaged.[49] From a later analysis of this action F.O. U-boats stated that the results were poor because of the numerical strength of the escorts, whose efficiency at pursuing, however, was not outstanding.

279. Collision during Convoy Battle

The danger always existed during large convoy battles that other U-boats attacking at night could not be seen. On the night of 8th December there was a collision between U.221 and U.254 while

---

49 British records show that only two ships were sunk in the convoy and one straggler.

both were manoeuvring for position near the convoy in squally weather. The ramming boat was practically undamaged but the other went down, and only four of her crew could be rescued. Under the circumstances no blame could be attributed to the ramming boat. But as a result of this incident it was decided that not more than 13 to 15 U-boats should be in the immediate vicinity of a convoy at any one time, so as to keep the danger of collision within reasonable limits.

280. Failure against HX 218, ONS 152 and ON 153

After the battle with HX 217, all boats were redisposed into two patrol formations, Ungestiim and Raufbold, which covered all the convoy routes leaving the North Channel in the sector between 240 degrees and 290 degrees. On 10th December we decrypted a British radio message giving several reference positions for an eastbound convoy, HX 218. Three boats from the former group Drachm, then east of Newfoundland, were drawn up ahead of the expected track of the convoy, into patrol-line Biiffel. At noon on the 13th, the convoy was sighted, as expected, by U.373, and in view of the precise data as to its future movements, the Ungestiim group was moved 300 miles westward at high speed. The three boats east of Newfoundland soon lost the convoy, nor did any other boats find it. Believing that

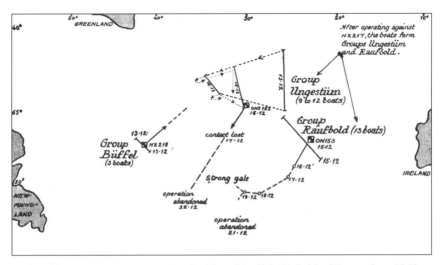

Plan 31. Groups Ungestum, Raufbold and Buffel, 13th-22nd December, 1942 .
Operations against HX 218, ONS 152 and ON 153

the convoy had been diverted to the south, they were told to proceed southeast at high speed on a new patrol line. But in fact the ships had slipped through without any diversion. U.373, instead of sighting an HX convoy, contacted ONS 152, apparently steering southwest in two groups. This now became the main target, but contact occurred for only a few hours. Further pursuit was handicapped by a violent westerly gale and extremely bad visibility, but the search was continued for stragglers, one of which was sunk. The operation was broken off on 22nd December.

The Raufbold group was more fortunate, for on 15th December ON 153 was contacted in the centre of the patrol line. On the first night it was possible to make some successful attacks, but the bad weather of the next four days prevented further attacks. The operation ended on 21st December when we had sunk three ships and damaged a fourth. One of the escorts of ON 153, H.M.S. Firedrake, was also sunk.

281. Attack on ONS 154

From 23rd December the Spitz group was lying in wait in the area previously occupied by Raufbold, hoping to contact the next westbound convoy. During the next few days Spitz gradually moved towards Ungestiim, which had been reformed after the attack on ONS 152. After 25th December the two groups between them covered a relatively wide area in mid-Atlantic.

On the afternoon of 26th December the left-wing boat of Spitz sighted ONS 154, which had been delayed two days by the storm. Both groups were ordered to attack, and in rather poor visibility some of them made contact, sinking four ships. On the morning of the 28th, U.260 made a steady contact which she maintained through hydrophone bearings, which proved of great use to the other boats, for it enabled them to penetrate the remote screen. When the weather cleared in the late afternoon, the boats were able to cope with the comparatively weak inner screen, and during the night they succeeded in sinking nine ships. When on 31st December the operation was broken off only five boats were still participating.

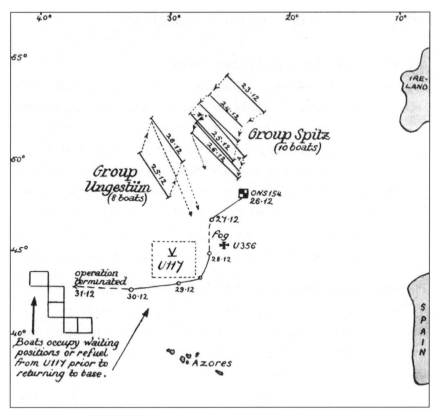

Plan 32. Groups Spitz and Ungestum, 23rd-31st December, 1942.
Operation against ONS 154

The remainder, having expended fuel .or torpedoes, had started on their return journey. The total losses in this convoy were thirteen ships, aggregating 67,000 tons sunk, and one damaged. A Special Service vessel of the convoy (H.M.S. Fidelity) was also attacked on the 29th by U.225, whose torpedo missed, and by U.615, which fired five single shots without result, as they were apparently held up by the vessel's torpedo nets. It was observed that this ship had an aircraft and that at night she lowered a small speed-boat. On the 30th, U.435 succeeded in sinking Fidelity. The U-boat later reported that between 300 and 400 survivors, probably including survivors from other sunken ships, were drifting on overcrowded rafts and that in the bad weather few would survive.

THE REMOTE AREAS

282. Reduction of Effort due to " Torch"

After the " Torch " landings the despatch of a number of boats to the Moroccan coast and to Gibraltar resulted in reduced activity, not only in the North Atlantic, but also in the remote areas, where a number of boats were due for relief. These had to refuel from U-tankers, and some of them remained in distant waters for three to five months. It was too long a period for efficiency, but we could not afford to abandon the Caribbean, the waters off Brazil, or the South African area. The total number of boats in all these regions began to fall, and by mid-December it was not more than twelve - the lowest for nearly a year.

283. Operations between St. Paul's Rock and Brazil

By the end of October conditions off Freetown were no longer satisfactory, and it was decided to order three boats, returning from there and from the Caribbean, to refuel from U.462 near Cape Verde, and then operate southwest of these islands. Here they sank a few independent ships. But they provided no intelligence of shipping between Freetown and Port of Spain, for all the ships sighted were heading either north or south.

Meanwhile, the tanker U.461 had newly arrived north of St. Paul's Rock, and refuelled the boats that were on both sides of the Equator, as well as the Eisbdr group, which was returning from the Cape via the Brazilian coast. She also refuelled U.161 and U.126. After their failure off the Congo Delta, these two had lain off Victoria, Lagos and Tacoradi, where they had sighted only two small convoys, from which they torpedoed two ships. From 25th November we thus had nine boats disposed between Fortalezza (Brazil) and a point 400 miles north of St. Paul's Rock. On 26th November, U.176 sank the Dutch Polydorus after a chase lasting 50 hours - the longest recorded pursuit of a single ship. But up to 8th December all these U-boats sighted (and sank) only three ships, and it seemed that nearly all the shipping in this area was now in convoy. While U.461 was refuelling boats north of St. Paul's Rock, intelligence from decryption at last gave us the position of a British convoy further north. U.172 encountered this westbound convoy on 12th December and scored two hits. Two further boats were sent to attack the same convoy in another reference position 600 miles east of Trinidad, where they found it on 15th December. They claimed two tankers sunk, which is not corroborated by British records.

The other boats, having refuelled from U.461, took up an extended patrol line on 12th December from St. Paul's Rock to the Brazilian coast. This disposition brought good results, for within four days seven ships had been sunk out of the east- and westbound traffic. As a result, F.O. U-boats planned to send a group of medium boats to this area in January, with their own U-tanker.

Towards the end of December only three boats were left in the equatorial zone, namely U.176, which had been damaged by aircraft bombs, and U.164 and U.507, which had been sent out as reliefs. Early in January, 1943, the two latter became casualties through attacks by American bombers north of Fortalezza. U.507 had only just reported making contact with an eastbound convoy.

In the region to the west of Trinidad the average number of U-boats declined from eight at the beginning of November to two in mid-December. We had to assume that here the enemy had now made good the deficiencies in A/S forces occasioned by Operation " Torch ". The comment on 22nd December, 1942, by F.O. U-boats was that: -

"Single ships arriving from the south are probably being assembled in Freetown and sent on in convoys to Trinidad... These measures will have an unfavourable effect on our rate of sinkings which, in the Trinidad area, have until now been very high."

After the return of the Eisbar boats from Capetown, only three large boats were still in that area. Their endurance allowed them to operate over wide areas along the southeast African coast as far as Lourenco Marques. Here they found plenty of targets, and by Christmas they had accounted for 20 ships. By the end of 1942 the last of these U-boats was on its way home.

JANUARY -MAY, 1943

JANUARY AND FEBRUARY, 1943
ATTACKS ON CONVOYS BETWEEN
U.S.A. AND BRITAIN

284. U-Boats from Northern Waters Reinforce Atlantic Operations

The highest rate of sinkings had been achieved during 1942. In that year the F.O. U-boats often had other commitments which prevented him from concentrating all his forces against shipping, yet he estimated that about 7.1 million tons (later revised to 6.3 million tons) had been destroyed. British records available since the war show the true figure to be 5.34 million tons (329). But even this amount had been achieved with an average of only 17 new boats each month, instead of the expected 20 or more (Section 165). The prospects for 1943 were not very promising, for to balance the expansion of U-boat numbers the enemy had used the 3l years to develop and perfect his A/S organisation. It would therefore require the utmost effort on our part to maintain sinkings at their existing rate.

1943 began with a relatively small number of boats available for Atlantic operations. In the last two months of 1942 newly commissioned boats had not sufficed to make good normal losses and reductions due to Mediterranean operations. Dönitz, who had foreseen this deficiency, sought approval on 8th December, 1942, to throw U-boats from Northern Waters into the Atlantic battle. Despite the importance of preventing supplies reaching Russia by the Northern sea route, it was evident that in this area the boats had not shown the results expected on the basis of available targets. This was largely due to the permanent winter night and the arctic conditions, whereas opportunities in the Atlantic had improved with the weakening of enemy A/S forces due to the North African operations.

The Naval Staff on 9th December decided that of the 23 U-boats then under the control of Naval Group Command North, only sufficient were to be retained to ensure six being immediately available against PQ and QP convoys. But in practice this decision resulted in the following weeks in only four boats being added to the Atlantic force. Thus in January, 1943, the average number of boats actually at sea in connection with Atlantic operations remained at 92, whereas during the previous four months it had been 99.

285. Conditions Unfavourable for Locating Convoys
After the successful operation against ONS 154, which ended on 31st December, 1942, only a few of the participating boats remained fit for further operations, and these tried to get in touch with the replenishment boat, U.117, which was waiting north of the Azores. The only U-boats fit for operations (Group *Falke*) had taken up a position 500 miles West of Ireland. In this rather southerly position they lay in wait for an ON convoy until 4th January, 1943, and then formed a north-south patrol line in the hope of catching the succeeding ONS convoy. As this also failed, the group proceeded further north on 16th January, and together with the southern group *Habicht* covered an area over 500 miles deep, between 53 degrees and 62 degrees North. Despite this extension of the search no westbound convoys were found, but only an eastbound convoy on 16th January, the attack on which was not pursued owing to its proximity to the air base in Iceland.

The weather was again the cause of failure. Already in September and October there had been lengthy periods of storm, and January was exceptionally bad, eating up the fuel, and shortening the operational period. But this factor alone could not account for the failure of these search operations against four westbound convoys, which F.O. U-boats attributed to another cause, as is shown by his comment dated 15th January:

"It is believed that the convoys, after six months of using certain

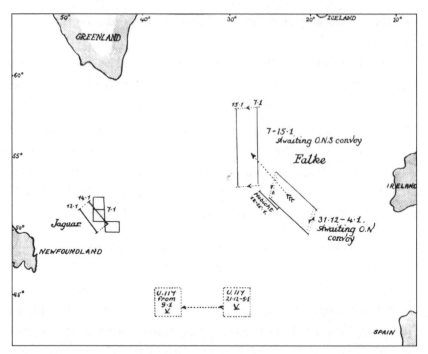

Plan 33. Groups Falke, Habicht and Jaguar, 31st December, 1942-15th January, 1943 Dispositions against ON and INS convoys

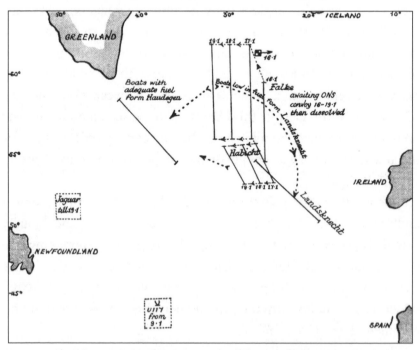

Plan 34. Groups Falke and Habicht, 16th-19th January, 1943

160

routes, have again changed their tracks. Such a development, most disadvantageous to our boats, was to be expected. Indeed it is quite surprising that for so many months the British used practically unchanging convoy tracks, for this made our task so much easier."

On 19th January, when our boats had still located nothing, it seemed that the convoys had been diverted northwards towards Greenland and Iceland. Accordingly the *Falke* and *Habicht* groups were dissolved, and a new group, *Haudegen*, was formed of boats with adequate fuel, which took up a patrol line extending 300 miles southeastward from Cape Farewell. The boats with less fuel stayed west of Ireland, forming the *Landsknecht* group.

286. Effects of Storms and Radio Uncertainties

The formation of a new western group of boats after refuelling from U.117 was much delayed by bad weather in the replenishment area, and it was not until 12th January that a small group (Jaguar) arrived in the attack area northeast of Newfoundland.

On 22nd January a U-boat returning to base reported to the *Haudegen* group that a British hunting group was in sight. As isolated hunting groups had not before been sighted in this area, it seemed that this might be the remote screen for an HX convoy then due in these waters. Accordingly F.O. U-boats ordered the *Haudegen* group to the southeast at high speed with a view to intercepting this eastbound convoy. Three of the boats, suspecting another convoy, remained behind, but nothing occurred, and they were later ordered to join the Jaguar group. The expected HX convoy was not in the vicinity of the British group, for on the same day it passed the western wing of the Jaguar group. Bad radio conditions, commonly experienced near Newfoundland, prevented the receipt of the sighting report by our shore radio station, so that it took 18 hours to inform F.O. U-boats that Jaguar was in pursuit of a convoy. The *Haudegen* group was at once ordered to form a long patrol line south of Cape Farewell. What with the delay in radio communications, and the smallness of the Jaguar group, contact with the convoy was lost on 23rd January, and heavy weather prevented the *Haudegen* group reaching its new position in sufficient time. It could now only try to intercept the convoy still further to the east. In spite of hydrophone reports of convoy noises, no ships were located, and a general search was ordered. At Headquarters it was thought that the failure to intercept was due to the inexperience of the young U-boat commanders and the unskilled interpretation of hydrophone noises. The case of U.201, who had pursued a school of whales for several hours, led to the embarkation in some boats of special ratings. These were to take gramophone records of the noises characteristic of schools of whales and dolphins. The noises were somewhat similar to propellor noises of a distant convoy or of a single steamship. The records were used in the training of U-boat officers and hydrophone operators. It was also possible that the enemy, in order to deceive U-boats, was using special buoys which simulated propeller noises.

The *Haudegen* group having failed to intercept, returned to its patrol line south of Cape Race, and on 1st February started to move towards Newfoundland. On the following day the most northerly boat sighted a small convoy steering north, presumed to be a Greenland convoy of the kind reported by our agents. This was SG 19. Five U-boats of the northern wing formed the Nordstrum group to attack the convoy, while the remainder continued to comb the area. After the American steamer Dorchester - carrying supplies and personnel to Greenland bases - was sunk, contact with the convoy was lost, and not regained before it reached the Greenland coast. For two days the boats patrolled in and off the fjord entrances without establishing the destination of the convoy, and they then rejoined the main *Haudegen* group in the direction of Newfoundland.

287. Action with SC 118

For a whole week the Landsknecht group had waited to the west of Ireland for an ON convoy, and on 28th January it was dispersed, only those boats with adequate fuel being attached to *Haudegen*, east of Newfoundland. One of the latter boats, in longitude 30 degrees West, sighted an eastbound convoy. But most of the other boats were already further west, so that only five could be concentrated for the attack.

162

U.456, commanded by Teichert, successfully shadowed during a heavy westerly gale over a period of three days, and attacked. This fortuitous operation resulted in the loss of one ship and damage to two others.

The early radio messages from U.456 showed that the ships belonged to a fast convoy, which in fact was HX 224. According to our plots the next SC convoy was due to pass the area two days later. It was presumed to consist of many ships with cargoes for Murmansk, which, according to our Radio Intelligence, had left New York on 24th January. Since the British knew that our boats had attacked HX 224, it was possible that they regarded the waters astern of this convoy as being clear of U-boats, and would therefore send the SC convoy along the same route. For this reason it was decided to form all the westbound Landsknecht boats into a reconnaissance patrol (*Pfeil*) to catch the SC convoy. On 4th February we received a radio report from U.632 that a large convoy would follow HX 224 on the same route. The Commanding Officer had obtained this intelligence from a survivor from a tanker sunk in the attack on HX 224. Only a few hours later this convoy, SC 118, passed through the centre of our reconnaissance line. As it was evidently an important one, efforts were made to concentrate all available U-boats. In addition to *Pfeil*, the five eastern boats of *Haudegen*, then 300 miles behind the convoy, were ordered to close it. Between 4th and 9th February 20 U-boats in all attacked the convoy, which was heavily protected by sea and air, and they claimed to have sunk 14 ships aggregating 109,000 tons. It is confirmed that 13 ships were sunk. The reconstruction of the action at Headquarters showed this to have been a violent battle, for three U-boats were lost, and of four attacked from the air two were damaged. Depth-charge attacks were made on 13 boats, of which two were seriously damaged. It was realised that only the most experienced attackers could achieve results in face of the formidable defences of this convoy.

The *Haudegen* group, having been weakened by sending boats against SC 118, was now dissolved, and from 6th February the

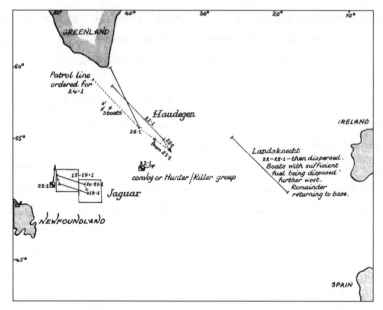

Plan 35. Groups Haudegen, Jaguar and Landsknecht, 18th-28th January, 1943.

Plan 36. Various groups, 28th January-13th February, 1943.
Operations against SC 118 and HX 224.

remainder were formed into a double line on an arc eastward of Newfoundland, being reinforced a few days later by the boats of Nordsturm coming from the Greenland coast.

Meanwhile an attempt was made west of the Biscay to intercept an HG convoy, reported by our Spanish agent as having left Gibraltar. A group of outward-bound boats (Hartherz) lay in wait for it from 4th to 7th February, but the search between 14 degrees and 19 degrees West longitude was fruitless. Our air reconnaissance also failed to sight the convoy, but spotted some single fast steamships and corvettes which were not considered worth attacking. The patrol line was therefore dissolved, the large boats heading for mid-Atlantic, while the medium boats made for the approaches to the North Channel.

288. Attack on Three Successive Convoys (ON 165 to 167)

By the middle of February a situation generally favourable to U-boat operations had developed. In addition to the two groups (Ritter and Neptun) which were forming between 25 degrees and 30 degrees West, the *Haudegen* group was positioned on the arc of a circle 300 miles northeast of Cape Race. On 15th February this group ended its patrol because of fuel shortage, and two days later one of the returning boats happened to sight a convoy steering southwest, which was ONS 165. Three hundred miles of sea room were available for pursuit to the west, and this provided a last chance for the returning boats and those of the *Haudegen* group which were still east of Newfoundland, now renamed Taifun. The boats were ordered to attack and refuel later for the voyage home. But in spite of almost continuous position reports and D/F bearings by the shadower over a period of two days, it was impossible in the prevailing storm to concentrate boats for the attack. The failure was attributed to the difficulties experienced by U-boats in fixing their positions in this area, where the Gulf Stream and the Labrador currents meet. The result of the operation - two ships sunk and two of our U-boats lost - was considered most unsatisfactory.

While ONS 165 was being pursued, the Paris radio intercepting centre of the *Luftwaffe* succeeded on 18th February in collecting

D/F bearings of the escorting aircraft of an outward-bound convoy, presumably ON 166 or 167. They indicated a position 300 miles west of the North Channel. Consequently the movements already started by Neptun and Ritter were cancelled, both groups being ordered to assume by 20th February an extended north-south line along the 30th Meridian. Some outward-bound boats were also ordered to form a line (Knappen) south of Ritter.

On 19th February the Radio Intercept Service deduced from further D/F cross-bearings that the convoy was heading southwest and it seemed advisable to extend the patrol line southward, but before this could be done Knappen sighted the enemy (ON 166). The Neptun group, too far astern to take part in the pursuit, formed a patrol line to the southwest. The other boats, pursuing the convoy from 21st to 25th February, covered 1,100 miles. It passed just to

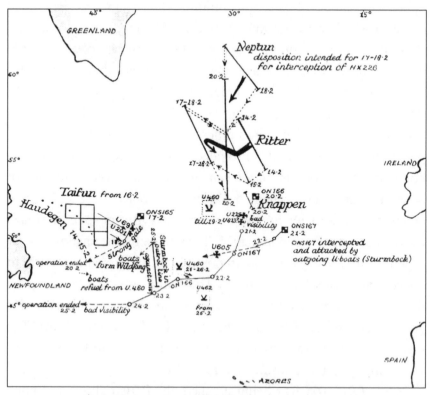

Plan 37. Various groups, 14th-25th February, 1943.
Operations against ON 166 and ONS 167.

the south of where U.460 was carrying out her replenishment task, and some of the *Haudegen* boats, having just refuelled, joined in the pursuit. " The result of the action, with only one boat lost of the 13 that participated, was particularly gratifying, 23 ships of 133,000 tons being sunk and seven torpedoed." The British records give only 14 ships of 88,000 tons sunk and one ship of 9,000 tons damaged.

The third westbound convoy - ONS 167 - was sighted on 21st February by an outbound U-boat about 150 miles east of ON 166. Several others, trying to close ON 166, were formed into group Sturmbock and diverted towards ONS 167. But the boats were very far apart, and only the shadower succeeded in sinking two ships. On 25th February the individual search for ONS 167 developed into an organised patrol line ahead of the presumed line of advance of the convoy, and later into a new line (*Wildfang*) east of Newfoundland.

The operations against ONS 165 and ON 166 with so many U-boats would have been impossible without the help of the U-tankers, U.460 and U.462. Between 21st February and 5th March these two tankers, lying 400 to 600 miles north of the Azores, refuelled 27 operational boats, some of which had almost exhausted their fuel. It remains a mystery why this activity was not interrupted by the enemy, who must have known of it through the heavy but unavoidable radio traffic that it involved.[50]

OPERATIONS AGAINST TRAFFIC TO THE MEDITERRANEAN

289. Influence on North Atlantic Operations

The attempt in December, 1942, to operate a U-boat group west of the Azores against the convoy traffic from the United States to the Mediterranean had failed (Section 275), and on 23rd December,

---

50 While the Germans mention the refuelling of their U-boats and the use of D.F. in connection with attacks on ON 166, it is worth noting that the escorts of this convoy were also refuelled from three attached tankers, and that the successful use of HF/DF by the escorts in anticipating the U-boat attacks led to the further development and use of the device.

as a result of the representations of F.O. U-boats, the Naval Staff cancelled the instruction that 12 boats were to be stationed between Spain and the Azores for attacking this shipping. F.O. U-boats fully realised the importance of sinking Mediterranean-bound shipping, but as his war diary shows, the number of boats available did not permit of simultaneous operations against this and the North Atlantic traffic.

"In the North Atlantic there are certainly about 16 convoys per month, whereas in the Azores area there are probably not more than three. Moreover the chance of picking up convoys north of 43 degrees North is far greater since the area is smaller... On the other hand the threatening situation in North Africa demands every effort against Allied supplies, and also requires that boats shall be available at short notice in the event of the Allies attacking the Spanish Peninsula" (330).

It was decided therefore that attacks on U.S.-Gibraltar convoys should not be undertaken unless and until reliable information was forthcoming as to their movements. It was not long before this situation arose.

290. Engagement with Tanker Convoy TM 1
On 26th December, 1942, a number of medium boats was assembling east of the Azores, with a view to making a sweep towards the Brazilian coast, accompanied by a U-tanker. But on 29th December, acting on Radio Intelligence, the boats were stationed on the great circle from the Azores to New York and told to sweep westward. When this westward sweep (*Delphin* in Plan 38) produced no results after four days, the group was redirected towards Brazil.

This change had barely been made, when U.514, returning from the Caribbean, sighted a tanker convoy (TM 1) about 900 miles south of the *Delphin* group, steering 070 degrees. This convoy was presumably on its way from Port of Spain to Gibraltar. The *Delphin* group was given an interception course, while U.514, and U.125 which happened to be in the vicinity, were ordered to shadow. It might appear rash to dispatch a group of U-boats over so great a distance on the chance of intercepting a convoy sighted only once. On the other hand in this southern area there had been, as far as was known, no marked re-routing of convoys, as had been the practice in the North Atlantic.

A few hours after these dispositions had been made, U.182, on her way to the Cape area, had sighted a Gibraltar-U.S. convoy about 600 miles southeast of the *Delphin* group, towards which the convoy was heading. The group was therefore directed to attack it. Meanwhile U.182, having made her first sighting report, was forced under water by depth-charge attacks, and lost contact. The *Delphin* group was now ordered to search on the anticipated line of advance of the convoy.

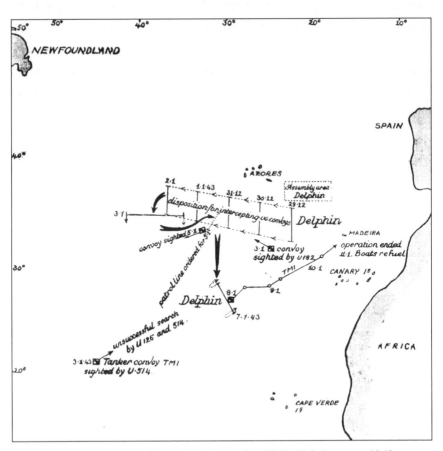

Plan 38. Group Delphin, 29th December 1942-11th January, 1943.
Operation against TM I.

169

Early on the morning of 5th January a fast westbound convoy was sighted at the southern end of the group, whose relative position was unsatisfactory for attack, and it was decided to pursue the original objective, namely TM 1. On 3rd January U.514, after obtaining one torpedo hit on a tanker of this convoy, had lost contact, and in spite of a search with U.125 lasting several days in the general direction of 060 degrees to 075 degrees, failed to relocate it. On 7th January the two U-boats joined up with the *Delphin* patrol line 600 miles west of the Canaries, and the following afternoon the convoy was sighted in the middle of the line. Some home- and outward-bound U-boats were collected into the group, making 12 boats available for the attack. Preoccupation with torpedoed tankers and enemy depth-charge attacks soon caused many of the attackers to drop astern, so that after the second day only four boats were still in touch, and the pursuit was abandoned on 11th January near Madeira. The convoy escort, consisting of old gun-boats and corvettes, was unpractised and lacked perseverance. The U-boats reported 15 tankers, aggregating 141,000 tons torpedoed, but in fact only seven were destroyed. This attack revealed the great capacity for survival of tankers, some of which required as many as five torpedoes to send them to the bottom. Nevertheless F.O. U-boats considered the results generally satisfactory, as more than 100 hours had elapsed between the original sighting and the contact.

291. Continuation of Operations South of the Azores

The successful action against this tanker convoy with its valuable cargo would probably affect Allied operations in the Mediterranean and benefit our Army in Africa. Hence it was decided to keep the *Delphin* group south of the Azores in the hope of further spoils. After refuelling from U-463, the group on 16th January took up a north-south patrol line ahead of the track of a UGS convoy which had been identified through a decrypted enemy signal. The group moved out to 35 degrees West, so as to gain space for the attack. On 25th January U.575, in the centre of the patrol line, sank a large transport, whose survivors confirmed that she belonged to the expected convoy,

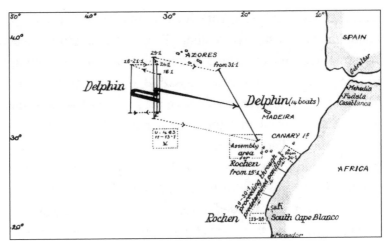

Plan 39. Groups Delphin and Rochen. 15th-31st January, 1943

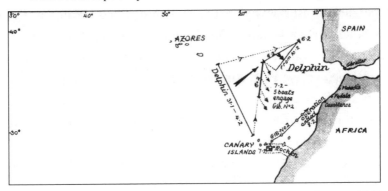

*Plan 40. Groups Delphin and Rochen, 31st January-10th February, 1943.
Operation against Gib. No.2*

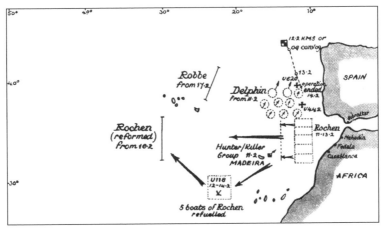

*Plan 41. Groups Deplphin and Rochen, 11th-16th February, 1943.
Operation against KMS or OG convoy*

which had sailed from New York for Casablanca, and had scattered on 22nd January in heavy weather. The boats therefore expected to find stragglers. By collecting additional boats and extending the patrol line north and south it was possible to intercept and sink two further stragglers. We decrypted one of the enemy's U-boat situation reports, which showed that the statements of the survivors were false. The convoy had not been dispersed, but had escaped to the north of the patrol line. This seemed to show that the enemy was fully aware of the position of the *Delphin* group, and consequently on 29th January it was decided to move our boats eastwards.

A small group of five boats had been assembling since 15th January west of the Canaries, in order to sweep southwards and later to operate against convoys between Trinidad and Freetown. Before these boats could assemble, French agents on the staff of F.O. U-boats had reported considerable north- and southbound shipping near Cape Blanco on the West African coast. Consequently the orders for the group {Rochen) were changed, and on 23rd January they were sent to this area. But when a Trinidad-Gibraltar convoy received orders (decrypted by us) to make its landfall north of Cape Blanco, the Rochen group was also sent north, and from 28th January swept towards the Canaries through pre-arranged positions.

Meanwhile the southern wing of the *Delphin* group had reached a position north of the Canaries. Between them the two groups formed an extended reconnaissance line from the Azores to the African coast, and, except for the gap formed by the Canary Islands, they should have been able to cover all routes converging on the Mediterranean from the south and the west. But no traffic was located. On 6th February fuel considerations compelled F.O. U-boats to move the *Delphin* group nearer to Gibraltar.

A German Consul had reported seeing convoys proceeding northwards near Santa Cruz, and the Rochen group was redisposed to cover the gap between the islands. The Consul's report proved correct, for on 7th February a small convoy (Gib. No. 2 - Port Etienne, Mauritania, to Gibraltar) was sighted between the islands heading for Gibraltar, and Rochen together with the five southern boats of *Delphin* operated against it. The powerful air escort - our Radio Intelligence had identified 44 aircraft between Gibraltar and the Canaries - and the A/S escorts with their radar made the approach very difficult, and the operation was abandoned on the following day, after one U-boat had reported one tanker and a corvette sunk, and a freighter probably sunk. Actually only the trawler Bredam was sunk. The author of the exaggerated report was once again U.521.

After a brief pursuit of a supposed convoy east of Madeira on 11th February, this turned out to be a hunting group. The Rochen boats having adequate fuel proceeded westward, while the remainder refuelled southwest of Madeira from U.118, rejoining the group on the 16th south of the Azores.

Meanwhile the northeast wing of the *Delphin* group was moved nearer Cape St. Vincent to intercept a convoy reported by our agent as westbound through the Strait of Gibraltar. It is thought that this convoy passed the gap between *Delphin* and the Portuguese coast. F.O. U-boats was about to order the group to return home when the Naval Staff directed that they should remain near the Portuguese coast, as an Allied landing was feared to be imminent. Consequently from 11th February the *Delphin* boats were disposed in attack areas to the west of Portugal, being reinforced by boats diverted from other tasks. On 12th February a southbound convoy was sighted 200 miles west of Cape Finisterre, and all these boats were ordered to close. The operation proved a distinct failure, for the convoy's air escort, becoming stronger as it approached Gibraltar, forced the boats to remain submerged day and night, so that they could not attain attacking positions, and we suffered two losses through aircraft bombs. "This again proves that running attacks on convoys near land, in areas heavily patrolled by aircraft, are no longer possible, because of the high performance of the enemy's sea- and airborne radar."

292. Chance Contact with UC 1

Our information about U.S.-Gibraltar convoys was still scanty, though we knew their approximate rhythm, from which F.O. U-boats deduced that one should be near the Azores on 17th February. It was considered useless to operate against it with less than two groups, one north and the other south of the Azores. Group Rochen was already assembling to the south, and the boats off Portugal would do for the north, if they could be spared from " anti-invasion " duties. The scare over the anticipated Allied landing in Portugal soon died down, and the waiting U-boats were formed into Group Robbe. From 17th February they combed the area north of the Azores while Group Rochen made a similar sweep south of the islands. When by 20th February neither group had located the convoy, the problem was how to use the boats in the interval, for 10 days would elapse before a further UG convoy was due. Meanwhile the situation in the Mediterranean had so deteriorated that Dönitz, in his capacity as C.-in-C. of the Navy, and against the advice of his U-boat Staff, ordered those Robbe boats having sufficient fuel to form a close patrol near Gibraltar by 28th February - the beginning of a new-moon period. The other group (Rochen) was also dispersed on 21st February, being ordered to refuel from U.461 about 200 miles south of Sao Miguel Island. But this did not occur, for on 22nd February U.522 to the east of the replenishment area, sighted a convoy steering southwest, probably heading for the Caribbean. All Rochen boats, and the two southern Robbe boats were ordered by radio to close the convoy, which was UC 1. U.461 was also ordered to follow behind the convoy to refuel boats after their attacks. The convoy's powerful screen of 10 warships used their very effective radar to ward off our scattered boats in their successive efforts to close, forcing them to submerge and to suffer depth-charge attacks. The first shadower was destroyed, and several U-boats were damaged. On the other hand the good visibility favoured the attackers, who remained in contact for five days. By 27th February fuel shortage and casualties left only two U-boats in pursuit of the convoy. The claims by attackers totalled seven ships, aggregating 50,000 tons, sunk. The true figures (three tankers sunk and two damaged) again emphasised the survival capacity of tankers in ballast.

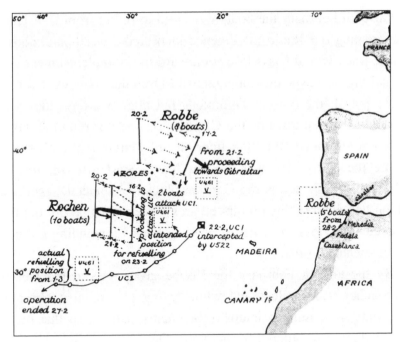

Plan 42. Groups Rochen and Robbe, 17th-28th February, 1943.
Operation against UC I

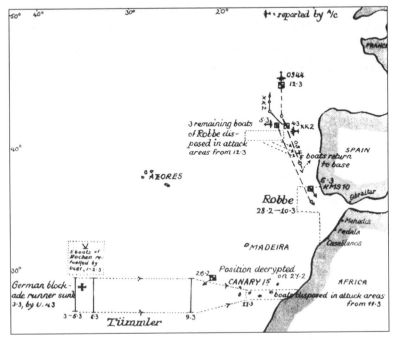

Plan 43. Groups Robbe and Tümmler, 28th February-12th March, 1943.
Operations against OS 44 and KMS 10.

On 27th February the boats were told to refuel from U.461, and that evening our Radio Intelligence identified a westbound convoy whose track would pass close southward of the replenishment area. Refuelling was expedited, and on 3rd March the boats were formed into a patrol line (Group Tiimmler), but after two days they were ordered to sweep towards the Canaries. U.43 later reported having sunk a northbound Blue Star liner on 3rd March. Not until shortly before the end of the war did our Naval Staff discover that the ship sunk by U.43 was the German blockade-runner Doggerbank, which had entered this prohibited area three weeks before the time ordered. This loss must be ascribed to her Commanding Officer's disobedience of orders.

By the end of February the Robbe group was at the western approaches to Gibraltar, and while trying to remain unobserved, the boats soon felt the intensity of enemy patrols, so that on 5th March they were ordered further west. On the next day U.410 came upon a small Gibraltar-bound convoy (KMS 10), sinking one ship, and damaging a second. The other boats, being low in fuel, were moved nearer their bases, to an area 200 to 400 miles southwest of Cape Finisterre, where our air reconnaissance was able to give them occasional help. By this means U.130 on 4th March contacted a northbound convoy (XK 2), scoring hits on four ships. On 12th March one of our FW 200 aircraft reported sighting a southbound convoy (OS 44) to the north of the Robbe group. U.107 contacted the convoy on the following day, scoring six hits which resulted in the destruction of four ships. Within a few days the last boats of the Robbe group returned to base.

REMOTE OPERATIONAL AREAS

293.Extension of Attacks on Convoys
Because of the shorter transit routes only Biscay-based U-boats were used against Mediterranean-bound shipping. But the Biscay ports

also had to provide the backbone of experienced U-boat groups against North Atlantic convoys and both demands could not be met. The only remedy was to use the large boats against Mediterranean-bound shipping, instead of in remote areas. The first of the U-cruisers (Type IXD, 1,200 tons), after operating in the Cape area, had to return home for lengthy overhaul. Further operations with this new type were delayed until April because of difficulties with their fast-running Diesel engines.

At the beginning of January, 1943, the situation in the remote areas was unsatisfactory compared with six months earlier. There were two boats off the Brazilian coast, one cruising between Freetown and Natal, and only four in the Caribbean zone. The concentration of boats at the focal point off Port of Spain had produced no noteworthy results, and it was now thought that eastbound shipping from this area had been formed into convoys. While operating against such a convoy off the Guiana coast on 9th January, U.124 successfully attacked four ships. Two further single ships were sunk farther to the northeast on the route to Gibraltar, one of these being the abandoned tanker British Vigilance from TM 1, which, torpedoed on 3rd January, had been drifting for over three weeks. In January another group (*Seehund*) was on passage to Capetown. Experience with the Eisbar group had shown that Type IXC boats, even if refuelled in the South Atlantic, could not last out in the Cape area until all torpedoes were expended. But since the Naval Staff attached importance to the interruption of shipping round the Cape to the Middle East, and as no U-cruisers were available, it was decided in January, 1943, to despatch four large boats and the U-tanker 459 (331). These refuelled about 600 miles south of St. Helena, and by the beginning of February were ready to operate off the Cape. But here also the situation had completely changed since December. Single ships were rarely encountered, while heavily escorted convoys were observed close along the coast, protected by air, sea and land radar, which prevented our boats from approaching. By the end of the month they had moved eastwards as far as Durban and Lourenco Marques.

JANUARY-MAY, 1943
IMPROVEMENT IN ENEMY A/S DEFENCES

294. Dönitz becomes C.-in-C. of the Navy

Dönitz was more than ever convinced that the only hope of preventing the United States from deploying their great fighting potential in Europe lay in vigorous attacks on the North Atlantic shipping. All indications pointed to the concentration of the American effort on the defeat of Germany before Japan. As a first step the United States were building up their base in the United Kingdom, and the excellence of the co-ordination of their sea and air effort towards this objective was most noticeable.

On the German side, however, similar co-ordination did not exist between the Navy and the *Luftwaffe*, so that the U-boat arm found itself virtually alone in meeting the crucial problem of the war on shipping. Meanwhile the demands on the German Navy in the various theatres of war had been extremely heavy, and it was essential to avoid wasting our limited resources on subsidiary tasks.

Dönitz faced continuous difficulties through the continental outlook of Hitler and the Supreme Command, who were not prepared to concede that for Germany the U-boat was the prior weapon. Those directing the German war effort failed to realise that U-boat operations produced a far greater effect on the enemy in relation to the effort involved than was the case with any other type of warfare. In Dönitz's view the Naval Staff also had failed to improve the top-heavy and over-organised departments of the Navy, such as armament production and development, dockyards and engineering works. When on 30th January he became Commander-in-Chief of the Navy, the staff of the U-boat Command had high hopes of a rapid development of the submarine as the paramount weapon. The new Commander-in-Chief believed that if adequate priorities had been given to this weapon during the past two years, results would have been immeasurable in the favourable conditions that then existed. It was a depressing thought that any steps taken now would be in the face of formidable counter-measures. For this reason he deprecated the propaganda that linked his new appointment with premature rejoicing over the anticipated results.

His past influence on the progress of the U-boat arm made it essential that Dönitz should retain control as Flag Officer U-boats, and this involved the transfer to Berlin of his U-boat Staff, which since the spring of 1942 had been located in Paris. The transfer occurred on 31st March, when the U-boat Staff were accommodated in a hotel at Charlottenburg, being incorporated as a division of the Naval Staff. This did not alter their functions, but allowed closer contact with other departments of the Admiralty.

295. Technical Progress with German Torpedoes

Since the summer of 1942 the most pressing task had been to obtain for the U-boats a torpedo which would be effective against the growing menace of surface escorts. But the difficulties encountered in designing this weapon - the G7s - made it doubtful whether it could be used operationally before the end of 1943. On the other hand the combined contact and non-contact pistol (Pi2) had become available in December, 1942, but it was not yet perfect, since it did not function when the track angle was under 30 degrees or over 150 degrees. The magnetic firing gear being very sensitive, the combined pistol could not be used as a non-contact pistol when the state of the sea was greater than 4 to 5, or when aircraft bombs or depth-charges were detonating in the vicinity. The greatest explosive effect was obtained when the torpedo exploded 1 to \\ metres below the keel of the ship. Should the torpedo's uneven depth-keeping cause it to pass more than 2 metres under the ship, then the pistol would not function. For this reason, and to avoid disappointment in the early use of the Pi2, instructions were given to set the depth to 1 metre less than the estimated draught of the target. It was realised that this would result in a majority of hits by *contact*.[51]

With insufficient workshop resources the monthly production of

---

51 It is interesting to compare these difficulties in developing the magnetic pistol with similar problems in the U.S. Navy in 1942 and 1943.

these pistols from December, 1942, onwards did not exceed 200, which were distributed first to the Mediterranean boats, then to the Atlantic, and last to boats in Northern Waters. By March, 1943, out of 30 hits obtained with Pi2, there were four definite cases of satisfactory functioning of the magnetic pistol. The evidence in each case was the breaking in half of the target ship, with only a small column of water resulting from the explosion. F.O. U-boats thereupon decided to order the use of non-contact firing with depth-setting 1 to 1 1/2 metres greater than the estimated draught of the target.

From December, 1942, the new G7a FAT[52] torpedoes were reaching the U-boat bases at the rate of not more than 100 per month. Originally it had been intended to supply these torpedoes only to U-boats fitted with radar. But the rate of production of radar sets lagged behind, and experience soon showed that the torpedo could be used effectively without radar. However, we had to stop using FAT torpedoes in the Mediterranean, where the bubble track was very conspicuous, for we wished to avoid compromising this new weapon.

The FAT torpedo could be regarded as highly successful, for it raised the number of hits in convoy attacks to 75 per cent, of shots fired. At first the U-boat crews were taken aback when the torpedo did not hit until perhaps the third or fourth loop. Commanding Officers were in the habit of turning away from the convoy immediately after firing, while the torpedo ran for eight to ten minutes ; hence there was even less accuracy than before in reporting results of attacks, particularly when several U-boats were involved.

If several boats were simultaneously attacking the convoy or found themselves within the screen, then they ran some risk from these FAT attacks. Boats intending to use FAT were told to send a warning signal on their special short wave, and such warning remained in force for 30 minutes. The order ran:

"Any boat receiving the warning while inside the convoy's

---

52 A torpedo destined to run in loops after reaching the track of the target.

perimeter should either clear out at high speed, or, if this is not possible, should dive to at least 50 metres. Boats attacking the convoy from outside its perimeter are to press home the attack, since the danger to other U-boats from FAT is then much reduced. Boats within a thousand yards in a forward firing position, or within two thousand yards in a rear firing position, are exposed to no greater danger than in normal attacks."

This order was of questionable value, for Commanding Officers, having once attained a good firing position within the convoy or within the screen, would be reluctant to abandon the attack merely because of the "FAT warning" from another boat. The war produced several cases of boats sighting bubble tracks of FAT torpedoes fired by another U-boat, yet there is no evidence of any self-inflicted loss from this cause.

It was anticipated that by April a trackless G7e FAT torpedo would become available, which could also be used as a circling torpedo for defence against a pursuing destroyer. But experience alone could show whether such tactics would be effective against the screen.

296. No Progress against the Air Menace

Against the enemy's aircraft we had been able to show no progress. In September, 1942, we had planned to arm the boats with two twin machine guns (1 -51 cm.) on the upper platform of the conning tower, and one 2 cm. twin machine gun (C/38) on the lower platform. But very soon it was realised that nothing less than 2 cm. barrels, or 3-7 cm. quick-firing cannon, would be effective. These weapons - 2 cm. quadruple mountings from army supplies, and 3-7 cm. cannon from naval sources - had to be treated with non-corroding coatings.

Starting in December, 1942, the obsolescent A.A. guns were gradually replaced by the new C/38, and the conning towers were rebuilt with two gun platforms. But U.553, the first boat to be fitted with these platforms, soon reported from sea that they were unsatisfactory, as the lower platform caused much spray, revealing the position of the boat. When submerged, the suction effect of the large bridge platform created difficulties in depth keeping. All this resulted in constructional modifications, and in January, 1943, the reconstruction of conning towers was widely put in hand. By April, 1943, all boats had been equipped with two 2 cm. machine guns (C/38). Too confident of the effectiveness of these new weapons, several boats ventured into gun actions with aircraft, which sometimes resulted in casualties to their guns' crews. The consequent decision to fit armoured doors to the after side of the conning tower for protection against machine-gun fire from astern was held up for some months owing to shortage of armour plating. Yet this new A.A. armament could hardly be considered as marking any real progress, for the 2 cm. calibre was quite inadequate against aircraft.

Even less satisfactory was the operation of our heavy fighters against the enemy's A/S aircraft. By the beginning of 1943 the few Ju 88 CVI aircraft that *Fliegerführer* Atlantic had been using were obsolete, and inferior to almost all enemy types. They had to operate in twos or even as a flight before tackling any four-engined enemy aircraft, and if *Beaufighters* were encountered, they had to clear off. Frequently our aircraft engaged in escorting damaged boats suffered losses, so that *Fliegerführer* Atlantic was reluctant to allow them to work even in the Bay of Biscay. Once again the enemy's A/S fighters could operate unmolested along the transit routes to the U-boat bases.

The *Fliegerführer's* repeated requests to Goring for more modern types were backed by Dönitz himself, but were useless, as the completion dates for the HE 177s had been indefinitely postponed.

297. Enemy A/S Developments

In contrast to these inadequate developments in German weapons, the enemy, vitally concerned with the protection of his shipping, had made rapid progress. Since the autumn of 1942 he had considerably increased the number of escort vessels and support groups for the protection of the convoy routes. From the beginning of 1943 we estimated that usually on the second day, and always on the third day after the convoy had first been attacked, one or more support groups would have come to its aid. These groups were observed not only south of Iceland and in the Bay of Biscay, but simultaneously off the east coast of Spain, northeast of Newfoundland and in the "Black Pit"[53]. We still wondered why the support groups were not active in the replenishment area north of the Azores.

F.O. U-boats had in the past been sceptical of reports from U-boats about alleged " Q " ships, but now there were instances of sighting fast vessels in the vicinity of convoys, which by skilled manoeuvring, using smoke and depth-charges, sometimes succeeded in luring even our experienced commanders away from the main objective. Auxiliary vessels that had been sighted near Cape Finisterre and off Freetown appeared on closer inspection to be decoys. They carried fast motor boats, which were used for attacking the U-boats. Conspicuously illuminated trawlers which had been seen south of Nova Scotia and west of Gibraltar dowsed their lights on the approach of the U-boats and operated their radar. Such methods contributed little to the destruction of U-boats, yet the frequent appearance of unidentifiable craft made our Commanding Officers extremely cautious at a time when the attainment of results demanded boldness.

British submarines also played their part in the general A/S organisation. They were to be found on patrol off our Norwegian and French bases and in the Bay of Biscay. Since the summer of 1942 we had lost only one boat through torpedo attack from an enemy submarine.[54] Our boats had to remain submerged on the transit routes, which were covered by enemy air patrols. The enemy's submarines were stationed in areas where 15 Group and 19 Group of the R.A.F. were active, and this required good radar recognition signals between the submarines and the aircraft. Here again the British methods were superior to ours. The opportunities for co-operation between the U-boats and the German Air Force were far too few.

---

53 In September, 1942, the first of the "Convoy Support Groups" was formed. Their primary object was the destruction of U-boats once they had been located in the vicinity of the convoy (C.B. 3304 (1), Section 80). The Germans use the English words "Black Pit" to describe the initially wide area north of the Azores in which air cover was not possible for convoys. This area became progressively smaller as air cover by V.L.R. aircraft was extended.

54 U. 335, sunk by H.M.S./M *Saracen* on 2nd August, 1942.

It seemed to us that the British submarines, finding few opportunities for attacking the U-boats approaching or leaving their bases, had moved further into the Atlantic. In November, 1942, there had been two unsuccessful attacks by British submarines on our U-boats southwest of the Cape Verde Islands. On 7th December we discovered from decryption that U.570, which fell into British hands in 1941, had been commissioned by the enemy for A/S purposes. All British submarines were easily recognisable by their conspicuous silhouettes and tall periscope sockets, but now the danger existed of sighting an enemy submarine with a German silhouette, and our U-boat commanders were warned accordingly.[55]

298. Enemy Air Patrols over the North Atlantic

The progressive westward extension of our operations had caused the enemy to develop his air bases in Newfoundland, and perhaps also in Greenland. By the beginning of 1943 Allied flying boats and land-based bombers were capable of reaching almost any point in the Atlantic north of 45 degrees North. But they were not able to remain for any length of time in the 400 mile wide " Black Pit " area north of the Azores, and F.O. U-boats therefore decided to move the boats further west into this area. Even on the fringes of the area our pursuit of convoys had only been successful when the weather conditions at the enemy air bases prevented the start of aircraft. Carrier-borne aircraft were first observed over a convoy in October, 1942. Press reports of increased air protection for convoys and of new escort carriers showed that the Allies were determined to close the gap in the " Black Pit ".

It was apparent from the *Luftwaffe*'s radio intelligence in January, 1943, that 19 Group of the R.A.F. was using about 35 to 40 aircraft each day for hunting U-boats in the Bay of Biscay. Whenever a Gibraltar convoy was passing the Bay, this number rose to 50 or 60. It may have been even higher, for we identified only those aircraft

---

55 From time to time during the Second World War British submarines were deployed for considerable periods against U-boats, but in British Home and Atlantic waters only five German and two Italian U-boats were destroyed by submarines before May, 1943 (C.B. 3304 (1), Section 146).

which used their radio. We estimated that from aerodromes in the southwest of England alone three to four times as many A/S aircraft operated as there were U-boats at the Biscay bases. All this revealed the immense effort that the enemy was putting into the business of impeding our boats.

299. Enemy Radar Developments

The original purpose of our *Metox* was to facilitate transit through the Bay of Biscay, but by October, 1942, this limited equipment had already indicated that in most areas enemy air and sea escorts were fitted with radar. The delicate aerials of the *Metox* were liable to give trouble. So great was the fear of surprise attacks from the air, that when their *Metox* was not functioning, the boats in the Caribbean and off the African coast were ordered to evacuate the operational area until they could obtain the necessary spare parts from a tanker ox from another boat. By the end of the year *Metox* was regarded as essential to the survival of boats.

The construction of radar stations along the enemy coasts proceeded with great speed. In September, 1942, U.69 had first observed such stations along the U.S. coast, and shortly afterwards similar stations were identified on the Moroccan coast and in the Caribbean. We had much information about the stations in the British Isles, but we did not realise their extent until we studied the log of U.404, which had been ordered to make an unobserved approach to Land's End for a surprise attack on the regular coastal convoys:

"2. 2.43. Near Wolf Rock, course 184 degrees, Longships bearing 048 degrees. My intention is to steam slowly up and down while charging batteries and waiting for an expected westbound convoy.

"2015. Surfaced. My Fu.M.B[56] registers an all-round search by land radar station, search period 10 to 15 seconds. 2050. A second station is observed giving a constant note. Dived. 2110. Surfaced. Can hear only commencement of radar sweep. 2122. Boat is again in the radar zone. Four radar stations were heard successively. I shall expect to be spotted or pursued very shortly. As I cannot move off or

---

56 This was the standard radar search receiver.

lie on the bottom because of the low state of the batteries, I decide to proceed at high speed on the surface, course 300 degrees.

"2130. I record the presence of eight simultaneous radar stations, distinguishable through pitch or wave length, apparently working in groups. Bearing 090 degrees, three aircraft searchlights approaching from low cloud, which force me to dive."

Observations of a similar kind were made by U.377 on 1st February and by U.376 on 6th February, 1943, when they attempted to approach the coast of Scotland near Peterhead for attacks on coastal convoys.

300. First Steps towards German Airborne Radar

After the introduction of Fu.M.B., F.O. U-boats collaborated with the Director of the Signal Division to organise an extensive listening service with a view to obtaining all possible information about enemy methods of location. Data collected from U-boats and other forces were systematically tabulated under carrier frequency, impulse frequency, and method of operating. There was some doubt as to whether the frequency range of our *Metox* - between 62 and 264 cms - was covering the whole range. New receivers with a wider frequency range would not be available until the summer. In February, 1943, some returning U-boats reported having been suddenly attacked at night by aircraft using searchlights, but apparently not using radar. These reports came from the Bay of Biscay and also from the Trinidad area. On 25th February the War Diary of F.O. U-boats stated: "Although the few cases reported so far may be due to failure in personnel or in equipment, these reports indicate that the enemy may have ordered extensive silent periods in order to deceive us" (332).

On 6th March one of our most experienced U-boat commanders, Hartenstein in U.156, reported "Between Port of Spain and Grenada very strong continuous note, with a new kind of radar, which *Metox* will not register, and accurate attacks without using searchlights." Such reports showed that the enemy was using new methods, which worried our hard-pressed scientists.

The War Diary of F.O. U-boats for 5th March states:

"1. The enemy is employing very high and also very low impulse frequencies which are barely audible. This is substantiated by the experience of U.124, where the P.O. Telegraphist, suspecting impulse frequencies beyond the range of the *Metox*, incorporated the " magic eye " of the general receiver into his apparatus, which enabled him to identify some radar activity. All boats due for sea are to have their receivers fitted with " magic eye ". A number of oscillographs are being sent to the boats in the western bases. Used in conjunction with the *Metox* they should indicate whether the enemy is indeed employing inaudible impulse frequencies. The boats have orders to report results by radio while still at sea.

2. The enemy is using carrier frequencies beyond the range of the present search receiver. So far the only confirmation of this comes from an enemy aircraft shot down over Holland, which apparently carried an instrument with a wave-length of 5.7 cm.[57] We must therefore assume that the enemy is working outside the range of our instrument.

3. The enemy switches on his search radar for only very short periods of two to three seconds. This confirms our previous observations of his economic use of radar and makes the identification so much more difficult. Theoretically we should deal with all three possibilities in the following way: Employment of an aperiodic or untuned receiver with optical indicator, which will show up every radar impulse, whether on carrier or impulse frequency. Use of a second tunable receiver for detailed observation of the radar transmissions. The appropriate organisation has been told to investigate whether such technical improvements are practicable."

No mention has been made here of steps to jam the enemy radar or to shield the U-boats against radar location, for it was believed that practical results in these fields would not be possible within a measurable time. The same applied to the protection of the U-boat through its own radar, and no progress had been made in this

---

57 This apparatus was later named *Rotterdamgeraet*, from the place where it was shot down.

direction. Since July, 1942, a few heavy Gema instruments with 80 cm wave-length had been put into boats, but proved so inadequate that the Commanding Officers usually dispensed with their use.

The desire of F.O. U-boats to experiment in U-boats with Hohentwiehl, which was the radar instrument of the *Luftwaffe*, using a 53 cm wave-length, had met with some opposition from the naval radar technicians, who were more interested in the Gema instrument, which had been their " baby ". But by the spring of 1943 Dönitz, who was now Commander-in-Chief, ordered trials with the *Luftwaffe* instrument.

CLIMAX OF THE BATTLE OF THE ATLANTIC

301. Radar, Radio Intelligence, Problems of Control

For three whole weeks in January, 1943, our system of search in the North Atlantic had produced no result.[58] In February a few convoys had been sighted, by chance, or by single boats at the extreme ends of our patrol lines. In all these cases it could be inferred from the tracks of the convoys that they were deliberately circumventing the dispositions and movements of our boats, about which they appeared to have precise information. As in the autumn of 1941, these circumstances led to a renewed suspicion that the enemy obtained his knowledge through treachery or through insight into our U-boat cyphers. The latter suspicion was accentuated by an incident on 12th January, 1943, when the U-tanker U.459, having taken up a pre-arranged position 300 miles east of St. Paul's Rock for the purpose of refuelling the Italian U-boat Kalvi, ran into searching enemy destroyers at the exact time of the rendezvous. This was indeed strange, for the locality was 800 miles from the nearest bases - Freetown and Natal - and far removed from any convoy routes.

Once again more stringent regulations for security were ordered

---

58 "In January, 1943, for the first time since the United States entered the war, merchant ship losses fell below one per day in all Atlantic areas, and below 200,000 tons per month." (Morsion, p. 312.)

for the staff of F.O. U-boats and for the few other centres which had knowledge of U-boat dispositions, and the Director of the Signal Division was instructed to examine our cypher security. He, however, persisted in his view that the enemy would not be able to decrypt the U-boats' radio messages, which were enciphered with Key M. Moreover, he could provide evidence which allayed our grave suspicions. After much searching and experiment the Radio Intelligence Service, which came under his control, had now succeeded in penetrating considerably into the enemy cyphers. More and more cypher messages and " U-boat situations " were decrypted and passed to F.O. U-boats. The author recollects that these routine " U-boat situations " were sent by the British Admiralty to Commodores of convoys. They contained data on the disposition of U-boats at fixed times, usually daily. In these reports the source of the information was sometimes given, as for example: " U-boats are patrolling, or are concentrating, data obtained from D/F bearings (or from radio location, or from dead reckoning, or estimation)." On the daily maps at U-boat headquarters were marked the positions of groups and single boats, with arrows indicating direction of movement, and also all the information that the enemy was assumed to have obtained about U-boats through sightings, D/F bearings and radio location. Since the boats did not use their radio in the operational area, they could not report at the time whether they had been located from aircraft, and these maps could not be fully analysed until the boats returned to base. Documents which had been found in a French agent's transmitting station in 1942 showed us that the enemy was receiving information not only of the times of departure of U-boats from bases, but also as to whether they were bound for the North or South Atlantic. It seemed therefore that he was in a position to estimate their movements with some accuracy.

On 5th March F.O. U-boats summed up the situation as follows:

"With the exception of two or three doubtful cases, enemy information about the position of our U-boats appears to have been obtained mainly from extensive use of airborne radar, and the resulting plotting of these positions has enabled him to organise effective diversion of convoy traffic. We were slow to realise the technical possibilities of ASV Radar and our counter-measures lagged behind."

Here is an example of the harmful effect of Hitler's order which excessively restricted the dissemination of secret technical information.

302. No help from Air Reconnaissance

It was reassuring that treachery, or insecurity of our cyphers, were apparently not the cause of the enemy's knowledge, yet it was disturbing that the British Commander-in-Chief, Western Approaches, who was in general charge of convoy routing, had so precise a picture of our U-boat positions. Airborne radar no doubt helped the British Admiral to obtain his information without delay, whereas F.O. U-boats had no air reconnaissance at his disposal, and it was sometimes weeks before all the details, collected from returning U-boats, enabled him to make an accurate estimate of the general position. Dönitz once compared his position to that of a card player with a mirror behind him, which discloses his secrets. The measures which, as Commander-in-Chief, Dönitz was able to introduce for better air reconnaissance would take months, perhaps even years to become effective. Meanwhile he had to resign himself to the realisation that while the air situation remained so unsatisfactory, the U-boats could never play their full part against the enemy's shipping.

303. Effective German Radio Intelligence

The summer of 1942, with its growing diversity and complexity of operations, demanded a clarification of the problems of the Battle of the Atlantic. By the spring of 1943 this clarification became even more necessary. The whole of our staff work took on the complexion of a game of chess, the opponent being the C.-in-C. Western Approaches. In estimating the opponent's reaction, his thought processes were classified into various stages, on the basis of his available information. Thus the first stage was the diversion of a convoy from the danger area, while the second was a further re-routing as soon as the British C.-in-C. realised that F.O. U-boats had adjusted the position of the boats to counter the original convoy diversion. Sometimes a third or a fourth stage followed, and always we tried to discover an underlying system in the re-routing of the convoys. In the first two months of 1943, for example, F.O. U-boats believed that the practice was to send four successive SC and HX convoys along the northerly route, followed by four convoys on the southerly route.

By March, 1943, however, the extent of the enemy's radar made this type of analysis redundant, for his knowledge of our U-boat positions was becoming so ubiquitous that he needed only to send the convoys through the gaps between our groups. Indeed, our handicap would have been hopeless, had it not been for the vital and timely assistance from our Decryption Service, which functioned with increasing speed as we penetrated into the British cyphers and completed their basic code book. We had reached a stage when it took one or two days to decrypt the British radio messages, and on occasions only a few hours were required between the time of original transmission and the arrival of the message in our intelligence centre. Thus, C.-in-C. Western Approaches now also had a mirror behind his cards, and we could sometimes deduce when and how he would take advantage of the gaps in our U-boat dispositions. Our function was to close these gaps just before the convoys were due.

It was almost entirely due to these outstanding achievements by our Radio Intelligence Service that the U-boats still succeeded in finding convoys.

304. Attempts to conceal Position of our Patrol Lines

On 5th March F.O. U-boats commented that: " The frequent appearance of the expression ' radio-located ' in the (British) U-boat situation reports complicates our problem of finding the convoys by means of the patrol lines, which until now has been our main method." Yet we could not abandon this method, which still offered the best chance of interception. We had to try every means of concealing this patrol line from the convoys, and with this object orders were issued on 5th March that: " As soon as enemy airborne radar has been identified, all boats are at once to dive for 30 minutes." Care was taken to form the patrol lines only just before contact was expected. Yet when the position of a patrol line had to be altered during bad weather, the speed of advance of the boats was so small in relation to the area covered by the enemy aircraft, that the patrol line could be regarded as almost stationary.

ACTIONS AGAINST U.S.-BRITISH CONVOYS

305. Summaries by Radio

It was essential to keep the U-boats up to date as to the latest A/S methods of the enemy. Ever since the outbreak of war Dönitz had insisted that the training organisation should make use of all the latest operational experience. Such discoveries were immediately sent by radio or teleprinter to the training flotillas and to the operational bases, and were supplemented by reports, extracts from the war diary, and lectures by experienced Commanding Officers. From 1941 summaries and appreciations were made on typical convoy operations, which not only kept the U-boat officers up to date on the general situation, but also served to acquaint them with the views of the F.O. U-boats, while officers were encouraged to advance their own views.

The increasing tempo of operations against convoys had produced a mass of observations concerning the ever-changing enemy tactics. These were sifted by the staff of F.O. U-boats, the more important being embodied in a printed series of standing orders which were distributed to the whole service.

306. Procedure against Radar used by Surface Escorts

The reports from operational boats since the autumn of 1942 were scanty as regards the enemy's method of using radar, for the winter weather had prevented careful observation because of the vulnerability of aerials. It was therefore difficult to give guidance on this problem (333). The following extracts from reports of convoy actions between January and March, 1943, illustrate the difficulty:

"7.2.43. Procedure against escorts of SC 118: On dark nights, when the enemy escorts can see the boat only at close range, say 200 to 300 metres, the Commanding Officer should always attempt to evade the approaching destroyers, for they have set their course as a result of radar, which however ceases to function at such short ranges. Thus if the boat evades at high speed and at right angles to the approach course, the destroyer will probably fail to keep the boat on the radar screen. Whenever possible the U-boat should head the sea, as this will complicate the A/S vessel's radar and lookout. If the destroyer opens fire, the result will often be ineffective, as he will not see the target. In such cases too, an attempt must be made to evade on the surface, for once the U-boat is forced under water it will never succeed in catching up with the convoy."

"25.2.43. No new lessons were learnt from the action against ON 166, but it seems that the effectiveness of the escort's radar ceased when range had closed to between 1,000 and 1,500 metres, particularly if the U-Boat evaded at right angles to the approaching destroyer. On dark nights this lateral evasion must always be attempted."

"18.3.43. Experience against SC 122 and HX 229. Some U-boats report that destroyers operating in daylight in fair weather have sometimes succeeded in shadowing U-boats, when the top of the shadowers' aerial arrays are only just visible above the horizon. In such cases they proceed directly towards the U-boat, but often give up the pursuit, as the narrow radar target presented by an escaping boat is seemingly more difficult to locate than a broad silhouette. Some U-boats took advantage of this while shadowing, and were able to remain on the surface. But this calls for close observation of the destroyer, so that whenever the latter alters course the U-boat can immediately change her angle of inclination. It was again found that in heavy weather the danger of radar location hardly exists."

FEBRUARY - APRIL, 1943

307. Tactical Problems of Convoy Operations

The numerical increase of escort vessels and their universal equipment with radar had greatly increased our difficulties and dangers in attacking convoys. The fact that the escort vessels could refuel from a ship in the convoy gave them an almost unlimited radius of action, and allowed the Commodores of the convoys to double their A/S screen, even in mid-Atlantic. Our boats experienced the greatest inconvenience from the outer screen, which was usually between 10 and 30 miles ahead of the main body. We found that the attempt to attain a forward position occupied far more time than formerly. Whenever an escort vessel or an aircraft appeared, the boats had to evade or dive, for depth-charge and air attacks invariably followed. When many U-boats were trying to attain the forward position, the escort vessels would not devote much time to any one U-boat, but after dropping one or two lines of depth-charges, would usually direct their attention to the next shadower, in order to force him under water.

If a boat were forced to submerge for 30 minutes, it would lose four miles in relation to the convoy, and since in the normally bad weather of the Atlantic its surface speed would not exceed that of the convoy by more than three or four knots, two or three hours would be needed to regain bearing. When the convoy had an air escort, it sometimes required one or even two days before the individual U-boats could reach an attacking position. It was therefore most important that the dispositions planned by F.O. U-boats should allow for at least one group of boats to be well ahead of the line of advance of the convoy.

Other tactical problems of this period are shown by the following extract concerning operations against SC 118, ON 166, SC 122 and HX 229:

"The basis of success against convoys is that they should be found quickly, and this is only possible if the navigation is accurate and information on the convoy tracks reliable... In using the numerous reports from our own boats, the reliability of their dead-reckoning, and the experience of individual commanders must be taken into account. As soon as the boat has sighted a convoy, it sends out shadowing reports, and compares the position of the convoy with the reports received from other boats. The shadower then increases the distance from the convoy to about 30 miles, to escape the attention of the escorts' radar, and maneuvers to attain a forward position. If within two hours no further sighting report is received, the shadower must again approach the convoy until mastheads are in sight, and then repeat the maneuver to gain position.

"When escort vessels are about, boats must try to remain on the surface as long as possible and must try to avoid being forced under water. They should try to escape on the surface from corvettes, over which they usually have the advantage in speed. The enemy will try, particularly at dawn and dusk, to send his escorts out from the convoy in order to force the greatest number of U-boats to remain submerged, and so remain unaware of the new line of advance of the convoy. If escort aircraft are met, particularly before dusk, they should be engaged with A.A. guns, so as not to lose the chance of a night attack on the convoy. Boats should only dive in the presence of aircraft, if they can reach a depth of at least 80 metres. In all doubtful cases they should remain on the surface and fight it out. The crews should be taught to do this, and the danger of being bombed at shallow depths must be explained.

"The best conditions for attack are nearly always at the beginning of an operation, when the enemy may still be unaware of the large number of U-boats present. Later on, with air support, he is usually able to operate offensively against the boats... On moonlight nights the enemy appears to station his escorts mainly on the down-moon side. Attacks from the direction of the moon are therefore often more promising, because the danger of radar location is reduced... Endeavour to make a submerged attack, for this offers at least as good prospects as a surface attack...

"Latest reports indicate that the sea and air escorts employ every means to deceive U-boats and to keep them submerged, thus preventing them from regaining contact with a convoy. For example, it is reported that the escorts drop buoys at the positions where U-boats dive. A series of explosions is emitted from the buoys to simulate depth-charge attacks. Escorts may also drop sonobuoys which either take D/F bearings of the U-boats or reproduce the noise of an escort vessel. Thus if a boat wishes to avoid dropping too far astern of the target, it must occasionally rise to periscope depth and proceed at silent running speed, in order to discover the true state of affairs."

It was essential for shadowing and attack that the convoys' defences should become dispersed and this could only be achieved by using a large number of U-boats. More than ever, therefore, F.O. U-boats had to press the armament industry to expand U-boat numbers.

308. Demands on U-boat Personnel

In the vicinity of a convoy, when boats were gaining bearing, attacking, or receding, their courses were governed almost exclusively by the tactical situation, and reduction of speed or alteration of course to avoid heavy seas was seldom possible. In the winter months in the North Atlantic the force of the wind was normally between 4 and 5, and the resulting spray was sufficient to interfere with the conning tower lookouts. In worse weather, it often happened that the belts by which the bridge personnel were strapped to the conning tower parted due to the force of the sea, the men being injured and sometimes washed overboard.

The engine room personnel could no longer count on odd half hours in the conning tower for fresh air, for the danger from aircraft restricted bridge personnel to the minimum. At any moment, by day or night, a boat on the surface might be attacked ; nothing was more enervating than a prolonged depth-charge pursuit, with batteries dwindling and the incessant leaks adding to negative buoyancy. Sometimes the pursuit lasted 8, 12 or even 20 hours.

The greatest strain devolved on the Commanding Officers who, even on the third or fourth night of a convoy operation, could never leave the bridge. Under such conditions great fortitude was required to resume the approach immediately after being attacked from the air. When Commanding Officers returning from operations explained that, after a certain period of this sort of existence, their efficiency became greatly impaired, it was certainly not for the office-bound staff officer to find fault.

309. Successes against SC 121

In February, 1943, 74 boats proceeded on Atlantic operations, being used to reinforce the groups on the eastern side.

Group Neptun, which did not take part in the attack on ON 166, had on 27th February contacted an eastbound convoy (HX 227). The group was proceeding southwestwards and contact was made on the northern flank. Although two ships, totalling 14,000 tons were sunk, the weather prevented the remaining boats of the group from reaching attacking positions, but on 1st March they temporarily contacted a westbound convoy. Since F.O. U-boats at this time lacked information on the true positions of the U-boats, it was left to the Commanding Officers to decide which convoy to attack. But the westbound convoy (ON 168) was lost, and two days later the search was abandoned.

Since 26th February a new group (Burggraf) was making a westward sweep, and from 4th March was joined by the *Wildfang* group, then east of Newfoundland. Together they formed a long, angled patrol line designed to catch an SC convoy on the following day. Not far to the north of this patrol line the boats of the Neptun group were in waiting positions. During the night the *Wildfang* and Burggraf groups steered northeast, but SC 121 slipped by, being sighted by one of the Neptun boats about 90 miles northward. Although the initial positions of the boats were unfavorable, F.O. U-boats decided to send 17 of them, drawn from all three groups, in pursuit, in the hope of catching the target within two days. On 8th March he also formed the 11 northerly boats of a new group Neuland into a patrol line west of Ireland, and ahead of the expected course of

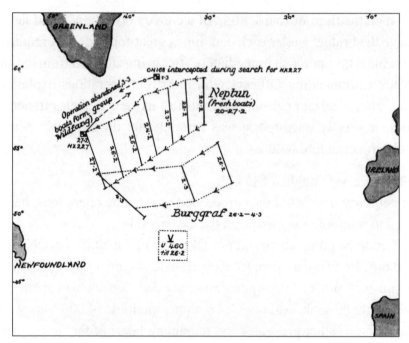

*Plan 44. Groups Beptun and Burggraf, 20th February-4th March, 1943.
Operations against ON 168 and HX 227*

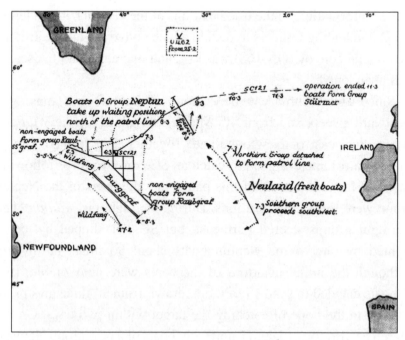

*Plan 45. Groups Burggraf, Wildfang and Neuland, 27th February-11th March,
1943. Operation against SC 121*

the convoy. The stormy weather caused a number of stragglers to fall victim to the pursuing boats, and the main body was also attacked. Without losing any U-boats, 13 ships totalling 62,000 tons were sunk and one ship torpedoed. The prevailing heavy seas probably hampered the enemy's escorts in the use of their surface and under water detection gear. This operation proved an exception to the dictum that the pursuit of convoys from an initially disadvantageous position was unrewarding.

Boats of *Wildfang* and Burggraf which had not joined in the pursuit of SC 121 were reinforced, and on 7th March were formed into a new group Raubgraf, intended for use against an HX convoy, which was expected to follow shortly in the track of SC 121 (Plan 46). The search for this HX convoy, as well as the northerly and westerly movements of the boats on 11th March to catch ONS 169 (reported by decryption as heading southwest) remained without result. On 13th March ON 170 was momentarily sighted in bad weather. Despite rain and snow it was decided to pursue the convoy in the hope of single targets, but the presence of strong air escorts, and particularly the receipt of radio intelligence concerning SC 122, caused abandonment of the pursuit.

310. Successful Attack on HX 228

Meanwhile by 7th March the remaining boats of Neuland had started moving west. On the 9th F.O. U-boats received a decrypted message giving the position of HX 228 on the previous day as 300 miles west of Neuland. Anticipating that the enemy would be aware of the group's position and would deviate to the north, the boats were immediately moved northward 120 miles, but the conjecture proved wrong, for on 10th March the convoy was sighted at the southern end of the patrol line. Within the next three days the U-boats claimed to have sunk six ships totalling 50,000 tons[59] and torpedoed others. U.221, commanded by Trojer, carried out a brilliant submerged attack which accounted for two and possibly three ships, and was very nearly lost through the explosion of an ammunition ship.

---

59 British records show only four ships sunk.

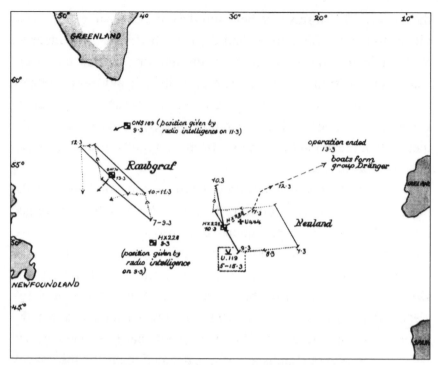

Plan 46. Groups Raubgraf and Neuland, 7th-14th March, 1943
Operations against ON 170 and HX 228.

311. The Biggest Convoy Operation of the War - Against HX 229 and SC 122

The operations in about 20 degrees West longitude against SC 121 and HX 228 had ended respectively on 11th and 13th March. As the boats still had sufficient fuel they were now formed into two groups, Sturmer on 14th, and Dranger on 15th March. It was intended that the latter should be used later against HX 229, whose position and course on the 13th (45° N., 50° W., 089°) had been derived from decryption. On the afternoon of the 14th we learnt from a further enemy signal that SC 122, which included at least 49 ships in 14 columns, had received orders on the 13th to steer 067 degrees from the position 49° N., 46° W. Under these circumstances it was essential to use the Raubgraf group (which had been looking for ON 170 northeast of Newfoundland) to close and shadow the SC convoy.

In heavy weather on the evening of the 15th one of the southern boats of this group sighted a destroyer steering northeast. Search measures yielded no result, but on the following morning a returning U-boat located a convoy not far to the southeast of the patrol line. This we presumed to be SC 122.

Further radio intelligence showed that HX 229 was being deliberately diverted from its original line of advance of 089 degrees to a course which followed the east coast of Newfoundland.[60] The original intention to use Dranger against this convoy was therefore cancelled, and with all other groups (totalling 40 boats) it now hurried to the attack of the presumed SC 122 .

Contact was made on the morning of the 16th, and by midday the first boats of Raubgraf had gone in to the attack. In the course of that day and the following night eight boats made contact with the convoy, and claimed sinking 14 ships and damaging six others. Three experienced commanders fully exploited this early opportunity of surprise by carrying out several attacks. One of these boats alone sank three ships and damaged three more. The second sank four, and the third sank three "and damaged one ship.

On the night of the 16th a second convoy was reported 120 miles ahead of the first. This second convoy being identified as an SC (SC 122), we now realised that the one we were attacking was an HX(HX229).

The speed of advance of SC 122 was 1 1/2 knots less than that of HX229. The two convoys were therefore closing, so.that towards the end of the operation, when separated by only a few miles, they formed a common objective to all boats. Since the convoys were not steering the same course, this had the disadvantage of confusing the objective to the searching boats, which in some cases failed to find it.

The following description of the subsequent course of the operation is taken from the diary of F.O., U-boats:

"After our successes of the first night, the enemy on the 17th used air escorts, which allowed only five boats to make submerged

<hr>

60 British records show that HX 229 did not in fact pursue the course indicated by German decryption, which may have been faulty. The Germans believed that the British might be using deliberate radio deception.

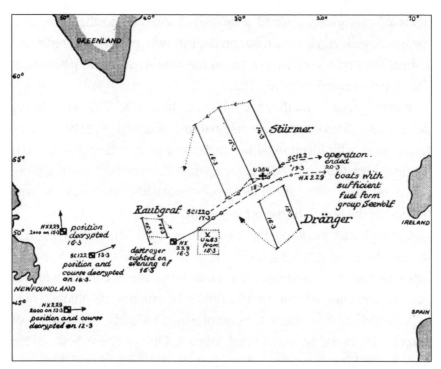

Plan 47. Groups Raubgraf, Strumer and Dranger, 15th-20th March, 1943.
Operations against SC 122 and HX 229

attacks, resulting in the sinking of eight ships and damage to four more. Four of those sunk had been damaged in the previous night's attack. The ever-increasing air defence caused us to lose contact with both convoys on the night of the 17th, and the operation became increasingly difficult owing to deterioration of weather and visibility, with the result that only one boat was successful against the SC convoy. Improved visibility on the 18th allowed nine boats again to make contact, of which one carried out a bold and successful underwater attack in the middle of the convoy, in high seas, and sank two ships. On the night of the 18th and during the 19th eight further ships and one destroyer were sunk by five of our boats. Two of these attacked the main convoy and three attacked the easterly convoy. On the morning of the 20th, in increasing difficulties, due at night to near-full moon and in daytime to stronger air defences, the operation had to be broken off..."

The boats claimed sinking 32 ships, aggregating 136,000 tons. They also sank the A/S trawler *Campo Bella*, and damaged nine ships.[61]

F.O. U-boats finally commented that this unprecedentedly successful convoy battle was all the more satisfactory in that only one of our boats was lost, while nearly half the participating boats had scored results.

312. First Use of an Escort Carrier for Convoy Protection - Operation against HX 230

A decrypted radio message of 20th March read: " That part of ONS 1 which comes from Iceland is to be in a position 60° 55' N., 22° W. at 0900 on 21 /3 to rendezvous with the main convoy." This precise intelligence gave us the opportunity of coming to grips at an early stage with an ON convoy, while still on the eastern side of the Atlantic (Plan 48). F.O. U-boats was anxious to give his boats some rest after the strenuous pursuit of SC 122, but such an opportunity could not be ignored. A number of the boats from the former Sturmer, together with some newly arrived boats south of Iceland, were formed into the patrol line Seeteufel, which would be able to cross the path of ONS 1, on 22nd March. U.168 was to proceed to the decrypted rendezvous, and was to shadow without attacking.

No sea or air escorts were observed either at the rendezvous of the two convoys or by our patrol line, and on the night of the 22nd Seeteufel proceeded along the estimated line of advance, and then further towards Cape Farewell. Here on the 26th, the search was extended by the new group Seewolf, and together these boats formed a line of nearly eight hundred miles southward from Cape Farewell, which line was to serve as a starting point for pursuit in either direction.

On the afternoon of the 26th many masts and an aircraft carrier were sighted in the centre of the Seeteufel line. Strong air and sea

---

61 According to British records only 21 ships were sunk, but they were aggregated 141,000 tons. "The Germans never came so near disrupting communication between the New World and the Old as in the first twenty days of March, 1943" (Admiralty Monthly A/S Report, December, 1943).

patrols prevented our boats from discovering the direction of advance of the convoy, and not until that night was it possible to identify it as an ON, and to organise interception courses accordingly.

To the southeast of the last indicated position of this ON convoy we assumed that there were also SC 123 and HX 230, whose Commodores, hearing the intense radio traffic of our boats closing on the ON convoy, would avoid the dangerous area by turning eastwards. In order to counter such escape, the Seewolf boats were ordered on the 26th to proceed northward at high speed, and the surmise proved correct, for within a few hours the most northerly boat reported an eastbound convoy.

Meanwhile, the Seeteufel group had failed to renew contact with the ON convoy and it was therefore concentrated on the new objective, HX 230. Once again initial conditions were unfavourable. Although on the 28th several boats were near the objective, the prevailing storm developed into a hurricane which precluded all

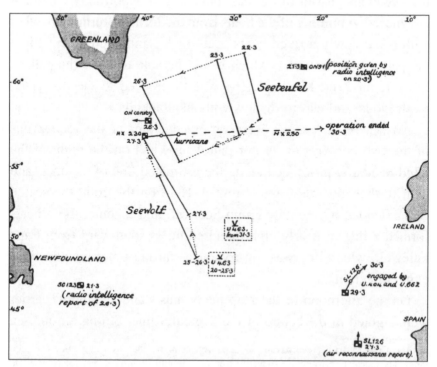

Plan 48. Groups Seeteufel and Seewolf, 22nd-30th March, 1943.
Operation against HX 230.

organised search. Though in the next few days the weather did not abate, the pursuit was continued in the hope of finding some stragglers, and this was justified. There was however only one victim because the heavy seas prevented the use of weapons. U.260 for example reported on 28th March that with wind W.S.W. and sea 9 she pursued an 8,000 ton steamer, and unsuccessfully fired one torpedo at her. The log states:

"At 2200 I abandond pursuit. In the attempt to run at high speed before the sea, the boat plunged twice. By means of extreme rudders, blowing tanks, and reduction of speed I succeeded in getting her to the surface. On the bridge the C.O. and the watch, after half an hour of this, are nearly drowned. In a very short period 5 tons of water were shipped through the conning tower hatch, voice pipe and diesel air intake."

F.O. U-boats was surprised to learn that the extremely bad weather did not interrupt the intense enemy air activity. Though it prevented the aircraft from making accurate attacks on our boats, their mere presence caused the boats to move eastwards even more slowly than the stragglers they were trying to attack. When eventually the weather moderated, the opportunities for attacking the convoy had passed. In spite of the poor result, the undertaking could not be regarded as wrong, for any slight improvement in the weather would probably have led to success.[62]

313. Last Satisfactory Convoy Battles -SL 126, HX 231, ON 176, HX 232

On 27th March a German aircraft on reconnaissance for a returning blockade-runner sighted a northbound convoy west of Cape Finisterre, and consequently a number of outward-bound U-boats were ordered to search for this target. U.404 and 662 found the convoy (SL 126) and in a successful surprise attack sank four and

---

62 "The cover given by U.S. escort carrier *Bogue* to SC 123 was the first instalment of continuous air cover for transatlantic convoys, which had been delayed by the diversion of the escort carriers to the North African operations. This cover came not a moment too soon, for convoy losses in the gap were mounting. With end-to-end air cover, the convoys could now take a more southerly route." (C.B. 3304 (1), Section 86).

damaged one ship. F.O. U-boats commented that the relatively weak escort of this convoy implied that in this area the British felt safe, and he hoped that standing air patrols could be established in order to drive them further west.

After the operation against HX 230 only one tanker (U.463) was available to replenish 16 boats due to return to base. This left only the single group *Löwenherz* for operations ; and on 3rd April its boats, 400 miles southeast of Cape Farewell, proceeded westward, making contact on the following day with HX 231. Their relative initial position was favourable; the weather was suitable, but the pursuit, lasting until the 7th, resulted in the sinking of only six ships, with damage claimed to one destroyer and three more ships. In this case U-boat numbers were adequate, but the relatively small result was ascribed to difficulty in attaining attacking positions owing to the presence of carrier-borne aircraft.

The eight boats of the *Adler* group, which meanwhile had been formed up south of Cape Farewell, were to commence a southward sweep on the 7th to intercept SC 125. An enemy hunting group was sighted steering north, and the resulting search for the convoy by three boats produced no result. The other boats were meanwhile moved northward. It was then discovered from decryption that on the previous day SC 125 had passed about 200 miles south of the *Adler* group. Since this convoy was now out of range, all we could do was to search for the succeeding HX 232 on the same route, and the boats therefore moved about 300 miles southeastward. During this sweep contact was made with ON 176, and nine of our boats, being favourably situated, were sent to attack. The remainder were formed into group *Meise* to continue the operation. To widen the area of search, the former *Löwenherz* patrol were formed into the *Lerche* group, adjoining *Meise*.

On the second day of the operation against ON 176 increased enemy air patrols prevented our boats reaching attacking positions, so that by the 13th the action had to be broken off. Our boats claimed nine ships sunk aggregating 56,000 tons. British figures, however,

206

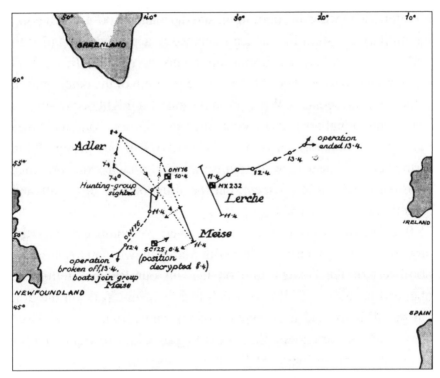

Plan 49. Groups Adler, Lerche and Meise, 7th-13th April, 1943.
Operations against ON and HX 232.

indicate that only two smaller ships were sunk out of ON 176 and
ONS 2 which was also in the vicinity.

Our assumption that HX 232 was following in the track of its
predecessor proved correct for, on 11th April it passed the newly
formed *Lerche* patrol. The latter sank four ships on the first night,
but found that fresh attacking positions were impossible, again due
to air patrols.

ATTACKS ON MEDITERRANEAN-BOUND
CONVOYS

314. Abandonment of Operations off U.S. Atlantic Coast

Results during the past eight weeks against convoys bound for the

Mediterranean were disappointing, and the main purpose of relieving the military situation in that sea remained unachieved. We failed to find a single U.S.A.-Mediterranean supply convoy. At this period everything had to be subordinated to the problem of the deterioration at the Tunis bridgehead. What could be done ? It might be possible to station individual boats as lookouts off Boston, New York, and other main ports, to report movements of convoys to our groups lying further east. This was an extreme measure, which from previous experience held little prospect, but the situation was desperate and something had to be tried.

Because of the long distances involved we could use only the large boats for this purpose. From 4th March they began to assemble northwest of the Azores, and on the 9th our Radio Intelligence obtained positions of UGS 6 which had left New York on the 5th. On the 10th we had a decryption of the entire route of this slow convoy and its stragglers, thus providing us with excellent data for an attack in mid-Atlantic. Hence the intention of proceeding to the American coast was abandoned and the six boats already northwest of the Azores were formed into a patrol line {Unverzagt) 500 miles southwest of the Azores. The remaining six boats were ordered south of the Azores and by the 13th assumed a patrol line (Wohlgemut) across the route of UGS 6. Unverzagt sighted the convoy on the evening of the 12th, 60 miles north of the position expected from decryption, when it was steering as if to evade this group. Apart from Wolhlgemut, the only other group available was Tilmmler, which was nearly 1,500 miles away, having arrived off the Canaries the previous day, and being occupied with a small southbound convoy. As the speed of the latter convoy was high, the group was immediately redisposed to intercept UGS 6.

The destruction of the first shadower of the big convoy (U.130) on the night of the 13th caused loss of contact until the 14th, after which is was maintained without interruption. In the first days there were usually six to seven, and later, nine boats in the vicinity of the convoy. Although not handicapped through enemy air patrols, or bad

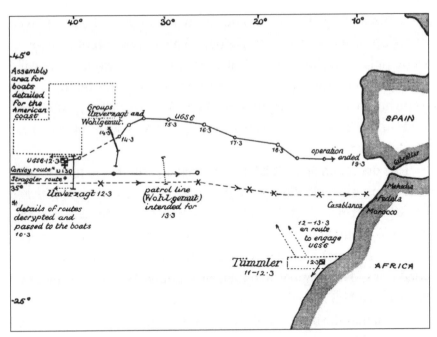

Plan 50. Groups Unverzagt, Wohlgemut and Tümmler, 12th-19th March, 1943.
Operations against UGS 6

weather, the boats were prevented from approaching the convoy by the remote screen which, using radar, spotted and pursued them with depth-charges while still 10 to 15 miles from the convoy.

On 16th March the Commanding Officers were instructed to confine themselves in future to distant shadowing, by watching the convoy's smoke or by noting on the Fu.M.B. the enemy radar activity. Later, when this achieved nothing, they were ordered to keep outside radar an visibility range of the screen, and to move ahead of the convoy guided by reports from the special detailed shadowers. The object was to dive before the remote screen came in sight, and attempt a submerged attack. It was realized that if during the submerged approach on an opposite course to the convoy the latter should zigzag, the target might be missed. Even so, this method was preferable to risking constant attacks by the screen while trying to haul ahead for the purpose c delivering a night attack.

The new procedure seemingly produced results, for on the 17th several submerged attack could be made, and the boats claimed five ships sunk and one torpedoed. The British record however show only one ship sunk. That evening air escorts in increasing strength reinforced the convoy so that by the 19th the operation came to an end. British figures show four ships of 28,000 tons sunk in all. This was valuable, as their cargoes were intended for the African front.

This operation against UGS 6 showed clearly that in fine weather it was most difficult, if no impossible, to approach a convoy protected by radar escorts. The prospects for the future were bleak, for in this case the availability of 20 boats with experienced commanders, who at first had no bother from air patrols, had provided excellent conditions. The original intention of sending the large (Type IXC) boats to the U.S. coast was now abandoned.

About half the boats employed against UGS 6 were now refuelled from the others in order to commence the homeward journey. The remainder proceeded southwards to occupy attacking positions west of the Canaries during the full-moon period. Our Radio Intelligence showed that RS 3 (a Rabat-Freetown convoy) was expected to pass between the Canaries and the mainland on 26th March, and these boats were formed into a patrol line 5 miles north of Cap Mogador. The convoy arrived two days later than expected, and the submerged attack resulted in the sinking of three ships. Thereafter the convoy had constant protection from shore-based aircraft, and although the pursuit continued until the 30th, no further results were possible. Nearly all the boats suffered from depth-charge and bombing attacks, and three of then had to give up because of severe damage.

We had too few boats in this area to justify continuing operations against convoys. Thre boats with adequate fuel were placed in the Dakar-Freetown area, the remainder stayec for some days off the Cape Verde Islands and then near the Canaries. On 5th Apri in this locality U.167 was so badly damaged by a bombing attack that she had to be scuttled. Th crew landed in Grand Canary, and were later taken back to France in U.159 and U.455. Ii addition to the U-boat activities already described, three U-boat minelaying operations were carriec out against the Mediterranean-bound shipping. In the first of these U.118 laid sixty moorec mines in short lines in the Strait of Gibraltar on the bank north of Cape Spartel on 2nd February 1943. These mines achieved some results according to our agent in Tarifa, but the; also damaged a Spanish, ship, and there was no repetition of the laying.

In April, 1943, the anchorages at Casablanca and Fedala were mined by U.455, using twelve mines from her torpedo tubes, and by U.117 using 60 moored mines in depths up to 100 metres. F.O. U-boats received no information on the results of these minefields, but believed that they had sunk at least one American ship.

OPERATIONS IN REMOTE AREAS

315. Enemy Derives Increasing Benefit from Radar

We had frequently adopted the procedure of suddenly re-occupying an area that had for some time been kept clear of U-boats. After a period of inactivity in such areas the enemy would reduce his A/S measures and the sudden re-appearance of our boats would provide us with initial advantages until he could organise counter-measures. The Freetown area provides an example of this policy of intermittent and sudden re-occupation by our U-boats.

It was this principle which prompted F.O. U-boats in March, 1943, to send a number of boats to the Caribbean. But this time the results were consistently adverse. Although we had made no attacks for over six months in the Gulf of Mexico, the Florida Strait, the Yucatan Channel or south of Cuba, our boats saw no relaxation in the enemy's A/S organisation. On the contrary, the period had been used to strengthen the radar organisation, for the better protection of shipping. Although air patrols in the Caribbean were weak, the surface escorts on the convoy routes and between the islands effectively hampered the movements of our boats. On the other hand, a chance contact with convoys, as on 10th and 13th March and 5th April, offered better prospects than in the North Atlantic, where the escorts were most powerful.

Even east of the Lesser Antilles prospects had deteriorated since the beginning of 1943. On 8th March U.510 found a convoy (BT 6) 70 miles off the coast of French Guiana opposite Cayenne, which was bound for Trinidad. In a pursuit lasting two days this U-boat, in the face of air and surface opposition, claimed to have sunk five ships and probably three more. Actually three ships totalling 18,000 tons were sunk, while five new Liberty ships, totalling 36,000 tons, were damaged. F.O. U-boats considered that this successful operation demonstrated the value of an efficient magnetic pistol.

U.518, which was patrolling off the Brazilian coast, sighted an eastbound convoy off Bahia on 28th February, 1943. Although the chances were favourable, this boat later reported that 8 out of 14 torpedoes fired at this convoy had failed to detonate, presumably because of faulty depth-keeping. After the boat had returned home, an enquiry revealed that the Commanding Officer had fired the torpedoes at excessive range, which was the cause of his failure. In contrast to this cautious conduct was that of the very able commander of U.160 - one of the *Seehund* boats operating off Capetown. On 3rd March he attacked the first convoy located south of Durban, sinking four ships and damaging two others. The remaining boats of this group were less successful and up to the middle of March sank no more than two or three ships each. As their fuel was running short, they were moved to the area between Capetown and Port Nollot. Although they remained here for a fortnight, searching as far north as Walvis Bay, they failed to locate the numerous small convoys that - according to our radio intelligence - existed in this area. In fact they torpedoed only two ships before leaving the area, which confirmed the generally unsatisfactory experiences of the *Seehund* group.

APRIL AND MAY, 1943
THE COLLAPSE OF THE
ATLANTIC CAMPAIGN

316.U-boat Losses up to March show no Increase

Officers of our surface ships were apt to look upon the U-boat arm as a privileged service as regards selection of personnel and award of honours. The pride of the U-boat personnel was indeed justified by the fact that they carried the main burden of the naval war, running far greater risks and suffering much heavier casualties than other branches of the Navy.

For the past nine months F.O. U-boats had shown increasing anxiety over developments in enemy A/S measures, and was aware of the general deterioration in the U-boat campaign, yet the sudden collapse of the operations in the Atlantic in May, 1943, took him by surprise. How did this occur ? Figures for U-boat losses issued by the U.S. and British Admiralties since the summer of 1942 had shown a steady increase, and from this it might be assumed that the U-boat menace would eventually be defeated. But in fact these figures bore no direct relation to the total number of U-boats involved in operations. The true criterion was the proportion of losses to the number of boats at sea, and the true picture is given by the following table which includes only boats operating in the Atlantic:

	1939	1940	1941	1942 Jan-June	1942 July-Dec	1943 Jan-March
Average actual monthly losses	3.0	1.9	2.7	2.7	8.1	10.3
Percentage of average number of boats at sea	17.5	13.4	11.4	3.9	8.9	9.2

The high percentage of losses in the early months of the war is attributable to the inexperience of crews and to technical deficiencies. In the first part of 1942 the percentage was very low, because of the " U-boat paradise " in the West Atlantic. Excluding these two phases, the average proportion of losses up to the end of 1942 had been

11-2 per cent, of boats at sea. In the second half of 1942 the losses, expressed as a percentage of the boats at sea, were actually less than the average for the first 3 years of war.

Since January, 1943, the proportion of boats participating in convoy actions had increased. This is illustrated by the following table which gives the ships sunk in Atlantic convoy, expressed as a percentage of the total shipping sunk in the Atlantic (334).

1942						1943				
July	Aug.	Sept.	Oct.	Nov.	Dec.	Jan.	Feb.	Mar.	April	May
25	35	39	44	37	58	67	84	75	5	46

From an average of 39 per cent, sunk in convoy during the second half of 1942 the figure had risen to 75 per cent, during the first quarter of 1943. In considering these figures, it must be remembered that convoy operations were more difficult and dangerous than individual attacks in remote operational areas. Moreover all boats leaving home ports on their first operation became involved in attacks on convoys, and their lack of experience was a serious matter as compared with easier conditions in the earlier stages of the war. In spite of this the percentage of U-boats lost in the first quarter of 1943 had hardly risen, and the above analysis alone could not presage the imminent collapse of the Battle of the Atlantic.

The real criterion for the effectiveness of the U-boat arm was the curve showing sinkings per boat per day. Disregarding the exceptionally favourable first half of 1942 the most effective month had been November, 1942, when we estimated that 329 tons per boat per day were sunk - the highest since July, 1941. By January, 1943, this figure had fallen to 129 tons, due to the effect of Operation " Torch " and the exceptional period of bad weather, but by March it had risen to 230 tons.[63]

At this time of course F.O. U-boats was still unaware of the true sinkings caused by the large convoy battles of March, 1943. The claims by the U-boats amounted to 780,000 tons sunk, but

63 British data, available since the war, reduce the figure for November, 1942, to 220 tons per day, for January, 1943, to 65 tons, and for March to 147 tons, as can be seen in PLan 60.

British post-war figures show only 500,000 tons. Thus our curve of effectiveness showed a positive tendency which concealed the true facts and gave F.O. U-boats no warning of the imminent collapse.

317. Hopes of Improvement through Increase in Number of U-Boats

According to German contemporary estimates the sinkings by U-boats in March, 1943, had reached the second highest peak of the war, and therefore the increasingly acute situation in the Atlantic was not fully appreciated. Moreover, the degree of exaggeration in claims by U-boats was not realised. In the operation against UGS 6 we had discovered that enemy destroyers could definitely locate a U-boat by radar when its conning tower was only just visible above the horizon. This was not considered very dangerous, for in the subsequent movements the boats had successfully used their Fu.M.B. to shadow the enemy radar transmissions and to keep out of sight while gaining position for eventual submerged attacks. These attacks on UGS 6 were reported as successful, for the boats claimed the sinking of six ships. But at the time F.O. U-boats was unaware that in reality only one ship had been sunk. Indeed this fact did not emerge until after the war, when the author compared the British and German figures.

The first that our boats saw of an enemy destroyer was the radar aerial at the masthead. As soon as this appeared on the horizon the U-boat had to turn away until the masthead just dipped below the horizon. As all convoys were protected by a remote screen, it became extremely difficult when mastheads were sighted to establish whether there was in fact a convoy behind them, and what course it was steering. The difficulty is shown by an episode on 25th/26th March. While the *Seeteufel* group was proceeding west, U.592 reported a large steamship and two destroyers 150 miles east of Cape Farewell.

"An earlier Special Intelligence report indicated that a damaged whale factory ship was in this area, and consequently three further boats were sent towards the target. U.592 pursued the ship but lost contact in rainstorms. On the 26th U.168 reported a large steamship that had been sighted earlier by U.592 and also one destroyer... Three hours later U.168 reported that the object was in fact an iceberg which had the appearance of a large ship and two destroyers."

The unreliability of sighting reports at such great distances forced us to employ more boats for confirmation of the sighting. This in turn involved heavy radio traffic, and we had to accept the undoubted risk of having these communications plotted by the enemy's D/F. We knew that in addition to the worldwide network of D/F stations for approximate cross-bearings of German naval transmissions, the escort vessels were fitted with HF/DF apparatus with which they obtained more accurate fixes. On the other hand frequent sending of shadowing reports by numerous boats would confuse the Commodore of the convoy when he tried to establish the position of individual U-boats.

In general the need to discover the convoy's course and to scatter the A/S defences required the employment of large numbers of boats. This also made the task of the convoy's air escort, usually comprising not more than two to three aircraft at any one time, more difficult. After two or three attacks from the air, an aircraft had usually expended its load of bombs, and its crew were unwilling to risk a gun duel with the U-boat. Experience in March and April was that even when the U-boats had only 2 cm. A/A guns, numerous air attacks were repelled, and aircraft were sometimes shot down. Much better results could be expected from May onwards, when boats would be equipped with 2 cm. quadruple mountings. Until then the U-boat crews had to be taught to remain on the surface to await and repel air attacks whenever the tactical situation required this, or when the proximity of an aircraft precluded diving.

318. Increased Losses in the Bay of Biscay
This procedure did not apply in the Biscay area, patrolled by units of Nos. 15 and 19 Groups of the R.A.F., which were highly trained in anti-submarine methods. They were treated with respect by our crews. The control of these air units was efficient, for the number of patrolling aircraft at any time bore a close relation to the number of

U-boats in the Bay. Moreover the attacks took place at times when the U-boats had to surface. If a U-boat in the Bay repelled an air attack using her A/A guns, a second or third aircraft would appear within a few minutes, against which the U-boat would be powerless. Therefore the boats remained submerged while in the Bay, but even so our losses increased. We suspected the enemy to be using radar frequencies inaudible to us, but we had no proof.[64]

On 9th and 10th March two U-boats had a curious experience in the vicinity of convoy SC 121. About 15 minutes after diving, and having been located - as they thought - by echo sounding buoys, they were attacked with bombs from the air. We did not know whether these attacks resulted from chance sighting of oil or air tracks, or whether there was some new method of echo location from aircraft. At this period the German scientists denied the possibility of an aircraft being able to fix the position of a submerged U-boat. They argued that it was difficult enough to locate a submerged U-boat with asdics, when hunter and hunted were both in the same medium. Nevertheless, the reports from these boats were perturbing, for they gave the first indication of a new enemy technique.

NORTH ATLANTIC CONVOY BATTLES

319. Greatest Number of U-Boats in the North Atlantic

Through damage, losses, and expenditure of torpedoes in the big convoy battles of March, 1943, many U-boats had dropped out, and it was important to fill the gaps without delay. Accordingly on 6th April F.O. U-boats ordered all the Type IXC boats originally destined for the south, to operate against North Atlantic convoys. Since much of the independently routed shipping formerly in the southern operational areas had now been incorporated into transatlantic convoys, the prospects in the south seemed correspondingly reduced, at least for

---

64 10cm. A.S.V. was in effective operational use for day air patrols in the Bay of Biscay by mid-February, 1943, but night patrols were not so equipped till a month later (*The R.A.F. in Maritime War*, Volume III, Chapter XII).

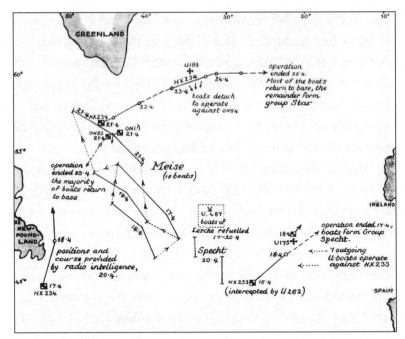

Plan 51. Groups Meise and various U-boats, 14th-25th April, 1943.
Operations against HX 233 and HX 234.

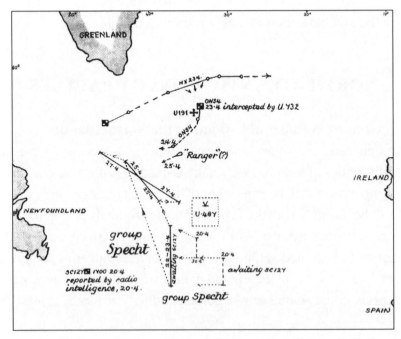

Plan 52. Group Specht and various U-boats, 22nd-27th April. 1943.
Operation against ONS 4.

218

the time being. The Atlantic U-boat bases were also ordered to hurry on the preparation of those boats which had returned since the end of March, for it was dangerous to let them lie in unprotected berths outside the U-boat bunkers.

These measures however took time, and meanwhile the number of operational boats in the North Atlantic temporarily fell. By the middle of April there was only one large group (*Meise*) northeast of Cape Race, lying in wait for the expected SC 126. At this time U.487 in the " Black Pit " began to refuel those boats of the *Lerche* group which after contact with HX 232 were still fit for action. Thus co-ordinated attacks with two or three groups, as in March, were not feasible. But in the latter part of April a stream of fresh U-boats flowed westward, either north round Britain, or from the Biscay ports, and if these should find an eastbound convoy, the situation would not be too bad. In the month of April 98 boats in all left for operations, of which 70 were involved in convoy operations. Whether the convoys chose the northern or the southern route, a proportion of these boats would be in a relatively favourable position.

320. Effective Escort for HX 233

Such an opportunity soon presented itself. On the night of 15th April U.262, while outward-bound on a special mission, sighted a convoy 400 miles north of the Azores, steering northeast (Plan 51). Having been attacked with depth-charges, she left the convoy and continued on her mission, but several other outward-bound boats were ahead of the target, and although rather close to the southern British air bases, they received the order to attack. The convoy was located after 24 hours ; four boats in succession attempted to attack, but each in turn was pursued by the escorts, and suffered continuous depth-charge attacks lasting up to 12 hours, during which U.175 was destroyed. U.628 succeeded in sinking one ship. The calm weather was against the U-boats, and we believed that the enemy was aware of the small number of U-boats involved since he used his escorts very persistently against them.

The mission of U.262 was to proceed to the Gulf of St. Lawrence to Prince Edward Island for the pre-arranged embarkation of a U-boat commander who was to escape from Canadian imprisonment. He had communicated his intention in a coded letter addressed to F.O. U-boats, but it is probable that this was intercepted by the Canadian authorities, for at the pre-arranged rendezvous U.262 found two patrol boats, which she managed to evade by lying on the bottom.

321. Disappointing Results against HX 234

A further convoy, possibly an SC, steering a similar course to HX 233, was sighted on 18th April, but was not attacked because of poor prospects. On that day we discovered through a decrypted message why these convoys were using such a southerly route. The message showed the enemy to be surprisingly well informed as to the number of *Meise* boats and their location (Plan 51). It seemed possible that further convoys would use this southern route, and hence a new group, Specht, was formed on 20th April, of boats that had refuelled after encountering HX 233. These were set up in two patrol lines 400 to 600 miles north of the Azores.

Meanwhile *Meise* remained northeast of Newfoundland until on the 20th our Radio Intelligence discovered that HX 234 had three days earlier been 150 miles south of Cape Race, whence it was to continue in a northerly direction. As this would lead it clear to the west of *Meise*, the group was moved 200 miles northwest at high speed, and on the 21st a convoy was sighted. About the same time one of the group sighted and attacked a convoy steering southwest, which was ONS 3. It was left to the boats on the spot to decide on which convoy to concentrate. Five of them became involved with ONS 3 and with a number of ships following 80 miles astern. That evening fog and snowstorms caused both convoys to be lost, and on the 23rd the search was discontinued. Three ships had been sunk. The remaining boats followed HX 234, U.306 carrying out most efficient shadowing and attacks on this her first operation, when she was commanded by von Trotha. On the 23rd eleven more boats made contact, but although they had seven hours of darkness that night, only two ships were sunk, and one torpedoed. This poor result was attributed to the rapidly changing visibility and to the inexperience of new commanders.

By the 24th the convoy's air protection was so strong that all boats lost bearing, and on the following morning operations were stopped.

322. Alleged Sinking of U.S.S. Ranger

U.732, which was closing HX 234 from the southeast, had on 23rd April sighted another southbound convoy (ONS 4), which was apparently attempting to evade the approaching pack of U-boats (Plan 52). Acting on U.732's sighting report, four further boats indicated that they were approaching the new target. F.O. U-boats now ordered the Specht group, then 600 miles further south, where it had waited in vain for SC 127, to proceed northwest at high speed, and on the 25th to form a patrol line at right angles to the line of advance of ONS 4. But this convoy was not found again. On the morning of this day U.404 sighted what she believed to be an aircraft carrier of the Ranger type, escorted by four destroyers. She claimed that her four torpedoes hit the carrier, but the circumstances were doubtful. This report was passed on to the German Supreme Command who released it to the public. F.O. U-boats did not uphold the claim and was irritated at the premature announcement.[65]

323. Minor Operations West of Finisterre

The small and fortuitous operations west and northwest of the Spanish coast against XK 2, OS 44 and SL 126 during the past weeks had produced good results considering the few boats employed. Consequently at the end of April the opportunity was taken to use a large number of outgoing boats for a controlled operation against an expected WS convoy. A patrol line (Drossel, was formed northwest of Cape Finisterre between the 14th and 19th meridians, but the air reconnaissance, provided by Fliegerfiihrer Atlantic, could find nothing in three days. It was not until 3rd May that an air patrol northeast of Drossel reported sighting eleven cargo ships and six escorts. Actually this was a southbound convoy consisting of 15

---

65 British records make no mention of such an attack.

coastal craft and two escorts. The Drossel group was immediately moved eastwards and located the convoy that afternoon. But it was not discovered until nightfall that these ships consisted of LCTs. In the existing state of the sea nothing was to be gained by firing torpedoes at these shallow-draught vessels, and the pursuit was abandoned. While in the vicinity of the convoy U.439 and U.659 came into collision, and both sank so quickly that there was no time to send off a short signal. Some survivors were picked up by an LCT. This was the second case of a collision between U-boats in the Atlantic.

The Drossel group was now moved 200 miles south in the hope of intercepting two northbound convoys which were expected on 5th May. On that day seven FW. 200 aircraft vainly searched the area south of the boats, which then turned north. On 6th May the aircraft located SL 128, but the beacon signals of the air shadower were not heard by the boats, and therefore F.O. U-boats ordered them to close the convoy, assuming that the position reported by the aircraft was correct. Later investigation, however, showed that the aircraft had been 30 miles in error in reporting the convoy's position, which the U-boats did not find until the morning of the 7th. During the day five boats made contact, but only one succeeded in sinking a ship of 4,000 tons. Within a few hours of spotting the U-boats, the convoy was provided with a continuous air escort so that on the following day the operation was abandoned and the boats were ordered to continue westward.

324. Serious Failure against Two Convoys

Strong reinforcements in the Atlantic now allowed the formation of two new groups, *Star* and *Amsel* (Plan 53). On 1st May no less than 60 boats in four groups were simultaneously involved in one operation. This was the highest number ever to participate in one convoy battle.

The most recently sighted ONS convoys (ONS 3 and ONS 4) had used a very northerly route. For this reason the *Star* group was sent to 30 degrees W. and as far north as 62 degrees N., but even this was not sufficient, for on 28th April ONS 5 passed its northern wing. The stormy weather and errors in dead-reckoning made it difficult to close this convoy, so that by the 29th only five boats had momentarily sighted it, and only one ship was sunk. On the evening of 1st May the pursuit was abandoned near Cape Farewell. To the south of the *Star* group, *Amsel* had begun a southwestward sweep on 26th April. The object was to prolong the attack on HX 235, in the event of Specht finding this convoy north of Newfoundland. On the night of the 27th the sweep was temporarily interrupted when U.377 reported hydrophone bearings of a convoy which could have been HX 235. On 29th April *Amsel* closed up with the left wing of Specht, and both groups were moved south. A partially decrypted message concerning SC 128, giving a position 200 miles east of Cape Race, induced F.O. U-boats to move both groups still further south. On the evening of 1st May, when U.628 reported sighting smoke,

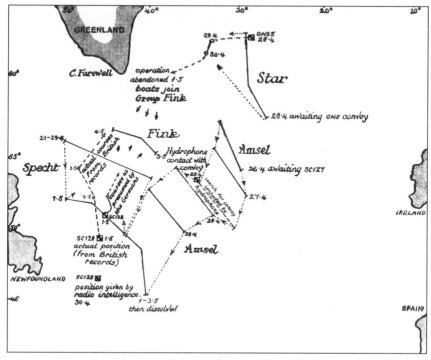

Plan 53. Groups Specht, Amsel, Fink and Star, 26th April-3rd May, 1943.
Operations against ONS 5 and SC 128

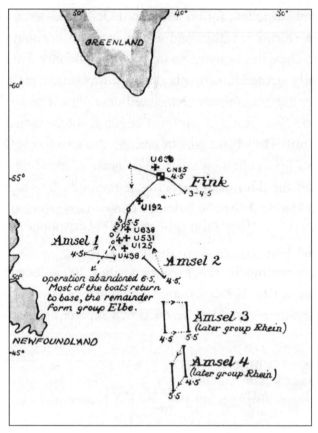

Plan 54. Groups Amsel and Fink, 3rd-6th May, 1943.
Operation against ONS 5

Specht was ordered to close the position indicated. The smoke was apparently moving northeastward and presumably came from SC 128 ; the thirteen *Star* boats at Cape Farewell were ordered to join in the pursuit. But on the first night contact was lost during a southerly gale, and when the situation had not improved by 3rd May a new patrol line, Fink, consisting of 29 boats, was formed out of *Specht* and *Star*. At the same time the *Amsel* group which had remained east of Newfoundland was formed into four sections forming an arc round Cape Race.

In spite of the boats in the Fink group being only eight miles apart, they had not located SC 128 by the afternoon of 4th May, and it was assumed that the convoy had taken bold avoiding action.

A well-executed feint, consisting of star shells fired by an escort group which had been moved out east from the convoy, deceived the U-boats. F.O. U-boats had just ordered a new disposition, when another convoy, steering southwest, was sighted in the centre of the Fink group. According to our reckoning this was ON 180, but it proved to be ONS 5 - much delayed by the storm.

The initial conditions for a convoy battle had never been more favourable. Thirty boats of the Fink group were in a patrol line, with gaps of only eight miles, and the convoy was sighted in the centre of this line. Moreover, 11 boats of *Amsel* 1 and 2 were ahead of the convoy. On the first night 11 boats located the convoy, and scored a number of hits, which apparently led to the dispersion of the convoy, for next day a number of separate groups of ships were seen, with their own escorts. British records show that 18 escort vessels in all were available for this convoy.

"During daylight hours of 5th May 15 boats made contact with the convoy, visibility being good and the sea calm. It seemed therefore that the ensuing night would bring particularly good results. But about two hours before darkness fog descended, which thickened rapidly, so that a great opportunity was lost. Nearly all the boats lost contact. At 0400 on the 6th the convoy was sighted for the last time under increasingly unfavourable conditions. In the fog the escorts succeeded in attacking 15 boats with depth-charges, and many found themselves suddenly and unexpectedly under fire from destroyers using radar. On the morning of the 6th the pursuit had to be abandoned."

325. Increasing Menace of Enemy Radar

Boats participating in this operation had sent a number of radio reports which showed F.O. U-boats how dangerous the situation had become during the night fog, and he anxiously awaited the short signals indicating the further state of readiness of our boats. Four of them reported heavy damage necessitating a return to base, while six were silent - they had been destroyed. In spite of the claim of 16 ships sunk, totalling 90,000 tons[66], and probable damage to several more, the heavy loss of U-boats compelled us to regard this operation as a reverse.

In the past F.O. U-boats had believed that the normal surface escorts of a convoy could be effectively scattered if sufficient U-boats were around. It had been constantly impressed on Commanding Officers that they should strive to deliver their attacks on the first or the second night, before air escorts appeared on the scene, for the latter would eventually force the boats to drop behind. Up to now it had seemed that the primary danger came from the enemy's air escorts and from bad weather. But in this last operation the surface escorts alone had sufficed to inflict grave losses on an exceptionally strong concentration of attackers. The U-boats were blind in the fog, whereas the escorts could attack them with radar-controlled gunfire. In short, unless U-boats had some means of countering the radar menace, their position would be desperate.

Two U-boats had been rammed in the fog, while others had been surprised at very short range, without any previous warning from their Fu.M.B. The enemy was evidently employing an impulse frequency which could not be recorded by our *Metox*. Perhaps they were also using instruments based on the principle of infra-red rays, or some other device. The diary of F.O. U-boats for 6th May mentions that " the scientists are working at high pressure to provide the U-boats with an apparatus which will register enemy radar, and also provide them with a protective covering and other means of misleading the enemy. On the solution particularly of the first problem depends the whole future of the U-boat war." So long as we had no suitable counter, we had to face the prospect of suspending operations against convoys whenever visibility was poor.

326. Enemy's Improved Under-water Location

The assumption that during operations against ONS 5 individual U-boats had been shot up in the fog, or rammed or destroyed by depth-charges while attempting to dive, proved correct, but a part of the

---

66 British records show 12 ships (55,000 tons) sunk.

losses occurred when there was no fog, presumably during a normal depth-charge pursuit. Reports on this and earlier operations showed that the more powerful depth-charges and the new methods of underwater location combined to make the attacks far more effective. For some time now the destroyers had been firing a complete broadside of depth-charges into a square, so that a "carpet" was laid without having to pass over the position of the U-boat. Our first knowledge of the "Hedgehog" came from decryption and from agents.[67] Information about "Mousetrap" did not reach us until much later.

It was of course impossible for the U-boat crews to distinguish between, or assess the importance of the various new methods, nor could they know whether the new effectiveness of depth-charges was due to some magnetic or induction firing mechanism. They were also baffled by what they believed to be a system of underwater location using some explosive body.[68] A further indication of the great accuracy of depth-charge attacks was the frequent damage that the U-boats now sustained to the upper deck containers for torpedoes, and this affected their diving capacity. In a Type IXC boat, for example, if four or six of these containers were suddenly flooded, the sinking of the boat could only be prevented by the immediate blowing of the diving tanks. On 30th April we had to order the removal of the upper deck containers on all operational boats. The resulting reduction of torpedo-carrying capacity was not serious, for the constant air danger had already discouraged boats from reloading at sea - a process that required a considerable time on the surface.

Experience during March and April, 1943, had shown that the more elaborate Type IX boat was more subject to damage from bombs and depth-charges than the Type VII. For every three Type VII boats on operations in April there was one Type IX, and yet

---

67 The first U-boat to be destroyed by Hedgehog was in November, 1942, in the Mediterranean.

68 The British Mark XXIV mine was introduced in March, 1943, and constituted a new method of attack on submerged U-boats. It may be that the German U-boats that survived attacks by this method were misled when they heard explosions on other U-boats in the vicinity. The Germans remained ignorant of the Mark XXIV mine throughout the war.

seven of the latter had been lost, of which five were during attacks on convoys. But only four Type VII had been lost, of which two were in attacks on convoys. We concluded that it was inadvisable to use any more Type IX boats in North Atlantic operations, for which we now possessed a sufficient number of Type VII boats. On 5th May all the Biscay flotillas were ordered to prepare their large boats for southern operations. New Type IXC boats leaving home bases were allowed to join in the convoy battles, but only for a limited period.

327. Renewed Successes off Freetown

On 16th April the large boats had been ordered to prepare for convoy operations in the North Atlantic (Section 319), and in the following four weeks most of them had sailed for this area, so that we could not augment the small number - about eight - operating on the fringes of the Central Atlantic.

At the beginning of April the greatest U-boat activity was centred southwest of Freetown. After the operations against RS 3 six boats had arrived in this area and were proceeding towards the Liberian coast. Our Naval Intelligence deduced from the frequent mention of Zone P in decrypted messages that this referred to an area off Liberia evidently containing much shipping. But our observations here did not confirm this deduction. When, on 19th April U-boats were allowed to operate in the central sector of route A between 10 degrees N. and 10 degrees S., F.O. U-boats took the opportunity of moving the boats to the southeast of St. Paul's Rock. But little traffic was found, so U.105 and U.126 were moved to Freetown, while U.154 joined U.128 for patrol off the Brazilian coast between Pernambuco and Bahia.

Once again the old battleground off Freetown, in which an average of four U-boats operated until the end of May, produced good results. The boats refuelled from U.460. Five independent ships were sunk southwest of the port, and U.515, commanded by Henke, scored a marked success on an incoming convoy. This convoy consisted of 14 laden ships with eight escorts, which included three destroyers. The U-boat log describes the attack as follows:

"30.4. At 2100 sighted the convoy 90 miles south of Freetown bearing 145 degrees, 15 miles, steering northwest. During a rainstorm I increased my distance, and established radar on *Metox*, strength 4, frequency 141 cm. As the convoy was well covered by the escorts ahead and abeam, I penetrated from astern.

"The night was dark with frequent lightning flashes. Between 2256 and 2301 I aimed six torpedoes, set to 5 metres, at five freighters and one tanker. All were hits. The starboard escorts fired star shell and illuminating rockets. One destroyer was coming towards me while two escorts lay to port. I dived to 170 metres, heard depth-charge explosions, and reloaded with three electric torpedoes.

"1.5. At 0130 surfaced and proceeded to the scene of my attack. Here a line of wreckage stretched from east to west and a large escort vessel was picking up survivors from rafts. My attempt to torpedo her failed... At 0513 I regained contact with the convoy, and entered it from astern. Seven minutes later I fired three torpedoes, set to 7 metres, at three freighters, which all began to sink. At 0549 in the light of star shells I saw two destroyers just ahead of me. I dived. Depth of water only 18 metres. Asdics and depth-charges. I moved along the bottom into deep water. The stratification of these coastal waters favoured me and I was not located. Noise of sinking ships to starboard and many remote depth-charge explosions."

The Commanding Officer claimed to have sunk eight ships out of this convoy, totalling 50,000 tons.[69] He was the officer who, off Gibraltar in November, 1942, had experienced failure with his torpedoes set at 2 metres. But in this very creditable attack off Freetown the Pi.2 magnetic pistol, with depth settings of 5 and 7 metres, achieved most satisfactory results.

328. Unsatisfactory Results off U.S. Coast

At the end of March U.161 and U.174 were sent to the west of the Azores, to rendezvous successively with the homeward-bound blockade-runners Regensburg, Karin, Pietro Orseolo and Irene and pass instructions to them. After each rendezvous the U-boats were to

---

69 According to British records this is correct.

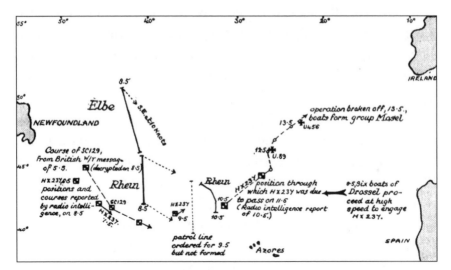

Plan 56. Groups Elbe, Isar, Ihn and Lech, 8th-14th May, 1943.
Operation against SC 129

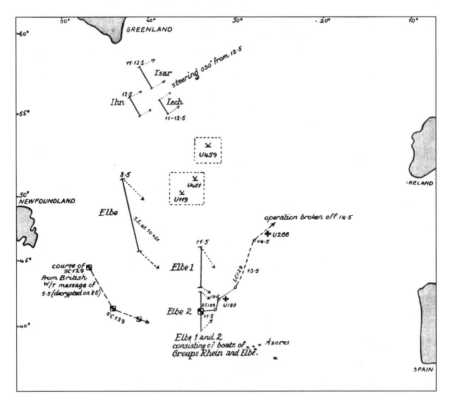

Plan 55. Groups Elbe, Rhein and Drassel, 7th-13th May, 1943.
Operation against HX 237.

move some distance west to report the expected time of arrival in the Bay of Biscay of each ship, in order to allow Group West to arrange escorts. This task having taken them far to the westward, the boats were ordered to the U.S. coast, there to be joined later by U.129. Early in April while still approaching the U.S. coast they noticed greatly increased activities by sea and air patrols. Enemy airborne radar in particular made it impossible for the boats near the coast to remain on the surface for any length of time, and only U.129 succeeded in torpedoing two ships southeast of Cape Hatteras. U.174 was sunk by air attack on 27th April while approaching a convoy south of Cape Sable, and U.176 suffered the same fate a fortnight later when passing the Florida Strait on her way to the Caribbean.

Six Type IXD boats were already on their way to the Cape area before we knew of the unsatisfactory experiences of Group *Seehund*, and as they carried large quantities of fuel - sufficient to enable them to reach Madagascar - it was decided to let them continue. On Hitler's instructions one of these boats, U.180, carried the Indian Chandra Bose and a friend, who on 25th April were transferred to a Japanese U-boat 300 miles south of Madagascar to continue the journey to India. The remaining U-boats proceeded on pre-arranged routes to survey the traffic situation 600 to 700 miles off the African coast. While on this task U.177 carried out the first trials with *Bachstelze*[70], which made thirty successful flights. But not a single ship was sighted. The South Atlantic was empty. This invention for extending the vision of U-boats came too late to be of value.

Some of the boats remained temporarily off Capetown, while the remainder patrolled between Madagascar and Lourenco Marques, and Port Elizabeth. By the end of May they had sunk eight ships of which three were in convoy.

329. Enemy Carriers Cause Failure against HX 237 and SC 129

After the attack on ONS 5 the surviving U-boats were aware that six others had been lost. But they had little time to consider

---

70 A kite, fitted with helicopter-type propeller blades, towed by the U-boat, which carried an observer.

the implications, for on 7th May - within 24 hours of the attack - they were ordered to form a new patrol line {*Elbe*) in longitude 42 degrees W., where two eastbound convoys were expected. The former Groups *Amsel* 3 and 4 prolonged the line to the southward and were now known as Group *Rhein*.

On 8th May we succeeded in decrypting a signal of the 7th giving the position and speed of the expected HX 237, and also a signal of the 5th giving the course of SC 129. These showed that the tracks of the two convoys ran far to the south of our dispositions, which occasioned the following comment by F.O. U-boats:

"The convoys have obviously taken steps to avoid the *Amsel* 4 position of 7th May, and also the dispositions ordered for the *Elbe* and *Rhein* groups on the same day. Once again we must question how it was possible for the enemy to learn of our dispositions... It is just possible that he knew these through his airborne radar, but we can hardly accept this. Moreover, it seems improbable that he has broken into our cypher system, unless, of course, one of our boats has been captured intact."

As soon as the decrypted signal was available, *Rhein* was ordered to head southeast at high speed and to assume a patrol line on 9th May. *Elbe*, which could no longer catch up with HX 237, also proceeded at high speed to the southeast to get ahead of SC 129, which was following astern. Drossel, having just finished the operation against SL 128, proceeded west at full speed. One of the *Rhein* boats sighted HX 237 on the 9th, but soon lost it in the deteriorating visibility. The boats searched independently, and on the following morning took up a close patrol on a quarter circle. At noon U.403 sighted an independent fast ship, and later an ocean-going tug proceeding east. By holding on to the latter, the U-boat made contact with the convoy in the afternoon. But as the convoy, steaming at 10 knots, was already 90 miles east of *Rhein*, this group was sent in pursuit of the slower SC 129, while U.403 and the Drossel boats were sent to attack HX 237. Again decryption aided us, by giving the position through which the latter convoy was due to pass on 11th

May. The boats closed this point and found the convoy at the time indicated. But even this valuable intelligence did not help, for the boats were held off by strong escorts and by carrier-borne aircraft which proved particularly dangerous. When on the morning of 13th May the operation was broken off, we had sunk three ships of 21,000 tons for the loss of three boats.[71] As soon as we realised that the HX convoy was out of range, *Rhein* and *Elbe* were ordered, on 10th May, to assume a new, extended patrol line - *Elbe* 1 and 2, and on the afternoon of the 11th while forming up, they passed SC 129. Only U.402 succeeded in sinking two ships, but she and U.223 were so heavily damaged by depth-charges that they returned to base. On 12th May the remaining boats again found the convoy in good visibility, and although it had no air cover, no less than 11 shadowers were driven off during daylight by the surface escorts. F.O. U-boats commented that this high proportion indicated improved enemy radar. Many of the boats received serious damage from depth-charge attacks, and U.186 was lost. The weather on 13th May was also favourable, but as meanwhile the carrier accompanying HX 237 had been sent to protect the SC convoy, we were forced to break off the operation.

330. Failure against SC 130

Acting on radio intelligence of the new southerly routes of HX 237 and SC 129, the U-boat Command now ordered fresh boats arriving in the Atlantic to form several groups southeast of Cape Farewell.

On 12th May, U.640, then southwest of Iceland, sighted a westward-bound convoy, presumed to be ONS 7 (Plan 57 overleaf), and other outgoing boats were ordered to shadow, as Group Iller. But on the following day U.640 lost contact and a new patrol in three sections (Iller, Donau 1 and 2) was set up east of the Greenland coast. As the convoy was not sighted by 15th May, the boats were sent west towards the Greenland coast, to await the passing of ONS 7 or HX 238. A decryption of 14th May had shown the latter to be

---

71 H.M.S. *Biter*'s aircraft were employed with great effect against U-boats attacking HX 237.

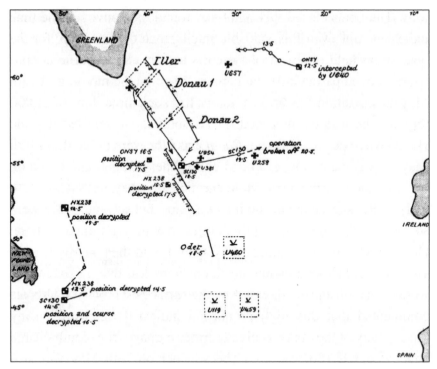

Plan 57. Groups Iller, Danau and Oder, 15th-20th May, 1943.
Operation against SC 130.

taking this northerly route. ONS 7 was not located, but a decryption of 17th May showed that at 2300 on the 16th it had already reached a position southwest of Donau 2, and must therefore have circumvented the patrol to the south. This was not surprising, for the decryption of the British " U-boat Situation '' showed that C.-in-C. Western Approaches had precise knowledge of the disposition of Iller and Donau. It was for the same reason that HX 238, instead of keeping to its northly course, had turned eastward when 360 miles north of Cape Race, and thereby passed to the southward of Donau 2. There was therefore no purpose in pursuit.

The position of SC 130 was also revealed by the British " U-boat Situation ". This convoy was 150 miles southeast of Cape Race, and its course of 067 degrees indicated a southerly route. But since the U-boats had not sighted HX 238, the U-boat Command concluded that SC 130 was following in its wake and the four groups were

234

therefore sent south in the hope of intercepting on this intermediate route, while newly arrived boats, forming Oder, were stationed as a precautionary measure along the 067 degrees track. The move was justified, for SC 130 was located on 18th May slightly to the north of the track of HX 237, and Iller and Donau were sent to attack. But from the second day the convoy had continuous air cover, and repeated surprise air attacks through low cloud made it impossible to shadow or close in to the attack. The most surprising feature of the enemy's success was that, according to our radio intelligence, there were never more than one or two aircraft in the air at the same time.[72] On 20th May we were forced to break off the operation with no result, having lost three boats, including U.954, in which Admiral Dönitz's second son was serving as watchkeeping officer. It is presumed that there was an error in our decryption of the ONS 7 position of 16th May, for British records show that this convoy had in fact made a detour to the north. It had passed the Iller patrol 60 miles southeast of Cape Farewell on the night of 17th-18th May. U.657 sighted the convoy, and scored one hit before being destroyed.

331. Further Failure against HX 239

Since the middle of April the convoy battles had produced very poor results, whereas our losses had been high. Nevertheless the U-boat Command decided to continue the operations, since the cause of failure had not been clearly established, and we still hoped that the timely and accurate reports from Radio Intelligence would enable us to attack a convoy successfully on the first night. It was the irony of fate that in this phase, when the boats were barely able to sustain the battle, our Radio Intelligence was giving us the location of most of the convoys heading for Britain.

On 19th May the U-boat Command already had information about HX 239. This convoy was 200 miles southeast of Cape Race on the 18th, from which position it was to steer an easterly and later a northerly course . We had sufficient time to reinforce the Oder group

---

72 SC 130, which arrived in the United Kingdom on 25th May, 1943, was the last convoy to be seriously threatened.

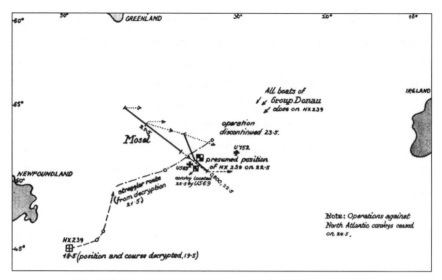

Plan 58. Groups Mosel and Donau, 21st-23rd May, 1943.
Operation against HX 239.

with a number of boats that had just refuelled, and together these were formed into Mosel, 400 miles south of Cape Farewell. On 21st May we discovered the route to be taken by the stragglers, which was far to the south of the Mosel line. As stragglers usually follow in the wake of the convoy, it was assumed that the latter would take the same route. So the southern half of Mosel was sent to intercept the stragglers, while the remaining boats were to steer east at high speed to join the Donau boats in an attack on the convoy itself.

At noon on the 22nd U.305, in the middle of the patrol line, sighted a destroyer, but immediately after reporting this she was forced by aircraft to dive. While submerged she heard a wide range of ship noises, and when later she reported this to the U-boat Command, a number of boats was sent east and northeast to search. But except for sighting one or two destroyers' masts, they established nothing, since they were repeatedly forced by carrier-borne aircraft to submerge. The numerous short signals from the boats, reporting attacks from the air, indicated how dangerous it was to linger in an area patrolled by carrier-borne aircraft, and under these circumstances F.O. U-boats was not prepared to organise further concentrated search.

On the evening of the 22nd U.569 reported sighting a convoy steering southwest, presumably ON 184. At least half of the Mosel group could have closed this convoy by the following day, but we still hoped that they would succeed in finding HX 239. This did not occur and although under cover of darkness the boats got well ahead, the cat and mouse situation between aircraft and U-boats started again at daylight. When several boats reported serious damage, and U.752 was lost through air attack, F.O. U-boats decided on the 23rd to discontinue the action and to send the boats westward.

332. Waning Prospects of Offensive Action

There had been several crises in the course of the U-boat campaign, such as the failure at the time of the Norwegian operations, and the sudden high losses in March and December, 1941. Investigation had shown that these setbacks were usually due to a combination of unfavourable circumstances rather than to any marked improvement in enemy A/S measures. But now, in May, 1943, things were very different, for our failure in a whole series of convoy battles had shown beyond doubt that the offensive power of the U-boat was incapable of dealing with the defence.

This situation was due firstly to outstanding developments in enemy radar, and secondly to effective co-operation between surface escorts, support groups, and carrier-borne aircraft. Moreover, we had numerous indications that the Allies' huge construction programme for escort carriers, escort vessels, and aircraft had not yet reached its peak. On the other hand, there was no increase in the destructive power of the U-boat. Yet the crux of the U-boat campaign was the maintenance of the offensive against the Allied life-line in the North Atlantic. But now the staggering realisation came upon us that we could no longer pursue this offensive in its existing form. Indeed, the latest experiences had shown that the striking power of the U-boat threatened to collapse in every theatre of war.

333. Temporary Evacuation of the North Atlantic

Since the beginning of May our losses in the North Atlantic had risen steeply. By the 22nd we had already lost 31 boats, while the fate of two others was in doubt after the attack on HX 239. An analysis of these losses is contained in the War Diary of F.O. U-boats for 24th May:

"Of the 31 boats lost up to 22nd May, 19, or about 60 per cent., were sunk either while proceeding to or from the operational area or while waiting in that area. Evidently only 12 boats, or about 40 per cent., were destroyed while engaging convoys, and of these, four or five were lost under the particularly unfavourable conditions of visibility which led to the abandonment of the attack on ONS 5.

"An analysis of the proportion of boats sunk respectively through enemy air and surface attacks gives the following:

17, or approx. 55 per cent., almost certainly sunk through air attacks,

6, or approx. 19-5 per cent., possibly sunk through air attacks,

8, or approx. 25-5 per cent., almost certainly sunk through surface attacks."

British post-war records show that F.O. U-boats was not far out in his contemporary analysis of the causes, particularly with regard to losses through enemy aircraft.[73] But, like the Commanding Officers of the U-boats, who suffered the full weight of the enemy's air effort, he perhaps overrated this factor in relation to the general crisis. This is shown by the secret order he issued to Commanding Officers on 24th May:

"In the last few months our serious U-boat losses can be mainly ascribed to the superiority of enemy radar equipment, which enables him to surprise our boats from the air while they are waiting in

---

73 Though not far out in his assessment of losses through air attacks, F.O. U-boats was wide of the mark as regards U-boats sunk in convoy battles. Research into British and German records has established that the 31 U-boats which formed the basis of F.O. U-boats' analysis were destroyed between 25th April and 20th May, 1943, and that 12 of these were sunk while proceeding to or from their respective operational areas in the Atlantic, or while waiting in their operational areas, and 16 while engaging convoys. Of these 31 losses air attacks accounted for 14 (7 in the Bay of Biscay and northern transit area, and 7 through attacks by convoy escorts), combined air/surface attacks by convoy escorts for 5, and attacks by convoy surface escorts for 9. Two U-boats were lost in collision during convoy battle, and one cause unknown.

the operational area or homeward or outward bound. This factor is responsible for more than half our losses, whereas in the actual convoy battles the losses are relatively small..."[74]

We estimated that in the first half of 1942 the loss of each U-boat was compensated by the sinking of 272,000 tons of Allied shipping. In the second half of 1942 the corresponding figure was 78,200 tons, and in the first quarter of 1943 it was 51,300 tons. But in May, 1943, we achieved the sinking of only one ship of 8,500 tons[75] for the loss of each U-boat.[76]

These disastrous figures and the hopelessness of the latest convoy battles obliged F.O. U-boats to take drastic measures until such time as his boats could be equipped with better offensive and defensive weapons. The first need was to prevent losses through air attack, not only while proceeding to or from the operational zone, but also in the waiting and attack areas.

On 22nd May the order went out that in bad visibility, all boats in the Atlantic operational area as well as the transit areas were invariably to remain submerged. In clear weather, when on the surface, they were to proceed at high speed with A.A. guns constantly manned, but at instant readiness to dive. At night, in order to hear approaching aircraft, they were to run as silently as possible on one electric motor, with diesels ready for use in case of an attack.

A further ominous decision had to be made. Hitherto convoy operations had taken place in the North Atlantic, where - with the exception of the transit areas - enemy air patrols were heaviest, and our boats were exposed to extreme danger through the excellent co-ordination between aircraft and support groups. But future operations

---

74 It is interesting that F.O. U-boats' analysis of U-boat losses gave:

    (a) 35 percent, lost in transit areas;

    (b) 26 per cent, lost in operational areas while awaiting convoys;

    (c) 38 per cent, in actual attacks on convoys.

But his secret order to commanding officers groped together the losses under (a) and (b), thus concealing from them that the danger was greatest during actual attacks.

75 The true figures, calculated from British records, were as follows: first half of 1942, 220,000 tons; second half of 1942, 55,600 tons; first quarter of 1943, 31,700 tons; May, 1943, 5,600 tons.

76 In May, 1943, the Germans lost 38 U-boats and sank 42 ships.

would have to be confined to areas less threatened from the air. For the boats already at sea there was only one possibility, namely, to send them to the southwest of the Azores, where they could operate against the US.-Gibraltar convoys. On 24th May those having adequate fuel were moved to that area. The boats with insufficient fuel remained on the North Atlantic convoy routes between 25 and 45 degrees West, with the thankless task of deceiving the enemy (by their mere presence) as to the date of our abandonment of North Atlantic convoy operations.

This was the first occasion in the war when the practice of suddenly evacuating an area because of the strength of the defences had to be applied to the vital battleground in the North Atlantic. As F.O. U-boats stated in his War Diary:

"This decision denotes a temporary abandonment of the fundamental principles which have so far governed the U-boat campaign. The change of policy is dictated by the need to avoid unnecessary losses in a period when our weapons are shown to be at a disadvantage. It must be realised, however, that as soon as our boats have been equipped with new weapons, the battle in the North Atlantic - the decisive area - will be resumed."

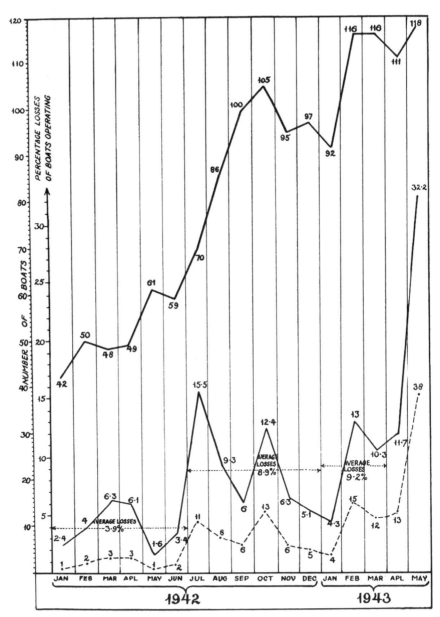

Plan 59. Analysis of U-boat numbers in the Atlantic (including the U.S. coast and West Indian zone), January 1942 to May 1943. Showing average monthly numbers of U-boats operating (top curve), actual monthly losses (dotted curve), and percentage losses of U-boats operating (middle curve)

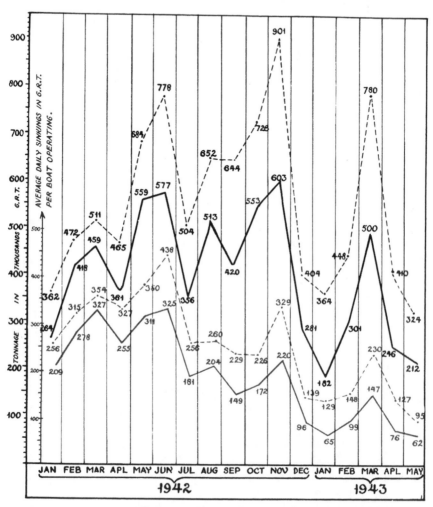

Plan 60. Sinkings in the Atlantic (including the U.S. coast and West Indian zone), January 1942 to May 1943. Showing German estimate (dotted curve), and the true figures, based on British and German records (solid curves).

AUTHOR'S NOTES AND LIST OF SOURCES

SECTION		NUMBER OF REFERENCE IN TEXT
164	German Naval Staff study *The State of the Battle in the Atlantic, July* 1941, PG 32615, page 10	(245)
164	German Naval Staff study *The State of the Battle in the Atlantic, July* 1941, PG 32615, page 9, and *Survey of the Situation on 20th October*, 1941, by the German Naval Staff, PG 32619, page 8	(246)
164	*Survey of the Situation* by the German Naval Staff, PG 32619, page 34	(247)
165	German Naval Staff study, PG 32615, page 39	(248)
165	Obtained from diagrams 8 to 14 at back of C.B. 4523(1) *The U-boat War in the Atlantic*, volume I, 1939–1941	(249)
165	Obtained from graph showing U-boats commissioned and lost from the outbreak of war to December, 1941, and diagrams 9 and 10 of C.B. 4523(1) *The U-boat War in the Atlantic*, volume I, 1939–1941	(250)
169	The subject was merely brought up in conversation	(251)
170	Log of U.203, PG 30191	(252)
173	War Diary of F.O. U-boats for 4th February, 1942	(253)
174	Files of *Skl. Iu Chefsache Allgem.*, PG 33416, pages 33–38	(254)
175	Files of *Skl. Iu Chefsache Allgem.*, PG 33416, page 17	(255)
176	Based on War Diary of F.O. U-boats for January to May, 1942, and Naval Staff War Diary, Part C IV, 1942, PG 32174, pages 9, 14, 15, 60–67, 70, and 79–95	(256)
177	Naval Staff War Diary, Part A, for 24th January and 2nd February, 1942. (*See also* British Admiralty edition of *The Führer Conferences on Naval Affairs*, volume 1942, page 8)	(257)
177	Naval Staff War Diary, Part C IV, 1942, PG 32174, page 14	(258)
178	War Diary of F.O. U-boats for 15th February, 1942	(259)
178	Naval Staff comments on War Diary of F.O. U-boats for February, 1942 (contained in War Diary of F.O. U-boats for 28th February, 1942)	(260)
179	Naval Staff War Diary, Part C IV, 1942, PG 32174, page 70	(261)
180	Naval Staff War Diary, Part C IV, 1942, PG 32174, pages 93 and 94	(262)
184	War Diary of F.O. U-boats for 15th and 19th April, 1942	(263)
188	War Diary of F.O. U-boats for 30th April, 1942	(264)
188	War Diary of F.O. U-boats for 9th May, 1942	(265)
188	War Diary of F.O. U-boats for 16th May, 1942	(266)
189	War Diary of F.O. U-boats for 1st May, 1942	(267)
191	This section is based on F.O. U-boats' notes for a conference with the *Führer* on 14th May, 1942 (contained in War Diary of F.O. U-boats for July, 1942)	(268)
191	*See* (268)	(269)
192	Naval Staff War Diary, Part C IV, 1942, PG 32174, page 133	(270)
192	War Diary of F.O. U-boats for 3rd June, 1942	(271)
192	Naval Staff War Diary, Part C IV, 1942, PG 32174, pages 148 and 149	(272)
193	From a memorandum to Section Iu of the German Naval Staff by Admiral Friedeburg, who was responsible for U-boat personnel and training. (Contained in files of 1 *Skl. U Allgem.*)	(273)
193	Based on statistics produced by the U-boat Command (contained in War Diary of F.O. U-boats for July, 1942)	(274)
194	This section is based on F.O. U-boats' notes for a conference with the *Führer* on 14th May, 1942, Naval Staff War Diary, Part C IV, 1942, and the British Admiralty publication B.R. 1337 *British and Foreign Merchant Vessels lost or damaged by Enemy Action during Second World War*	(275)
195	From F.O. U-boats' notes for a conference with the *Führer* on 14th May, 1942	(276)
195	Files of *Skl. Iu Allgem.*, PG 33349, pages 86 and 87	(277)

DATES ON WHICH THE U-BOATS SAILED AND RETURNED TO BASE, AND THE BASES USED

(December, 1941 to May, 1943)

(H = Base in Germany ; F = Base in Western France ; N = Base in Norway)

U-BOAT	SAILED		RETURNED		U-BOAT	SAILED		RETURNED	
U.43	H	30.12.41	F	22. 1.42	U.92	F	12. 8.42	F	25. 9.42
	F	4. 7.42	F	15. 8.42		F	24.10.42	F	28.12.42
	F	23. 9.42	F	9.12.42		F	12. 4.43	F	26. 6.43
	F	9. 1.43	F	31. 3.43	U.93	F	23.12.41	sunk	15. 1.42
U.66	F	25.12.41	F	10. 2.42					
	F	21. 3.42	F	27. 5.42	U.94	H	12. 1.42	H	30. 1.42
	F	26. 6.42	F	29. 9.42		H	12. 2.42	F	2. 4.42
	F	6. 1.43	F	24. 3.43		F	4. 5.42	F	23. 6.42
	F	29. 4.43	F	1. 9.43		F	2. 8.42	sunk	28. 8.42
U.67	F	19. 1.42	F	30. 3.42	U.96	H	31. 1.42	F	23. 3.42
	F	20. 5.42	F	8. 8.42		F	23. 4.42	F	1. 7.42
	F	16. 9.42	F	21.12.42		F	24. 8.42	F	5.10.42
	F	3. 3.43	F	13. 4.43		F	26.12.42	F	5. 2.43
U.68	F	11. 2.42	F	13. 4.42	U.98	F	18. 1.42	F	27. 2.42
	F	14. 5.42	F	9. 7.42		F	31. 3.42	F	6. 6.42
	F	20. 8.42	F	6.12.42		F	22.10.42	sunk	19.11.42
	F	3. 2.43	F	8. 5.43	U.103	F	3. 1.42	F	1. 3.42
U.69	F	18. 1.42	F	26. 1.42		F	15. 4.42	F	22. 6.42
	F	31. 1.42	F	17. 3.42		F	21.10.42	F	29.12.42
	F	12. 4.42	F	25. 6.42		F	7. 2.43	F	26. 3.43
	F	16. 8.42	F	5.11.42		F	24. 4.43	F	26. 5.43
	F	2. 1.43	sunk	17. 2.43	U.105	F	26. 1.42	F	8. 2.42
U.71	F	18.12.41	F	21. 1.42		F	25. 2.42	F	15. 4.42
	F	23. 2.42	F	20. 4.42		F	23.11.42	F	14. 2.43
	F	11. 6.42	F	20. 6.42		F	16. 3.43	sunk	2. 6.43
	F	4. 7.42	F	15. 8.42	U.106	F	3. 1.42	F	22. 2.42
	F	5.10.42	F	17.11.42		F	15. 4.42	F	29. 6.42
	F	23.12.42	F	12. 2.43		F	23. 9.42	F	26.12.42
	F	27. 3.43	F	30. 4.43		F	17. 2.43	F	4. 4.43
U.73	F	4. 1.42	Mediterranean		U.107	F	7. 1.42	F	7. 3.42
U.82	F	11. 1.42	sunk	6. 2.42		F	21. 4.42	F	11. 7.42
U.84	F	21.12.41	F	7. 2.42		F	15. 8.42	F	18.11.42
	F	17. 3.42	F	14. 5.42		F	30. 1.43	F	25. 3.43
	F	10. 6.42	F	13. 8.42		F	24. 4.43	F	26. 5.43
	F	29. 9.42	F	7.12.42	U.108	F	12. 1.42	F	4. 3.42
	F	7. 2.43	F	4. 5.43		F	30. 3.42	F	1. 6.42
U.85	F	10. 1.42	F	23. 2.42		F	13. 7.42	F	10. 9.42
	F	21. 3.42	sunk	14. 4.42		F	25.10.42	F	26.11.42
U.86	F	27.12.41	F	15. 2.42		F	20. 1.43	F	24. 2.43
	F	25. 3.42	F	26. 5.42		F	1. 4.43	F	15. 5.43
	F	2. 7.42	F	18. 9.42	U.109	F	27.12.41	F	23. 2.42
	F	30.10.42	F	7. 1.43		F	25. 3.42	F	3. 6.42
	F	24. 2.43	F	16. 4.43		F	18. 7.42	F	6.10.42
U.87	H	27.12.41	F	29. 1.42		F	28.11.42	F	23. 1.43
	F	22. 2.42	F	27. 3.42		F	3. 3.43	F	1. 4.43
	F	19. 5.42	F	8. 7.42		F	28. 4.43	sunk	7. 5.43
	F	31. 8.42	F	20.11.42	U.116	N	25. 4.42	F	5. 5.42
	F	9. 1.43	sunk	4. 3.43		F	16. 5.42	F	9. 6.42
U.89	H	14. 5.42	F	27. 5.42		F	27. 6.42	F	23. 8.42
	F	6. 6.42	F	21. 8.42		F	22. 9.42	sunk	19.10.42
	F	4.10.42	F	19.11.42	U.117	H	12.10.42	F	22.11.42
	F	24. 1.43	F	28. 3.43		F	25.12.42	F	17. 2.43
	F	25. 4.43	sunk	12. 5.43		F	31. 3.43	F	14. 5.43
U.90	H	30. 6.42	sunk	24. 7.42	U.118	H	19. 9.42	F	16.10.42
U.91	H	15. 8.42	F	6.10.42		F	12.11.42	F	13.12.42
	F	1.11.42	F	26.12.42		F	25. 1.43	F	26. 2.43
.	F	11. 2.43	F	29. 3.43		F	25. 5.43	sunk	12. 6.43
	F	29. 4.43	F	7. 6.43	U.119	F	6. 2.43	F	1. 4.43
						F	25. 4.43	sunk	24. 6.43

|--------|--------|----------|--------|--------|----------|
U.123	H 23.12.41	F 9. 2.42	U.157	H 30. 4.42	F 10. 5.42
	F 2. 3.42	F 2. 5.42		F 18. 5.42	sunk 13. 6.42
	F 16. 5.42	F 29. 5.42	U.158	H 2. 2.42	F 31. 3.42
	F 5.12.42	F 6. 2.43		F 4. 5.42	sunk 30. 6.42
	F 13. 3.43	F 8. 6.43	U.159	H 22. 4.42	F 3. 5.42
U.124	H 21. 2.42	F 10. 4.42		F 14. 5.42	F 13. 7.42
	F 4. 5.42	F 26. 6.42		F 24. 8.42	F 5. 1.43
	F 25.11.42	F 13. 2.43		F 4. 3.43	F 25. 4.43
	F 27. 3.43	sunk 2. 4.43	U.160	H 24. 2.42	F 28. 4.42
U.125	F 18.12.41	F 23. 2.42		F 20. 6.42	F 24. 8.42
	F 4. 4.42	F 13. 6.42		F 23. 9.42	F 9.12.42
	F 27. 7.42	F 6.11.42		F 6. 1.43	F 10. 5.43
	F 9.12.42	F 19. 2.43	U.161	H 3. 1.42	F 15. 1.42
	F 13. 4.43	sunk 6. 5.43		F 24. 1.42	F 2. 4.42
U.126	F 2. 2.42	F 29. 3.42		F 28. 4.42	F 7. 8.42
	F 25. 4.42	F 25. 7.42		F 19. 9.42	F 9. 1.43
	F 19. 9.42	F 7. 1.43		F 13. 3.43	F 7. 9.43
	F 20. 3.43	sunk 3. 7.43	U.162	H 7. 2.42	F 18. 3.42
U.128	F 8. 1.42	F 23. 3.42		F 7. 4.42	F 10. 6.42
	F 25. 4.42	F 22. 7.42		F 7. 7.42	sunk 3. 9.42
	F 14. 9.42	F 15. 1.43	U.163	H 21. 7.42	F 16. 9.42
	F 6. 4.43	sunk 17. 5.43		F 17.10.42	F 6. 1.43
U.129	F 26. 1.42	F 5. 4.42		F 10. 3.43	sunk ? 3.43
	F 20. 5.42	F 21. 8.42	U.164	H 18. 7.42	F 7.10.42
	F 28. 9.42	F 6. 1.43		F 29.11.42	sunk 6. 1.43
	F 11. 3.43	F 29. 5.43	U.165	H 7. 8.42	sunk 27. 9.42
U.130	F 27.12.41	F 25. 2.42	U.166	H 30. 5.42	F 10. 6.42
	F 24. 3.42	F 6. 6.42		F 17. 6.42	sunk 1. 8.42
	F 4. 7.42	F 12. 9.42	U.167	H 21.12.42	F 16. 1.43
	F 29.10.42	F 30.12.42		F 27. 2.43	sunk 5. 4.43
	F 28. 2.43	sunk 12. 3.43	U.168	H 9. 3.43	F 18. 5.43
U.132	N 15. 1.42	F 8. 2.42	U.169	H 18. 3.43	sunk 27. 3.43
	F 10. 6.42	F 16. 8.42	U.171	H 17. 6.42	sunk 9.10.42
	F 6.10.42	sunk 5.11.42	U.172	H 22. 4.42	F 3. 5.42
U.134	H 18. 5.42	F 1. 6.42		F 11. 5.42	F 21. 7.42
	F 11. 6.42	F 1. 9.42		F 19. 8.42	F 27.12.42
	F 15.10.42	F 19. 1.43		F 21. 2.43	F 17. 4.43
	F 6. 3.43	F 2. 5.43	U.173	H 15. 6.42	F 20. 9.42
U.135	H 24.12.41	F 31. 1.42		F 1.11.42	sunk 16.11.42
	F 22. 2.42	F 3. 4.42	U.174	H 30. 7.42	F 6. 9.42
	F 26. 4.42	F 5. 7.42		F 8.10.42	F 9. 1.43
	F 8. 8.42	F 3.10.42		F 18. 3.43	sunk 27. 4.43
	F 21.11.42	F 25.12.42	U.175	H 15. 8.42	F 27.10.42
	F 24. 1.43	F 10. 3.43		F 1.12.42	F 24. 2.43
U.136	H 22. 1.42	F 1. 3.42		F 10. 4.43	sunk 17. 4.43
	F 24. 3.42	F 20. 5.42	U.176	H 21. 7.42	F 2.10.42
	F 30. 6.42	sunk 11. 7.42		F 9.11.42	F 18. 2.43
U.153	H 18. 5.42	F 30. 5.42		F 6. 4.43	sunk 15. 5.43
	F 6. 6.42	sunk 6. 7.42	U.177	H 17. 9.42	F 22. 1.43
U.154	H 7. 2.42	F 1. 3.42		F 1. 4.43	F 1.10.43
	F 11. 3.42	F 9. 5.42	U.178	H 8. 9.42	F 9. 1.43
	F 4. 6.42	F 23. 8.42		F 28. 3.43	Penang 29. 8.43
	F 12.10.42	F 7. 1.43	U.179	H 15. 8.42	sunk 8.10.42
	F 20. 3.43	F 6. 7.43	U.180	H 9. 2.43	F 2. 7.43
U.155	H 7. 2.42	F 27. 3.42			
	F 20. 4.42	F 14. 6.42			
	F 9. 7.42	F 15. 9.42			
	F 7.11.42	F 30.12.42			
	F 8. 2.43	F 30. 4.43			
U.156	H 24.12.41	F 10. 1.42			
	F 19. 1.42	F 17. 3.42			
	F 22. 4.42	F 7. 7.42			
	F 20. 8.42	F 16.11.42			
	F 16. 1.43	sunk 8. 3.43			

U-BOAT	SAILED		RETURNED	
U.181	H	12. 9.42	F	18. 1.43
	F	23. 3.43	F	14.10.43
U.182	N	9.12.42	sunk	16. 5.43
U.183	H	19. 9.42	F	23.12.42
	F	30. 1.43	F	13. 5.43
U.184	N	9.11.42	sunk	20.11.42
U.185	H	27.10.42	F	1. 1.43
	F	8. 2.43	F	3. 5.43
U.186	H	31.12.42	F	5. 3.43
	F	17. 4.43	sunk	12. 5.43
U.187	H	12. 1.43	sunk	4. 2.43
U.188	H	4. 3.43	F	3. 5.43
U.189	H	3. 4.43	sunk	23. 4.43
U.190	H	20. 2.43	F	30. 3.43
	F	1. 5.43	F	19. 8.43
U.191	H	11. 3.43	sunk	23. 4.43
U.192	H	13. 4.43	sunk	5. 5.43
U.195	H	20. 3.43	F	23. 7.43
U.196	H	13. 3.43	Japan	
U.197	H	3. 4.43	sunk	20. 8.43
U.198	H	9. 3.43	F	25. 9.43
U.201	F	24. 3.42	F	11. 5.42
	F	27. 6.42	F	8. 8.42
	F	6. 9.42	F	26.10.42
	F	3. 1.43	sunk	17. 2.43
U.202	F	1. 3.42	F	26. 4.42
	F	27. 5.42	F	25. 7.42
	F	6. 9.42	F	25.10.42
	F	12. 1.43	F	26. 3.43
	F	29. 4.43	sunk	1. 6.43
U.203	F	26.12.41	F	29. 1.42
	F	12. 3.42	F	30. 4.42
	F	3. 6.42	F	29. 7.42
	F	15.10.42	F	6.11.42
	F	6.12.42	F	7. 1.43
	F	3. 4.43	sunk	25. 4.43
U.209	H	6. 4.43	sunk	19. 5.43
U.210	H	18. 7.42	sunk	6. 8.42
U.211	N	26. 8.42	F	6.10.42
	F	16.11.42	F	29.12.42
	F	13. 2.43	F	25. 2.43
	F	13. 5.43	F	16. 7.43
U.213	H	24. 1.42	F	19. 3.42
	F	23. 4.42	F	21. 6.42
	F	19. 7.42	sunk	31. 7.42
U.214	H	18. 5.42	F	2. 6.42
	F	13. 6.42	F	17. 6.42
	F	9. 8.42	F	9.10.42
	F	30.11.42	F	24. 2.43
U.215	H	9. 6.42	sunk	3. 7.42
U.216	H	29. 8.42	sunk	20.10.42

U-BOAT	SAILED		RETURNED	
U.217	H	14. 7.42	F	16.10.42
	F	24.11.42	F	23. 2.43
	F	19. 4.43	sunk	5. 6.43
U.218	H	25. 8.42	F	29. 9.42
	F	7. 1.43	F	10. 3.43
	F	20. 4.43	F	2. 6.43
U.221	H	1. 9.42	F	22.10.42
	F	23.11.42	F	23.12.42
	F	27. 2.43	F	28. 3.43
	F	3. 5.43	F	21. 7.43
U.223	H	12. 1.43	F	6. 3.43
	F	15. 4.43	F	24. 5.43
U.224	H	17.10.42	F	9.12.42
U.225	H	5.12.42	F	8. 1.43
	F	2. 2.43	sunk	21. 2.43
U.226	H	31.12.42	F	10. 3.43
	F	10. 4.43	F	17. 5.43
U.227	H	24. 4.43	sunk	30. 4.43
U.228	H	6. 2.43	F	29. 3.43
	F	4. 5.43	F	19. 7.43
U.229	H	20. 2.43	F	17. 4.43
	F	11. 5.43	F	7. 6.43
U.230	H	4. 2. 43	F	31. 3.43
	F	25. 4.43	F	24. 5.43
U.231	H	13. 4.43	F	30. 5.43
U.232	H	8. 5.43	sunk	8. 7.43
U.252	H	26. 3.42	sunk	14. 4.42
U.253	H	12. 9.42	sunk	23. 9.42
U.254	H	14. 7.42	F	19. 8.42
	F	21. 9.42	F	22.10.42
	F	21.11.42	sunk	8.12.42
U.256	H	28. 7.42	F	3. 9.42
	F	21. 9.42	F	18.10.42
	F	22.12.42	F	12. 2.43
U.257	N	21. 9.42	F	18.10.42
	F	22.12.42	F	12. 2.43
	F	14. 3.43	F	7. 5.43
U.258	H	1. 9.42	F	27.10.42
	F	2.12.42	F	6.12.42
	F	10. 1.43	F	4. 3.43
	F	1. 4.43	sunk	20. 5.43
U.259	H	29. 8.42	F	5.10.42
	F	5.11.42	Mediterranean	
U.260	H	10. 9.42	F	15.11.42
	F	14.12.42	F	3. 2.43
	F	12. 3.43	F	22. 5.43
U.261	H	8. 9.42	sunk	15. 9.42
U.262	H	3.10.42	F	9.12.42
	F	16. 1.43	F	15. 2.43
	F	6. 4.43	F	25. 5.43
U.263	H	27.10.42	F	29.11.42
U.264	H	3.11.42	F	4.12.42
	F	10. 1.43	F	5. 3.43
	F	8. 4.43	F	1. 6.43

U-BOAT		SAILED		RETURNED
U.265	H	21. 1.43	sunk	3. 2.43
U.266	H	22.12.42	F	17. 2.43
	F	14. 4.43	sunk	14. 5.43
U.267	H	12. 1.43	F	18. 2.43
	F	23. 3.43	F	21. 5.43
U.268	H	2. 1.43	sunk	19. 2.43
U.270	N	23. 3.43	F	15. 5.43
U.273	H	8. 5.43	sunk	19. 5.43
U.301	H	1.10.42	F	6.11.42
	F	3.12.42	Mediterranean	
U.303	H	31.12.42	F	8. 3.43
U.304	H	27. 4.43	sunk	28. 5.43
U.305	H	27. 2.43	F	12. 4.43
	F	12. 5.43	F	1. 6.43
U.306	N	9. 3.43	F	9. 5.43
U.332	F	27. 1.42	F	8. 2.42
	F	17. 2.42	F	10. 4.42
	F	24. 5.42	F	1. 8.42
	F	5. 9.42	F	6.12.42
	F	28. 1.43	F	24. 3.43
	F	26. 4.43	sunk	2. 5.43
U.333	H	27.12.41	F	9. 2.42
	F	30. 3.42	F	26. 5.42
	F	1. 8.42	F	24. 8.42
	F	1. 9.42	F	23.10.42
	F	20.12.42	F	5. 2.43
	F	2. 3.43	F	13. 4.43
U.335	H	31. 7.42	sunk	3. 8.42
U.336	H	28.11.42	F	8. 1.43
	F	2. 3.43	F	11. 4.43
	F	8. 5.43	F	17. 7.43
U.337	H	24.12.42	sunk	15. 1.43
U.338	H	23. 2.43	F	24. 3.43
U.340	H	29. 4.43	F	31. 5.43
U.352	H	15. 1.42	F	26. 2.42
	F	7. 4.42	sunk	9. 5.42
U.353	H	22. 9.42	sunk	16.10.42
U 356	H	3. 9.42	F	4.11.42
	F	5.12.42	sunk	27.12.42
U.357	H	15.12.42	sunk	26.12.42
U.358	H	12. 1.43	F	8. 3.43
	F	11. 4.43	F	16. 5.43
U.359	H	4. 2.43	F	18. 3.43
	F	19. 4.43	F	20. 5.43
U.373	F	25.12.41	F	15. 1.42
	F	1. 3.42	F	17. 4.42
	F	19. 5.42	F	8. 7.42
	F	6. 8.42	F	4.10.42
	F	22.11.42	F	3. 1.43
	F	25. 2.43	F	13. 4.43
U.376	N	30. 1.43	F	13. 3.43
	F	6. 4.43	sunk	10. 4.43
U.377	N	30. 1.43	F	18. 3.43
	F	15. 4.43	F	7. 6.43
U.378	N	12. 4.43	F	4. 6.43
U.379	H	25. 6.42	sunk	8. 8.42
U.380	N	22. 8.42	F	7.10.42
	F	5.11.42	Mediterranean	
U.381	H	1.10.42	F	21.11.42
	F	19.12.42	F	19. 2.43
	F	31. 3.43	sunk	19. 5.43
U.382	N	19. 9.42	F	31.10.42
	F	8. 2.43	F	8. 3.43
	F	8. 4.43	F	24. 4.43
U.383	H	17.10.42	F	9.12.42
	F	6. 1.43	F	10. 3.43
	F	17. 4.43	F	25. 5.43
U.384	H	12.12.42	F	3. 2.43
	F	6. 3.43	sunk	19. 3.43
U.386	H	15. 4.43	F	11. 5.43
U.402	F	11. 1.42	F	11. 2.42
	F	26. 3.42	F	20. 5.42
	F	16. 6.42	F	5. 8.42
	F	4.10.42	F	20.11.42
	F	14. 1.43	F	23. 2.43
	F	20. 4.43	F	26. 5.43
U.403	H	24. 2.42	Northern waters	
	F	9. 1.43	F	2. 3.43
	F	19. 4.43	F	31. 5.43
U.404	H	17. 1.42	F	1. 2.42
	F	14. 2.42	F	3. 4.42
	F	6. 5.42	F	14. 7.42
	F	23. 8.42	F	13.10.42
	F	21.12.42	F	6. 2.43
	F	21. 3.43	F	3. 5.43
U.405	H	26. 2.42	Northern waters	
	N	7. 2.43	F	23. 3.43
U.406	H	4. 4.42	F	19. 4.42
	F	5. 5.42	F	1. 7.42
	F	9. 8.42	F	8.10.42
	F	14.12.42	F	12. 1.43
	F	22. 2.43	F	30. 3.43
	F	25. 4.43	F	11. 5.43
U.407	H	15. 8.42	F	9.10.42
	F	2.11.42	Mediterranean	
U.408	H	21. 5.42	Northern waters	
U.409	H	18. 8.42	F	9. 9.42
	F	13.10.42	F	5.11.42
	F	7.12.42	F	6. 1.43
	F	14. 2.43	F	12. 4.43
U.410	H	27. 8.42	F	28.10.42
	F	3.12.42	F	4. 1.43
	F	9. 2.43	F	27. 3.43
	F	26. 4.43	Mediterranean	
U.411	H	18. 8.42	F	30. 9.42
	F	7.11.42	sunk	28.11.42
U.412	H	17.10.42	sunk	22.10.42
U.413	H	22.10.42	F	25.11.42
	F	27.12.42	F	17. 2.43
	F	30. 3.43	F	13. 6.43

U-BOAT	SAILED		RETURNED	
U.414	H	7. 1.43	F	19. 2.43
	F	1. 4.43	Mediterranean	
U.415	N	7. 3.43	F	5. 5.43
U.418	H	24. 4.43	sunk	1. 6.43
U.432	F	21. 1.42	F	16. 3.42
	F	30. 4.42	F	2. 7.42
	F	15. 8.42	F	4.10.42
	F	30.11.42	F	5. 1.43
	F	14. 2.43	sunk	11. 3.43
U.435	H	20. 1.42	Northern waters	
	N	30.11.42	F	10. 1.43
	F	18. 2.43	F	25. 3.43
	F	20. 5.43	F	9. 7.43
U.436	H	2. 2.42	Northern waters	
	H	6.10.42	F	12.11.42
	F	17.12.42	F	19. 2.43
	F	25. 4.43	sunk	26. 5.43
U.437	H	4. 4.42	F	16. 4.42
	F	29. 4.42	F	18. 5.42
	F	6. 6.42	F	12. 8.42
	F	17. 9.42	F	15.11.42
	F	3. 2.43	F	5. 3.43
	F	26. 4.43	F	30. 4.43
U.438	H	1. 8.42	F	3. 9.42
	F	6.10.42	F	19.11.42
	F	9. 1.43	F	16. 2.43
	F	31. 3.43	sunk	6. 5.43
U.439	H	12.11.42	F	24.12.42
	F	22. 2.43	F	29. 3.43
	F	27. 4.43	sunk	3. 5.43
U.440	H	1. 9.42	F	21. 9.42
	F	19.10.42	F	13.11.42
	F	12.12.42	F	26. 1.43
	F	27. 2.43	F	11. 4.43
	F	26. 5.43	sunk	31. 5.43
U.441	H	17. 9.42	F	7.11.42
	F	13.12.42	F	22. 1.43
	F	27. 2.43	F	11. 4.43
	F	22. 5.43	F	13. 7.43
U.442	H	17. 9.42	F	16.11.42
	F	20.12.42	sunk	12. 2.43
U.443	H	1.10.42	F	4.11.42
	F	29.11.42	Mediterranean	
U.444	H	17.12.42	F	3. 2.43
	F	1. 3.43	sunk	11. 3.43
U.445	H	3.11.42	F	3. 1.43
	F	7. 2.43	F	27. 3.43
U.447	H	20. 2.43	F	24. 3.43
	F	27. 4.43	sunk	7. 5.43
U.448	H	30. 1.43	F	25. 3.43
	F	17. 4.43	F	26. 5.43
U.454	H	4. 7.42	F	17. 8.42
	F	26. 9.42	F	7.12.42
	F	18. 1.43	F	8. 3.43
	F	17. 4.43	F	23. 5.43
U.455	H	15. 1.42	N	28. 2.42
	N	21. 3.42	F	30. 3.42
	F	16. 4.42	F	16. 6.42
	F	22. 8.42	F	28.10.42
	F	29.11.42	F	29. 1.43
	F	20. 3.43	F	23. 4.43

U-BOAT	SAILED		RETURNED	
U.456	H	3. 1.42	Northern waters	
	N	13. 1.43	F	26. 2.43
	F	24. 4.43	sunk	13. 5.43
U.458	H	21. 6.42	F	26. 8.42
	F	1.10.42	Mediterranean	
U.459	H	21. 3.42	F	15. 5.42
	F	6. 6.42	F	19. 7.42
	F	21. 4.43	F	3. 6.43
U.460	H	7. 6.42	F	31. 7.42
	F	1. 9.42	F	12.10.42
	F	11.11.42	F	19.12.42
	F	31. 1.43	F	5. 3.43
	F	24. 4.43	F	25. 6.43
U.461	H	21. 6.42	F	16. 8.42
	F	7. 9.42	F	17.10.42
	F	19.11.42	F	3. 1.43
	F	20. 4.43	F	30. 5.43
U.462	H	23. 7.42	F	21. 9.42
	F	18.10.42	F	7.12.42
	F	19. 2.43	F	11. 3.43
	F	1. 4.43	F	24. 4.43
U.463	H	11. 7.42	F	3. 9.42
	F	28. 9.42	F	11.11.42
	F	6.12.42	F	26. 1.43
	F	4. 3.43	F	17. 4.43
	F	8. 5.43	sunk	15. 5.43
U.464	H	4. 8.42	sunk	20. 8.42
U.465	H	29.10.42	F	21.12.42
	F	16. 1.43	F	18. 2.43
	F	7. 4.43	F	14. 4.43
	F	29. 4.43	sunk	5. 5.43
U.466	H	12. 1.43	F	11. 2.43
	F	17. 4.43	F	26. 5.43
U.467	N	20. 5.43	sunk	25. 5.43
U.468	H	28. 1.43	F	27. 3.43
	F	19. 4.43	F	29. 5.43
U.469	H	16. 3.43	sunk	25. 3.43
U.487	H	27. 3.43	F	11. 5.43
U.488	H	18. 5.43	F	9. 7.43
U.502	F	19. 1.42	F	16. 3.42
	F	22. 4.42	sunk	5. 7.42
U.503	H	15. 2.42	F	22. 2.42
	F	28. 2.42	sunk	15. 3.42
U.504	H	6. 1.42	F	20. 1.42
	F	26. 1.42	F	1. 4.42
	F	2. 5.42	F	7. 7.42
	F	19. 8.42	F	11.12.42
	F	19. 1.43	F	24. 3.43
	F	21. 4.43	F	28. 5.43
U.505	H	19. 1.42	F	3. 2.42
	F	11. 2.42	F	7. 5.42
	F	7. 6.42	F	25. 8.42
	F	4.10.42	F	12.12.42
U.506	H	2. 3.42	F	25. 3.42
	F	6. 4.42	F	15. 6.42
	F	28. 7.42	F	7.11.42
	F	14.12.42	F	8. 5.43

U-BOAT		SAILED		RETURNED	U-BOAT		SAILED		RETURNED
U.507	H	7. 3.42	F	25. 3.42	U.533	H	15. 4.43	F	24. 5.43
	F	4. 4.42	F	4. 6.42	U.552	F	25.12.41	F	27. 1.42
	F	4. 7.42	F	12.10.42		F	7. 3.42	F	27. 4.42
	F	28.11.42	sunk	13. 1.43		F	9. 6.42	F	19. 6.42
U.508	H	25. 6.42	F	15. 9.42		F	4. 7.42	F	13. 8.42
	F	17.10.42	F	6. 1.43		F	10. 9.42	F	15.12.42
	F	22. 2.43	F	15. 3.43		F	4. 4.43	F	13. 6.43
U.509	H	25. 6.42	F	12. 9.42	U.553	F	31.12.41	F	3. 2.42
	F	15.10.42	F	26.11.42		F	24. 2.42	F	1. 4.42
	F	23.12.42	F	11. 5.43		F	19. 4.42	F	24. 6.42
U.510	H	7. 7.42	F	13. 9.42		F	19. 7.42	F	17. 9.42
	F	14.10.42	F	12.12.42		F	16. 1.43	sunk	23. 1.43
	F	16. 1.43	F	16. 4.43	U.558	F	10. 2.42	F	11. 3.42
U.511	H	16. 7.42	F	29. 9.42		F	12. 4.42	F	21. 6.42
	F	24.10.42	F	28.11.42		F	29. 7.42	F	17.10.42
	F	31.12.42	F	8. 3.43		F	9. 1.43	F	29. 3.43
	F	10. 5.43	Japan			F	8. 5.43	sunk	20. 7.43
U.512	H	15. 8.42	sunk	2.10.42	U.561	F	3. 1.42	Mediterranean	
U.513	H	7. 8.42	F	22.10.42	U.563	F	21. 1.42	N	3. 2.42
	F	20. 2.43	F	14. 4.43		H	9.12.42	F	14. 1.43
U.514	H	12. 8.42	F	9.11.42		F	21. 3.43	F	18. 4.43
	F	9.12.42	F	12. 2.43		F	29. 5.43	sunk	31. 5.43
	F	15. 4.43	F	22. 5.43	U 564	F	18. 1.42	F	6. 3.42
U.515	H	12. 8.42	F	14.10.42		F	4. 4.42	F	5. 6.42
	F	7.11.42	F	6. 1.43		F	9. 7.42	F	18. 9.42
	F	21. 2.43	F	24. 6.43		F	27.10.42	F	30.12.42
U.516	H	12. 8.42	F	14.11.42		F	11. 3.43	F	15. 4.43
	F	23.12.42	F	3. 5.43	U.566	F	15. 1.42	F	9. 3.42
U.517	H	8. 8.42	F	19.10.42		F	8. 4.42	F	30. 6.42
	F	17.11.42	sunk	21.11.42		F	6. 8.42	F	5. 9.42
U.518	H	26. 9.42	F	15.12.42		F	28.10.42	F	1.12.42
	F	11. 1.43	F	27. 4.43		F	6. 2.43	F	25. 3.43
U.519	H	17.10.42	F	29.12.42	U.569	F	26. 2.42	F	2. 4.42
	F	30. 1.43	sunk	10. 2.43		F	4. 5.42	F	28. 6.42
U.520	H	3.10.42	sunk	30.10.42		F	4. 8.42	F	8.10.42
U.521	H	3.10.42	F	8.12.42		F	25.11.42	F	28.12.42
	F	7. 1.43	F	26. 3.43		F	8. 2.43	F	13. 3.43
U.522	H	8.10.42	F	2.12.42		F	19. 4.43	sunk	22. 5.43
	F	31.12.42	sunk	23. 2.43	U.571	F	21.12.41	F	27. 1.42
U.523	H	9. 2.43	F	16. 4.43		F	10. 3.42	F	7. 5.42
	F	22. 5.43	F	24. 5.43		F	11. 6.42	F	7. 8.42
U.524	H	9.11.42	F	9. 1.43		F	3.10.42	F	14.11.42
	F	3. 3.43	sunk	22. 3.43		F	22.12.42	F	19. 2.43
U.525	H	15.12.42	F	3. 3.43		F	25. 3.43	F	1. 5.43
	F	15. 4.43	F	26. 5.43	U.572	F	7. 1.42	F	10. 2.42
U.526	N	11. 2.43	sunk	14. 4.43		F	14. 3.42	F	13. 5.42
U.527	H	9. 2.43	F	12. 4.43		F	30. 6.42	F	3. 9.42
U.528	H	15. 4.43	sunk	11. 5.43		F	12.10.42	F	22.11.42
U.529	H	30. 1.43	sunk	15. 2.43		F	23.12.42	F	11. 2.43
U.530	H	20. 2.43	F	22. 4.43		F	10. 3.43	F	13. 4.43
U.531	H	13. 4.43	sunk	6. 5.43	U.575	F	14. 1.42	F	26. 2.42
U.532	H	25. 3.43	F	15. 5.43		F	24. 3.42	F	13. 5.42
						F	10. 6.42	F	7. 8.42
						F	19. 9.42	F	8.11.42
						F	17.12.42	F	18. 2.43
						F	22. 4.43	F	11. 6.43
					U.576	F	20. 1.42	F	28. 2.42
						F	29. 3.42	F	16. 5.42
						F	16. 6.42	sunk	15. 7.42
					U.578	H	15. 1.42	F	26. 1.42
						F	3. 2.42	F	25. 3.42
						F	7. 5.42	F	3. 7.42
						F	6. 8.42	sunk	10. 8.42
					U.581	F	11. 1.42	sunk	2. 2.42

U-BOAT	SAILED	RETURNED	U-BOAT	SAILED	RETURNED
U.582	H 20.12.41	F 7. 2.42	U.604	H 4. 8.42	F 8. 9.42
	F 19. 3.42	F 24. 5.42		F 14.10.42	F 5.11.42
	F 22. 6.42	F 26. 6.42		F 26.11.42	F 31.12.42
	F 27. 6.42	F 12. 8.42		F 8. 2.43	F 9. 3.43
	F 14. 9.42	sunk 5.10.42			
			U.605	H 28. 7.42	F 4. 9.42
U.584	H 5. 5.42	F 16. 5.42		F 4.10.42	Mediterranean
	F 25. 5.42	F 22. 7.42			
	F 24. 8.42	F 10.10.42	U.606	N 17.10.42	F 5.12.42
	F 30.12.42	F 21. 2.43		F 4. 1.43	sunk 22. 2.43
	F 23. 3.43	F 24. 5.43			
			U.607	H 9. 7.42	F 16. 8.42
U.586	H 12. 1.42	N 12. 2.42		F 8. 9.42	F 23.10.42
				F 2. 1.43	F 9. 3.43
U.587	H 8. 1.42	F 31. 1.42		F 24. 4.43	F 2. 6.43
	F 12. 2.42	sunk 27. 3.42			
			U.608	H 20. 8.42	F 24. 9.42
U.588	H 8. 1.42	F 30. 1.42		F 20.10.42	F 9.12.42
	F 12. 2.42	F 27. 3.42		F 20. 1.43	F 29. 3.43
	F 19. 4.42	F 7. 6.42		F 15. 5.43	F 18. 7.43
	F 14. 7.42	sunk 31. 7.42			
			U.609	H 16. 7.42	F 10. 9.42
U.589	H 24. 2.42	Northern waters		F 6.10.42	F 22.10.42
				F 30.11.42	F 23.12.42
U.590	H 4. 4.42	F 17. 4.42		F 16. 1.43	sunk 7. 2.43
	F 3. 5.42	F 26. 6.42			
	F 11. 8.42	F 23. 8.42	U.610	H 12. 9.42	F 31.10.42
	F 27. 8.42	F 24.11.42		F 22.11.42	F 26.12.42
	F 22. 2.43	F 12. 4.43		F 8. 3.43	F 12. 5.43
U.591	H 15. 1.42	N 20. 2.42	U.611	H 1.10.42	sunk 10.12.42
	N 1.12.42	F 12. 1.43			
	F 17. 2.43	F 7. 4.43	U.613	H 22.10.42	F 27.11.42
	F 12. 5.43	F 16. 5.43		F 9. 1.43	F 18. 2.43
				F 25. 3.43	F 6. 5.43
U.592	N 9. 3.43	F 18. 4.43			
			U.614	H 9. 1.43	F 26. 2.43
U.593	H 2. 3.42	F 28. 3.42		F 12. 4.43	F 24. 5.43
	F 20. 4.42	F 17. 6.42			
	F 22. 7.42	F 19. 8.42	U.615	H 5. 9.42	F 30.10.42
	F 3.10.42	Mediterranean		F 25.11.42	F 9. 1.43
				F 18. 2.43	F 20. 4.43
U.594	H 14. 3.42	F 30. 3.42			
	F 11. 4.42	F 25. 6.42	U.616	H 6. 2.43	F 26. 3.43
	F 4. 8.42	F 28. 9.42		F 19. 4.43	Mediterranean
	F 30.12.42	F 18. 2.43			
	F 23. 3.43	F 14. 4.43	U.617	H 29. 8.42	F 7.10.42
				F 2.11.42	Mediterranean
U.595	H 23. 7.42	F 6.10.42			
	F 31.10.42	Mediterranean	U.618	H 1. 9.42	F 27.10.42
				F 25.11.42	F 18. 1.43
U.596	H 25. 6.42	H 2. 7.42		F 21. 2.43	F 7. 5.43
	H 25. 7.42	N 28. 7.42			
	N 8. 8.42	F 3.10.42	U.619	H 10. 9.42	sunk 15.10.42
	F 4.11.42	Mediterranean			
			U.620	H 12. 9.42	F 12.11.42
U.597	H 27. 6.42	F 16. 8.42		F 19.12.42	sunk 14. 2.43
	F 16. 9.42	sunk 12.10.42			
			U.621	H 29. 9.42	F 5.11.42
U.598	H 7. 7.42	F 13. 9.42		F 5.12.42	F 5. 1.43
	F 26.12.42	F 8. 2.43		F 1. 2.43	F 23. 3.43
	F 6. 3.43	F 13. 5.43		F 22. 4.43	F 3. 6.43
U.599	H 27. 8.42	sunk 24.10.42	U.623	H 5.11.42	F 26.12.42
				F 2. 2.43	sunk 21. 2.43
U.600	H 14. 7.42	F 22. 9.42			
	F 22.11.42	F 27.12.42	U.624	H 10.10.42	F 4.12.42
	F 11. 2.43	F 26. 3.43		F 7. 1.43	sunk 7. 2.43
	F 25. 4.43	F 11. 5.43			
			U.626	N 8.12.42	sunk 15.12.42
U.602	H 26. 9.42	F 6.11.42			
	F 1.12.42	Mediterranean	U.627	H 15.10.42	sunk 27.10.42
U.603	F 7. 2.43	F 26. 3.43	U.628	H 28.11.42	F 8. 1.43
	F 5. 5.43	F 16. 7.43		F 1. 2.43	F 9. 3.43
				F 8. 4.43	F 19. 5.43
			U.630	H 18. 3.43	sunk 4. 5.43

U-BOAT	SAILED			RETURNED	
U.631	H	19.12.42	F	4. 2.43
	F	6. 3.43	F	10. 5.43
U.632	H	24.12.42	F	14. 2.43
	F	15. 3.43	sunk	6. 4.43
U.633	H	20. 2.43	sunk	7. 3.43
U.634	N	18. 2.43	F	23. 3.43
	F	15. 4.43	F	23. 5.43
U.635	H	16. 3.43	sunk	6. 4.43
U.636	N	2. 5.43	F	8. 6.43
U.638	H	4. 2.43	F	31. 3.43
	F	20. 4.43	sunk	5. 5.43
U.640	H	1. 5.43	sunk	17. 5.43
U.641	H	20. 2.43	F	11. 4.43
	F	9. 5.43	F	16. 7.43
U.642	H	20. 2.43	F	8. 4.43
	F	4. 5.43	F	6. 7.43
U.645	H	24. 4.43	F	22. 6.43
U.646	N	12. 5.43	sunk	17. 5.43
U.648	H	3. 4.43	F	19. 5.43
U.650	H	10. 4.43	F	28. 5.43
U.653	H	16.12.41	F	13. 1.42
	F	31. 1.42	F	30. 3.42
	F	25. 4.42	F	6. 7.42
	F	5. 8.42	F	31. 8.42
	F	27.10.42	F	29.12.42
	F	28. 1.43	F	31. 3.43
U.654	N	15.12.41	F	25.12.41
	F	3. 1.42	F	19. 2.42
	F	21. 3.42	F	29. 5.42
	F	9. 7.42	sunk	22. 8.42
U.656	H	15. 1.42	F	28. 1.42
	F	4. 2.42	sunk	1. 3.42
U.657	N	4. 5.43	sunk	14. 5.43
U.658	H	7. 7.42	F	12. 9.42
	F	6.10.42	sunk	30.10.42
U.659	H	15. 8.42	F	16. 9.42
	F	13.10.42	F	5.11.42
	F	12.12.42	F	5. 1.43
	F	8. 2.43	F	20. 3.43
	F	25. 4.43	sunk	3. 5.43
U.660	H	25. 7.42	F	5. 9.42
	F	3.10.42		Mediterranean
U.661	H	5. 9.42	sunk	15.10.42
U.662	H	22. 9.42	F	18.11.42
	F	19.12.42	F	7. 2.43
	F	23. 3.43	F	19. 5.43
U.663	H	5.11.42	F	31.12.42
	F	10. 3.43	F	4. 4.43
	F	5. 5.43	sunk	7. 5.43
U.664	H	20.10.42	F	10.11.42
	F	5.12.42	F	13. 1.43
	F	14. 2.43	F	28. 3.43
	F	29. 4.43	F	9. 6.43
U.665	H	20. 2.43	sunk	22. 3.43
U.666	H	25. 2.43	F	10. 4.43
	F	6. 5.43	F	9. 7.43
U.701	H	27.12.41	F	9. 2.42
	F	26. 2.42	F	1. 4.42
	F	19. 5.42	sunk	7. 7.42
U.704	H	30. 6.42	F	16. 8.42
	F	5.10.42	F	23.11.42
	F	7. 1.43	F	12. 2.43
	F	14. 3.43	F	10. 4.43
U.705	H	1. 8.42	sunk	3. 9.42
U.706	H	22. 9.42	F	7.11.42
	F	8.12.42	F	13. 2.43
	F	15. 3.43	F	11. 5.43
U.707	H	12. 1.43	F	8. 3.43
	F	12. 4.43	F	31. 5.43
U.709	H	13. 2.43	F	18. 3.43
	F	15. 4.43	F	23. 5.43
U.710	H	15. 4.43	sunk	24. 4.43
U.731	H	29. 4.43	F	12. 6.43
U.732	H	8. 4.43	F	15. 5.43
U.751	F	14. 1.42	F	23. 2.42
	F	15. 4.42	F	15. 6.42
	F	14. 7.42	sunk	17. 7.42
U.752	H	4. 2.42	F	13. 3.42
	F	28. 3.42	F	22. 5.42
	F	2. 7.42	F	4. 9.42
	F	22.10.42	F	3.11.42
	F	9. 1.43	F	15. 2.43
	F	22. 4.43	sunk	23. 5.43
U.753	H	17. 1.42	F	1. 2.42
	F	26. 2.42	F	26. 3.42
	F	22. 4.42	F	25. 6.42
	F	20. 9.42	F	8.12.42
	F	28. 1.43	F	10. 3.43
	F	5. 5.43	sunk	15. 5.43
U.754	H	30.12.41	F	9. 2.42
	F	7. 3.42	F	25. 4.42
	F	19. 6.42	sunk	31. 7.42
U.755	H	4. 8.42	F	5.10.42
	F	1.11.42		Mediterranean
U.756	H	15. 8.42	sunk	3. 9.42
U.757	N	26. 9.42	F	24.10.42
	F	22. 2.43	F	18. 3.43
U.758	H	14.11.42	F	24.12.42
	F	14. 2.43	F	30. 3.43
U.759	H	2. 2.43	F	14. 3.43
U.760	H	29. 4.43	F	31. 5.43
U.951	H	13. 5.43	sunk	7. 7.43
U.952	H	22. 4.43	F	31. 5.43
U.953	H	13. 5.43	F	22. 7.43
U.954	H	8. 4.43	sunk	19. 5.43
UA.	F	14. 3.42	H	24. 4.42
UD.3	H	3.10.42	F	7. 1.43
UD.5	H	27. 8.42	F	12.11.42

MORE FROM THE SAME SERIES

Most books from the 'World War II from Original Sources' series are edited and endorsed by Emmy Award winning film maker and military historian Bob Carruthers, producer of Discovery Channel's Line of Fire and Weapons of War and BBC's Both Sides of the Line. Long experience and strong editorial control gives the military history enthusiast the ability to buy with confidence.

The series advisor is David McWhinnie, producer of the acclaimed Battlefield series for Discovery Channel. David and Bob have co-produced books and films with a wide variety of the UK's leading historians including Professor John Erickson and Dr David Chandler.

Where possible the books draw on rare primary sources to give the military enthusiast new insights into a fascinating subject.

For more information visit www.pen-and-sword.co.uk